an aesthetics of
junk fiction

an

aesthetics

of

fiction

· ·

THOMAS J. ROBERTS

The University of

Georgia Press

Athens and London

© 1990 by the University of Georgia Press
Athens, Georgia 30602
All rights reserved
Designed by Richard Hendel
Set in Bodoni Book
The paper in this book meets the guidelines for
permanence and durability of the Committee on
Production Guidelines for Book Longevity of
the Council on Library Resources.

Printed in the United States of America

94 93 92 91 90 5 4 3 2 1

Library of Congress
Cataloging in Publication Data
Roberts, Thomas J. (Thomas John)
    An aesthetics of junk fiction / Thomas J.
Roberts.
        p.   cm.
    Bibliography: p.
    Includes index.
    ISBN 0-8203-1149-9 (alk. paper)
    1. Fiction—20th century—History and
criticism.   2. Popular literature—History and
criticism.   3. Literary form.   I. Title.
PN3503.R59   1990
809.3—dc20   89-4911
CIP

British Library Cataloging
in Publication Data available

This book is for our sons

Tom and Mark and Dan.

Sometimes our life together

is more interesting than any

of us wants it to be, but it

is always fascinating.

I would not have missed it.

contents

· · · · · · · · · ·

acknowledgments

. . . .

My friend John Fraser and I have been talking about junk fiction in all its many forms ever since we were students together in the 1950s. We swapped titles, shared readings, gave useful warnings-against, and fruitfully disagreed. His sense of the merits and defects of these materials is the sanest and soundest I have ever known—as is evident in his *Violence in the Arts*, the most thoughtful inquiry into that much-vexed matter that has yet appeared. We do have different theories about these materials, however, and he should not be thought a coconspirator. Indeed, one of the pleasures I anticipate is the long period of happy disagreement that will follow his reading of these pages.

It would be futile to try to name all the other people who have helped me, but some have given me especially steady and gratifying assistance. Philip Stevick, Herbert Weil, and Milton Stern helped me win fellowship support. Irving Cummings, Jack Davis, Thomas Jambeck, Samuel Pickering, and Roger Wilkenfeld—among many other colleagues—shared in the reading of paperback fiction and in the viewing of films and television: we almost never agreed about anything, which, of course, is the happiest situation for someone who is trying to think his way through some confusing matters. My classes in science fiction have always attracted quarrelsome and opinionated students who, bless them, never hesitated to offer competing observations. There have been many occasions when I entered the classroom with one opinion and left it an hour later with a completely opposite opinion.

Others helped more than they ever knew and in ways they never suspected. My nephew Donald Friedlander has for many years been a sure guide in the intricacies of the world of the comic book, for instance. Of those who helped me think my way into science fiction, I owe a special acknowledgment to Paul Walker and John J. Pierce. Some of the theories I offer here appeared first in their brief-lived fanzine *T.A.D.* (*Tension, Apprehension, and Dissension*), and Pierce's monumental history of the genre has changed my opinions about individual writers and books and has saved me much embarrassment. In other ways and at other times other friends helped me too: Carol Horn Frazer, Lynne Kelson, Jon Tydor, and Howard Weinstein, especially over the last few years.

Most helpful, and for a long time, was Bernhard Kendler, who gave unfailingly useful advice. He saved readers much that was awkward, distracting, and even irrelevant. I owe separate recognition to Madelaine Cooke and Joanne S. Ainsworth, whose editorial skills have also come between me and the legitimate annoyance of readers on many occasions. They have rescued phrases, buried silliness, corrected faulty bibliographic citations, and brought whole paragraphs back from the dead. Their copy editing has been a joy to the soul.

It was the National Endowment for the Humanities that helped me get started on this book by awarding me a year's fellowship. The University of Connecticut later gave me sabbatical leave, and the Department of English twice eased my teaching load so I could continue with the writing. The university's Research Foundation provided financial help when I needed it and assigned a private study to me, away from friendly students and safe from the press-gangs of the university's many committees. Linda Polcari and Richard Schimmelpfeng of the University of Connecticut Library never failed me when I asked for their help, and I often did ask for help.

Oh, yes. Thanks, Betty, for all the many years that have passed and for all the many years to come.

an aesthetics of
junk fiction

. . . .

introduction

. . . .

In this introduction, I take up three questions: What does the term *junk fiction* mean in these pages? Does the formal study of junk fiction offer opportunities for new kinds of inquiry into literature and the other arts? What do the chapters in this book contain?

We readers divide printed fiction in many different ways. We distinguish between learned and popular fiction, between the fiction of the past and current fiction, between hardbound and paperback fiction, and on and on. Underneath all these variously useful, variously contradictory distinctions that we honor, however, there lies a simple, widely recognized division into four broad classes. We recognize two types of learned fiction and two types of popular fiction.

1. *Canonical fiction* is one of those two parts of learned fiction. It is probably best defined as that part of the fiction of the past that still interests us: Henry Fielding's *Tom Jones*, Laurence Sterne's *Tristram Shandy*, George Eliot's *Middlemarch*, and so on. We meet this fiction in the classroom; and, since we all spend a good many years in classrooms, canonical fiction is the most widely known of these four types: *Great Expectations* and *Silas Marner* have been in the hands of more readers than even the novels of a Harold Robbins or a Sidney Sheldon. It is in the classroom, too, that we learn—or at least are told—to feel that these stories require a highly specialized response, one marked by deep respect, by close attention, and by careful rereading. When we are students we do not call this kind of response *reading*, we call it *studying*.

2. *Serious fiction* is the other part of learned fiction. It is one of the three types of contemporary fiction, but it is written for its own small,

highly educated readership: James Joyce's *Ulysses* and Virginia Woolf's *Mrs. Dalloway*, now accepted as canonical fiction, were once thought of as serious fiction. The writers of serious fiction are not primarily concerned about popularity. Their readers are to be found in and around the universities, and their own most cherished goal is to have their books match the success that *Ulysses* and *Mrs. Dalloway* had in winning acceptance into canonical fiction. Writers of serious fiction do expect more of their readers than the writers of popular fiction do, of course. They want their books to be given the same thoughtful attention—that is, the same study —that those readers give canonical fiction.

3. *Plain fiction* (also awkwardly named *best-seller fiction*) is the more respectable of the two kinds of contemporary popular fiction. Plain fiction is the most widely read part of contemporary fiction, and sometimes the readerships are immense. Harriet Beecher Stowe's *Uncle Tom's Cabin*, Margaret Mitchell's *Gone with the Wind* and Mario Puzo's *Godfather* were each in its day accepted as plain fiction. Plain fiction's readers think of themselves as a sanity that lies midway between decadence and brutishness—between what they think of as the hyperintellectuality of serious readers and the baser appetites of the readers of junk fiction.

Some observers would claim that there is no plain fiction, that bestsellers are nothing more special than those few books that find readers outside their target readerships. There does seem to be such a class in fact as well as in name, however. First, many readers do identify themselves as members of the group that gives its primary reading loyalties to this plain fiction. Second, some writers regularly do produce hugely successful books: they know how to find that group of plain readers. This in itself suggests that there may be an algorithm for cross-genre success in the writing of stories. Finally, there is at least one genre that is unique to the plain reader—that tradition John G. Cawelti named and so brilliantly described: *social melodrama* (Cawelti 260–95).

Plain fiction does not ask to be read more than once: it certainly does not expect to be studied. In this respect, it is unlike serious fiction and is like junk fiction.

4. *Junk fiction* is the other part of popular fiction. It has many names, each with its own nuance: genre fiction, vernacular fiction, category fiction, paperback fiction, and others besides. It includes popular fantasy,

the western, science fiction, the mystery, the romance, and much more. This junk fiction is not so different from its contemporary rivals, serious and plain fiction, as is supposed. Like plain fiction, it is read rather than studied; but, unlike plain fiction, its writers assume that their readers already know earlier stories within the same tradition, for, like serious fiction, it requires its own sort of (unadmitted, invisible) learnedness.

As its title indicates, this book is a study of this fourth type of fiction, of the materials that usually appear first in paperback format. I have chosen to refer to these stories as *junk fiction*, but not without misgiving and regret; for the phrase is offensive to the very writers whose minds and work I admire deeply and seek to defend. They certainly do not need yet another dismissal, and nothing I can say here will give some of those writers solace, of course. I can ask them to read the pages that follow and judge for themselves whether I do indeed feel that their stories are the junk that the unsympathetic say they are. I could invite them to look into my notes on my reading to see how many other stories and writers won my admiration even though I could not find an excuse to talk about them in this book. None of that will seem an excuse for the insult, I am sure; I know that it would not satisfy me if I were a writer of science fiction or detective stories or romances and was not specifically praised here. (It is not impossible that one or two of the writers I cite have another reason for protesting: that they do not want their books associated, under any label whatsoever, with some of the other books I describe here. That sort of protest does not discourage me. It delights me.)

I did not choose that phrase *junk fiction* lightly. I chose the phrase because it makes us face the problem of these stories honestly. It is not because my tastes are so catholic and because I deeply admire and enjoy everything I read that the word *junk* makes me uncomfortable, then. Far from it. I have never been a member of that Father Flanagan school of literary criticism whose motto is, "There is no such thing as a really bad book." Whether one novel is better than any other novel in an absolute sense—independently of a human observer—is a fascinating question, but it is irrelevant in this study. What is important is that we individually perceive books as better and as worse than one another and that we ourselves sometimes choose the books that we think are poorer over the books that we think are better. I do feel that much of what I hear, see, and read does indeed deserve to be called junk. This includes much of paperback fiction as well as some canonical fiction, some serious fiction, and much plain fiction. Almost all of the books I quote or cite in this study, though, are books that I admire, for one reason or for many. Still, as I show later, even the other stories, the stories that truly do seem bad to me, are rewarding. Indeed, my purpose in this book is to show how it is that good readers find deep pleasure and lasting satisfaction not only when they are reading the good stories their favorite genres produce but even when they are reading the stories they feel are poor.

I speak of these materials as junk fiction because it faces that problem squarely, then, and also because the phrase suggests similar stories that come in other formats: comic books, movies, television shows, for instance. (As some readers of these pages have helpfully remarked, much of what I say is true of junk nonfiction, too.) I also use other phrases: *paperback fiction*, for instance. All printed fiction today appears in paperback format at one time or another, of course, and especially canonical fiction when it is published for the schools. Still, there are stories, like those of John D. MacDonald and Isaac Asimov and Barbara Cartland, which may make brief, strategic appearances in hardback format but are written especially to sell to the people who buy only paperbacks.

Two terms that are especially useful are *vernacular fiction* and *genre fiction*. The phrase *vernacular fiction* reminds us that some excellent writers validly choose not to conceive of their stories in terms of the monumentality that is the goal of the serious author and, consequently, that their own vernacular stories are an expression of a profoundly different aesthetic. The term *genre fiction* serves somewhat the same purpose. It reminds us that it is sometimes useful to say of certain stories that they were written by a tradition rather than by an individual and that their readers' interest lies rather in that dynamic tradition than in the writers who have chosen to serve as that tradition's voices. The terms *vernacular fiction* and *genre fiction* make us continuously aware that these materials —in paperback format or some other—are the product of a different aesthetic, one barely recognized in traditional literary studies. The phrase *junk fiction*, when understood as I should like it to be understood here, reminds us that this vernacular aesthetic achieves its successes by means of stories that, for excellent reasons, are usually inferior—as stories—to the stories we find in the lists of canonical, serious, and plain fiction. It is for this reason that we can say of it that it is authentically a *literature* that deserves the respect that word connotes today, but that it is a *literature without texts*. This is to say that it is a literature even when it is not giving us stories that are distinguished in their own right.

Junk fiction has two readerships. I am interested in both of these groups, but I give my attention to only one of them. The readers I study are the people who are well read. They have read, and they continue to read, far outside the boundaries of junk fiction. They see that much of this junk fiction is junk, and yet they continue to read it. The other readership comprises the people whose reading is confined exclusively to these materials, the people who may be more intelligent than some of the well-read people reading the same materials they do, and who may be wiser, and who may be better, but who are not as widely experienced with books.

There is some amusement to be found in the study of well-read people who are enjoying stories that they cannot find it in them to respect and who must invent casually plausible explanations for themselves, but I did not choose to study these readers because of the ironies implicit in the contradictions between their private tastes and public protestations. I chose to study them because we cannot dismiss them as readers. We know that they have good taste, for we can see that if they are taking deep and lasting satisfaction from junk fiction they are also taking deep and lasting satisfaction from canonical and serious fiction. These readers have earned the right to be treated seriously. If people who read Goethe and Manzoni and Richardson and Lady Murasaki and Pushkin with pleasure are also reading detective stories with pleasure, there is more in the detective story than its critics have recognized, perhaps more than even its writers and readers have recognized. If we can identify what it is in the detective story that satisfies experienced readers, we have gained an insight into those other readers of the detective story, too.

The pages that follow are not eccentric, I trust, but they are different from what other students of junk fiction have been writing. They are different because I feel strongly that the study of these traditions in fiction is still tied too closely to the study of canonical fiction.

What shall we say is the difference in literary studies between a *disci-*

pline and a *fan club*, however learned? This difference, at least, is worth noticing: a *fan club* says, "What we love you should love, too," but a *discipline* says, "What we are discovering about what we love will be useful to you in your investigations of what you love." If one of the many groups studying the oeuvre of John Milton or of the detective story or of the oral culture of the Ashanti makes no larger claim than that it finds that oeuvre deeply rewarding and that we others are at fault for not recognizing its merits also, then that group—be it ever so learned and ever so honored and ever so wise—is a fan club and only that. The whole of literary study can be described as a network of such sharings of delight in a common love. Why, after all, should readers give their time to the study of something they do *not* love? Groups of this character can become solidly entrenched, but they become living parts of literary studies only when they move beyond love. That is, when the Miltonists and the students of the detective story and the anthropologists discover something— some lesson, some form of inquiry, some attitude—that those who love other things will also find helpful, then those students have joined literary studies as functioning parts.

Studies of junk fiction can be brilliant, and they are becoming more rigorous as their writers have moved beyond the excitement of sharing their enthusiasms as readers. But they are still modeled on forms of inquiry that were developed in the study of canonical literature. Whatever interest students of literature may have in junk fiction itself, they have no interest in books written about it. So far, those books have provided nothing new, nothing that the study of canonical literature does not already know. When we examine them we find such well-established practices as the study of individual writers, the study of dominant themes, and the writing of histories of the individual genres that give familiar emphasis to great names and great titles. Each of the vernacular traditions in fiction certainly can be studied in these familiar ways, but vernacular materials equally certainly do not invite those types of study. I show how junk fiction resists these lines of approach, and I suggest other lines of inquiry and other features of our reading that, in fact, are not being studied in competing pockets of reading enthusiasm. My hope was to show that the study of the vernacular genres need not be the province of fan clubs, that it has the potential to become a discipline in its own right. That is why, wherever I had the choice, I always elected to examine a familiar object in ways others had not looked at it. That is why I always asked myself the most difficult questions I could imagine.

Alas, I found that some questions were too difficult for me and that other matters required more space than I had available. I still find it intriguing to ask why it is that some of us turn to one form of junk fiction and others turn to other forms, for instance. Why is it that you prefer the spy story and I prefer science fiction? It is easy to find answers offered to this sort of question; but, for all my efforts, I was unable to find answers that satisfied me either in any of the other studies I examined or in my introspective inquiries. The more closely I examined my own patterns of interest the less confident I became of explanations I encountered or devised. Someone somewhere once spoke of questions where an endless debate goes on "between those who do not know and those who do not know they do not know." My impression is that those who do not know they do not know what the attractions of any vernacular genre are have the best chances of getting into print. (I include in this group many of the Freudians. Perhaps nowhere are certain fundamental sillinesses in applied Freudianism so evident as in its commentary on the vernacular arts.)

Another example, this one of a road not taken: I am interested in traditions of traditions, bundles of genres that have a kinship but appear in different media. It is helpful to speak of a *genre* as a medium-bound tradition and of a *kind* as a bundle of such medium-bound traditions. The *kind* of the western, then, includes the genres of the western in film, in print, on television, in comic books, in commercials, in tourist attractions, in songs, and no doubt in other mediums as well. Not only would the exploration of this matter of the kinds and genres have taken more time and space but it would have been an additional distraction from the main line of the argument of these pages. The matter of kinds and genres is not trivial, however. The confusion of genres within a kind is a continuing source of error—most notoriously, perhaps, in the impressions people form of prose science fiction from their experiences with film science fiction. Certain curious features of genre loyalties become evident —as when we find that intellectuals of the 1940s and 1950s admired the western in film but not in print, the detective story in print but not in film, and so on. There are indications that fiction makers are beginning to conceive of their works in the mode of the kind (as central texts and their spin-offs), as when editors, publishers, writers, and film producers plan works that will be successful first as books, then as films, and then as television series and will also generate successful lines of ancillary toys and memorabilia. This sort of thing makes most readers uneasy, but it is a recognition of styles of fiction perception that have only recently become common. It may be a symptom of a significant change in artists' modes of conception and of new opportunities for artists with several talents.

No one who has puzzled about matters like these while working on the canonical arts will feel that they are unimportant to our understanding of the role of the arts in human existence. For example, studies in the inter-relations of the arts—music, poetry, painting—have had great difficulty in becoming established. As René Wellek and Austin Warren observed many years ago, the different arts work within different traditions, or systems (125–35). The study of the interrelations of vernacular genres within vernacular kinds, however, offers some promise, for here, too, we have systems interacting with systems. The differences between two vernacular genres (say, film and print) within a single vernacular kind (say, the western) are minimal and would permit us to develop a vocabulary for describing system-to-system interactions, a vocabulary that could later be enriched to accommodate studies of such widely separated systems as modernist music and modernist poetry.

These and other matters—a dozen, perhaps two dozen—that seem equally important and promising were beyond my powers as a writer to present usefully. Some are still beyond my powers of understanding. As every writer knows, when a book has to be given a usable shape it seems always to be the brightest pages that have to be sacrificed. I feel that keenly when I reflect upon how little of what I have written in preparation for this book actually appears in these pages. What remains is, however, what seems most to need saying now.

This book, *An Aesthetics of Junk Fiction*, explains why we have mis-understood junk fiction and its readers in the past, then, and what it is we find when we look at it with fresh eyes.

Chapter 1 reminds us of the materials we encounter in paperback fiction and shows that one of its attractions is that it mirrors back our own times in some unexpectedly useful ways. Chapters 2 and 3 turn from the readers and the materials they are reading to the images we have inherited of junk fiction and of those who use it. (An interest in people who are secretly ashamed of their taste is evident as early as Plato, for instance.) Chapter 4 distinguishes five types of readers that a paperback genre recognizes—ranging from the people who will read nothing else to the people who are violently allergic to anything that the genre produces.

Chapter 6, "Textures, Designs," shows that a work of junk fiction is as form-intensive as a sonnet or a villanelle and that it is read in part for the formal pleasures it provides. These pleasures include, most notably, variations in verbal textures and intricacies of narrative design. Chapter 7, "Thinking with Tired Brains," argues that junk fiction carries in it chunks of raw information that is valued for its own sake and also that it provides a range of alter egos, counter egos, and alternate egos with which its readers' minds play—but that a genre's greatest value to its readers lies in its definition and dramatization of problems. Chapter 8, "Reading in a System," shows that readers of a paperback genre are less usefully thought of as reading stories than as reading *by means of* stories. (This is a criterial distinction between the people who read plain fiction and those who read junk fiction. The first group reads by story; the second reads by genre. This difference makes the phrase *popular fiction* inappropriate for these pages, for that term covers two fundamentally different types of materials.) The chapter proposes that the absurdities of the junk genres are literary conventions that writers have invented to enable the genres to explore new areas of form and thought and that junk genres deal successfully with complexities by means of the very simplicities that so disappoint us when we first look into these genres.

Chapter 9 compares the literary and the paperback bookscapes and outlines certain valid differences between them. Chapter 10 compares *study reading* and *thick reading*, the modes of response that the two bookscapes teach.

Chapter 11 extrapolates the findings of the preceding chapters in two directions. It suggests, first, that professional students of literature are probably reading literary scholarship and criticism in the same style that they read paperback fiction; and it suggests, too, that what is true of paperback fiction is probably true also of vernacular fiction in other mediums—television fiction, especially.

the stories of
our times

. . . .

*If youre a show man then what ever happens is took in to your
figgers and your fit up its took in to your show. If you dont
know whats happent sooner youwl hear of it later youwl hear
your figgers tell of it 1 way or a nother. That boar kicking on
the end of my spear hewl be in my shows I dont know how but
hewl be there. That crow what callit, "Fall! Fall! Fall!" and
my smasht father that greyling morning at Widders Dump
and that old leader with his yeller eyes and woar down teef.*
—*Russell Hoban*, Riddley Walker

We all read junk fiction—detective stories, spy stories, romances, science fiction, the daily comic strips—or watch those half-hour
television programs or run out for a quick film. Not all junk fiction comes
in paperback format, but the stories are pretty much the same, and they
are all doomed. The great works will live forever, we have been told,
whereas the meretricious Zane Greys and Agatha Christies win brief
attention and then disappear utterly, while the serious writer, creating for
the happy few, finds each year a larger and more appreciative attention. It
is not quite true, of course. Where are the novels of Dorothy Richardson
today? Some paperback writers do better than the serious artists—even,
alas, with the happy few. All of Zane Grey's novels and all of Agatha
Christie's can be purchased as sets even now, though Christie's early
novels are over sixty-five years old and Grey's best-known novel, *Riders of*

the Purple Sage, appeared in 1912, almost eighty years ago. E. E. (Doc) Smith's science-fiction novel *Skylark of Space* first appeared in 1928, but every few years it blooms again on the drugstore racks. These stories too will disappear, of course.

We grant it freely: paperback stories are doomed. Why is it fatal for their readers to admit this? We are all of Yeats's dying generations. If we knew that a century from now no one would have any interest in the great art of the past, would we lose interest in *The Magic Flute?* If we decided that we would not waste our time with anyone who was not among the Truly Great, with whom would we share our lives? Few of us have more than a dozen friends who are the equals of Dante, Shakespeare, Newton, Einstein, Vermeer, Raphael, Spinoza, Alexander the Great, and Abraham Lincoln. And some of us suspect that our friends are not yet persuaded that we ourselves belong in that company. If we looked too closely at one another with only the highest standards, we could all become a little lonely.

Whatever it is, paperback fiction is of our time: it is ours. Its very time-boundedness gives it a special value. *Riders of the Purple Sage* and *The Murder of Roger Ackroyd* and even the sadly dated *Skylark of Space* are intelligible only to readers of this century. Cicero could not have imagined us, and the Time Travelers' Eloi will not remember us. Whatever we say about these books, in the whole stretch of time between the big bang and the final whimper these are some of the only stories that will ever have understood us.

We know them but we do not always speak sensibly about them. We say that we read them for the plots, but this is manifestly untrue. All the writers use the same plot lines, but we do not like all their works equally. It is not the plots which bring us back; it is what the plots are carrying. They are nets that have been used over the centuries—they were used in the streets that Tiglath-Pileser ruled—and in each period caught pieces of the life of a dying generation. The plots are seining from our own lives just as effectively as they did for all those earlier generations and will for all the generations to come—even the bookless generations.

In this chapter, we look at the materials that come uniquely from our century: the incidents, ideas, and scenes that no other generation could understand. I divide them according to their sources: the bits from our own newspapers, the materials from the literary past as our generation has defined it, the scenes only this century has witnessed, the kinds of people we meet or think we meet. It is this feature—its solid basis in our shared life—that makes these materials so easy for us to read, that will make the stories so difficult for our grandchildren to puzzle out. When readers can no longer understand these books, they will no longer understand us.

Newspaper Reality

In George V. Higgins's *Rat on Fire*, Proctor, an arsonist, is explaining to Fein, his client, that there are rats in Fein's building and that this is good news. He will have a rat set the fire. Fein is puzzled. How can one get a rat to set a fire?

"Very simple," Proctor said. "You catch the rat. Just to be on the safe side, you catch maybe a dozen rats. This is not very hard. You just go down to the fuckin' dump and catch a few rats and you put them inna cage. Then you take the cage fulla rats to the place that's got rats and you put the cage down onna floor and you take a can of gasoline and you pour it all over the rats while they're in the cage.

"They don't like it," Proctor said. "Makes their skin sting or something. And they start to go nuts. Then you take the fuckin' cage over to where the wallboard starts, and you open it up, and them rats're all running around in there and they're looking for a place to run away to, and you just give it to them. Except just as they're starting out, what you do is drop this here lighted match in there, in that cage, and all of a sudden those rats've got more'n stinging skin to look out for, because they are on fire."

"Ah," Fein said.

"And those rats that're on fire go running right up inside all those walls where the wiring is, and they set the building on fire."

"And anybody," Fein said, "that was looking at it, they would think that it was probably the wiring."

"See?" Proctor said. "That is why rats're good news."

"Finally," Fein said. "Finally, I am gonna get even with the rats."

(61–62)

Is this passage something only our generation would write? One simple way of discovering this is to ask ourselves what the scholars, our grandchildren, will be saying about it if they come across it fifty years from now.

They will explain to their students that a national concern about professional arsonists emerged in the late 1970s. They will cite the word *fuckin'*, which did not become common in print until our period. They will dissect the speech rhythms: "'Just to be on the safe side, you catch maybe a dozen rats. This is not very hard. You just go down to the fuckin' dump and catch a few rats and you put them inna cage.'" Those rhythms, common enough today and probably common enough in everyday speech a century ago, did not appear earlier in fiction. Finally, they will remark on the national interest given a few years ago to slum children fighting rats, echoed in Fein's delight at the scheme: "'Finally,' Fein said. 'Finally, I am gonna get even with the rats.'" These indications will be as telling to a scholar as a fingerprint is to a detective.

They are the materials netted by the story, in outline a familiar pattern of a criminal enterprise gone wrong. The writer, Higgins, knows what interests us; he is interested, too. He reads the same newspapers we read.

Newspaper reality is as good a term as any for that continuously changing image of reality we put together from all the sources reporting on events we do not actually see for ourselves: the newspapers, the magazines, the radio and television broadcasts, the books on crime and science and history. We read the books of the past, we see things for ourselves, and we have our own contacts with people; but we carry a newspaper reality in our heads as well, and the writers of our time share it. (This has always been true of the novel, in all of its forms. We do not see the newspaper realities of the times of Charlotte Brontë in her novels, but the specialists do.)

Science fiction shows us that we cannot escape from our newspaper reality. Since so much of science fiction is about the future or about the past—a flight, it is supposed, from our own present—the signs of the moment of the writing are especially telling.

Sprague de Camp's *Lest Darkness Fall* was written in 1941; it tells about a man who travels back to the Roman empire of 535 A.D. and introduces brandy, double-entry bookkeeping, and a primitive telegraph. John Brunner's *Stand on Zanzibar* was written in 1968; it tells about life in America in 2010. Neither tells about events in the year it was written, and yet *Lest Darkness Fall* could not have been written in 1967 and *Stand on Zanzibar* could not have been written in 1941.

It is not only slang that dates each story, though that is important. For *The Good Old Stuff*, a reprint of some of his work for the pulps, John D. MacDonald reviewed stories he had written thirty-five years earlier and found that he had to update them. "I changed a live radio show to a live television show. And in others I changed pay scales, taxi fares, long-distance phoning procedures, beer prices, and so forth to keep from watering down the attention of the reader" (xiv). In Hammett's *Red Harvest* of 1929 the detective smokes Fatimas, and Dinah Brand drives a Marmon, neither of which is much in evidence anymore. These date indicators are important, too, but more so is the writer's conception of the situations the stories present. De Camp, living inside the newspaper reality of 1941, could not have conceived of the kinds of future or past Brunner could conceive of in 1967, and Brunner, from inside his newspaper reality, could not have felt the resonance De Camp felt for sixth-century Rome.

In 1941, Europe was at war, and with the triumph of Nazi Germany newspapers were warning about the return of barbarism to Europe and the fall of cultural darkness over the world. De Camp's choice of sixth-century Rome was appropriate, for it was in that century that the barbarians descended upon Rome and Rome fell finally from its eminence. The cultural crises of 1941 and 535 were just parallel enough for the one to resonate to an account of the other. Twenty-six years later the counterculture seemed to be sweeping all before it, terrifying an older generation with a new style of dress, new attitudes toward sex, its radical politics, and its discovery of LSD. America was apparently going insane: the protest movements had become violent; the Vietnam adventure was treated as an obscenity; even minimal faith had been lost in the institutions of government. Brunner, writing brilliantly from this moment, projected a future in which lines of social and political division already evident were combined with ecological near-disaster, even greater intrusion into private lives, and faint indications of hope that solutions would be found, if anywhere, in Africa and the East, echoing the interest the counterculture was then showing in Eastern religions. The two writers looked backward and forward to other years, but they were looking with minds shaped by the news sources of their day.

This is not unique to pulp fiction, of course. Historians assure us that all the stories from the past carry in them explicit and implicit references to the newspaper realities of their own times. There is some reason to think that pulp fiction is more closely tied to its own times than other forms of fiction, however—so closely tied, in some cases, that it has trouble freeing itself from its own times.

We are already reading *Lest Darkness Fall* and *Stand on Zanzibar* from inside a different newspaper reality, and they are already losing their power to entertain. Our grandchildren will find these stories as puzzling as we find stories from the last century that told about young immigrants working their way to honest wealth and about ministers torn with doubt by science. Future generations of readers will be eavesdropping. Only our generation can actually hear these stories.

Literary Reality

The stories are part of our generation's dialogue with itself about current events but also about the honored past. Readers in 2089 will have no more interest in these stories than we have in the dime novels of 1889, of course, but scholars in 2089 will insist that though in turning to the paperbacks we seemed to be turning away from literature we were in fact evincing our continuing interest in it.

Paperback writers read good books, too: that ought to be kept in mind. It was not the newspapers that got them started on careers that, contrary to all myth, are usually ill-paid. Perhaps because we are always comparing their books unfavorably to the best of the past, they are always referring to the books that came before. If in some selective catastrophe all evidence of formal literary criticism were to disappear, our grandchildren could reconstruct literary reality as we know it merely through references in paperbacks to what we have begun lately to call the *literary canon*.

Like all writers, paperback writers too sometimes groan under the burden of the past. George Alec Effinger's "Ghost Writer" tells of a future in which writers can tune into the past and make brief contact with the minds of such masters as Shakespeare and Defoe, and bring some of their lost words into that far-distant present; though they do not know it, they are cousins of the *rhapsodes* Socrates questioned in the *Ion*. The most popular of these writers confesses that he has been writing his own materials and only pretending to make contact with the past: his horrified audience does away with him.

We will examine the paperback's quarrel with high literature in the two genres where we least expect to find it: in the western and in science fiction. Benjamin Capps's *Trail to Ogalalla* is a western talking back to Melville. One of the cowhands, the Professor, is a former schoolteacher working now on a cattle drive. "He rode beside the string of cattle as it wound about among the hills and occupied his mind with a whimsy. He had read Melville's *Moby-Dick* several times, and it pleased him to compare man's mastery of whales with man's mastery of longhorn cattle" (45). He half-seriously compares the weight of a whale with the weight of the cattle and decides that the herd is the equal of twelve whales, one for each member of the crew, that it will be driven 1,800 miles, and that each drover will ride three or four times that far circling the herd and chasing cattle. Capps explains that these are not the contented cows of nursery stories.

> So the herd was mixed. . . . The precise mixture, the unpredictable mixture, that the herd turned out to be would have been appreciated by no one. It was mixed with more than females and castrated males. Some of them were hill cattle out of the Balcones Escarpment; others had been born in the bush much farther south. Some of them, frightened by loboes or a panther, would have run for cover in the brush; others would have headed for open ground. And their blood was mixed, in the individual and in the herd. Some of them were obviously Spanish or Moorish, some even pure black of the strain that makes fighting bulls; these were fierce with keen horns. Others were Mexican cattle, identified farther north as "Texas longhorns," themselves a mixture of big oxen and the smaller fighting cattle from the old world, but a mixture that had grown wild and primitive in the new world, a reversion to ancestors so ancient that they did not

. . . .

admit the dominion of man. The cattle were of all ages within the
limits of the contract. The young heifers were also fierce and quick,
with bright, suspicious eyes.   (46)

The Professor is unimpressed by Melville's account of the dangers of the
whale hunt. "'And note, Ishmael, no blubber. It's all horn and rawhide,
lean muscle, sinew, bone. No, you soft fellows can go whaling, Ishmael,
but we who are tough, who love hard work and a hard life . . .'" (47). In
one sense, the Professor is absurd. What makes *Moby-Dick* distinctive is
the epic response of Melville to the whale hunt, not the whale hunt itself.
In another sense, the Professor is dead on the money. For though the cattle
drive and the whale hunt disappeared at about the same time, the whale
hunt left no fictional tradition behind—there is no whale-hunt genre. The
image of the cattle drive, however, is still charged with enough energy to
foster hundreds of stories in the twentieth century. Capps's book—a good
book—is not the equal of Melville's, but his quarrel with a great writer
is valid.

We all recognize these quarrels with the past, though they are not
inevitably so explicit as this one. Less evident—and not apparent at
all to the occasional reader—is the interplay inside the genres, which
is more important. To the experienced reader, there is not a page in a
new paperback that does not echo, answer, vary (or, sometimes, fatally
ignore) pages written earlier. Everything that occurs within an intensely
self-conscious, self-referential, and aggressively literary subculture has
its exact parallel in paperback fiction.

In John Varley's "Persistence of Vision," a drifter falls by chance upon
a commune whose members are deaf and blind. They are the human
detritus of a rubella epidemic, but it is likely that the Thalidomide horrors
lie somewhere in the background of the fictional situation. The young
man discovers that the deaf and the blind, freed from dependence upon
their eyes and ears, have developed a rich physical, intellectual, and
spiritual life.

It is a piece of its time, this story, with young men wandering aimlessly
in search of meaning and with a commune finding happiness; but it is also
a reply to H. G. Wells's "Country of the Blind," published eighty-three
years earlier. In that story a young man falls into an Andean valley and

finds a blind people who have managed to devise a satisfactory life and have even developed a philosophical and scientific explanation for events they do not understand. Wells's young man finds that his sight gives him no advantage, that his claims are disbelieved, and that he will be permitted to stay only if the tumors—his eyes—are removed. He chooses to climb and die on the heights. Wells's story, sometimes misread, is a parable of the talented living among the untalented who cannot credit the existence of gifts they do not share.

Varley's wanderer leaves, but he is unable to find peace and so returns. A friend tells him that the people he knew best are gone. They have disappeared into some other form of existence by means she cannot understand or explain; they were deeply happy. He is certain he has lost his chance at Brigadoon. But this story ends differently. His friend takes pity on him.

> "I will give you a gift."
> She reached up and lightly touched my ears with her cold fingers. The sound of the wind was shut out, and when her hands came away it never came back. She touched my eyes, shut out all the light, and I saw no more.
> We live in the lovely quiet and dark. (272)

Whatever the sequence in which we come across the two stories, they end up talking to one another in our minds, for the question is not so easily settled as Wells's story proposed. And that, of course, is what Varley intended. For, as every reader of these stories knows, paperback stories are not self-sufficient, monumental. Wells's story is simple enough; Varley's story is simple. Neither story is much of anything in itself, but it does not stand by itself. When a group of writers are working successfully against and off one another, the simple stories they write create something larger, something which may be monumental. James Gunn once suggested that in order to understand science fiction it was enough to read about one hundred books. That seems about right. Some of the fun comes immediately, with the first book—if that is a happy selection—but most of the pleasure for experienced readers lies in listening to the stories talk to one another. As readers of westerns recognized, Benjamin Capps's *Trail*

. . . .

to Ogalalla is an answer to Melville's *Moby-Dick* but is also an answer to a genre classic: Andy Adams's *Log of a Cowboy*, published half a century earlier. In that competition, it comes off very well indeed, complementing though not replacing Adams's fine novel.

This aspect of paperback fiction is not given sufficient attention. Its interplay with the art of the past is pervasive. Roger Zelazny's "For a Breath I Tarry" offers a science-fiction variation on the story of Satan's efforts in the book of Job. It is a new treatment which draws some of its power from our familiarity with Job and with the prologue to Goethe's *Faust*. Zelazny frequently uses situations drawn from the reading he did during his graduate studies in literature. His *Lord of Light*, for instance, offers a variation on demonic possession in which the demon protests that he is being corrupted by his victim. The victim has acquired a taste for cruelty, but the demon has developed pangs of conscience. In Cordwainer Smith's prologue to *Space Lords*, a collection of five of his stories, Smith explicitly identifies his inspirations. One story is a reinvention of the story of Ali Baba and the forty thieves, another is "a rendition of the true narrative of Joan of Arc," a third—"Drunk Boat"—is "a rendition of some of the life and experience of Arthur Rimbaud," a fourth is "loosely inspired by some of the magical and conspiratorial scenes in *The Romance of Three Kingdoms*," and the fifth is a science-fiction recreation of scenes from Dante's *Inferno* (224). De Camp's *Lest Darkness Fall*, examined earlier in connection with 1941 newspaper reality, is also a tacit comment on Mark Twain's *Connecticut Yankee in the Court of King Arthur*.

We see all of this fear, love, rivalry, resentment—this brooding awareness of our literary past—captured in a single image taken from another western, Williams Forrest's *White Apache*. We are following the flight of a band of Apaches, and we are in the hands of a skillful craftsman working in the bent-twig school of the western.

> The immediate back trail was narrow because they had passed single file, Tesca in the lead; and she led well. It was comparatively simple for him to erase signs for the last few miles, those leading from the stone and water to the initial ascent of the mountain. Because the horses were unshod or shod with leather, there were no chips on rocks, and Tesca had avoided most of the vegetation except in

the places where that was impossible. And then all of them had moved their horses in a sideways manner, so that stems bent but did not break. This was of great importance. A broken stem could not be remedied; it had to be carefully removed, and even so, an experienced reader of signs would know if he used enough patience. Stems of branches that pointed your way must be coaxed back into position or, that failing, made to point in the opposite direction. A wound on a tree or bush must be transformed into the act of an animal, and this was done by biting or scratching.

Forrest describes Blanco's study of the earth disturbed by the horses and his blowing of dust into the cuts left by the hooves, but Blanco's job is not finished.

After he had done with the back trail, his task became more difficult. Although at a distance the mountain seemed fairly bald, the scrub at a higher level was not spaced so far apart as it had been farther down. This is why Tesca and the girls had moved apart and made individual trails. If three had gone through the same spaces, the damage would have been irreparable.

Blanco found himself remolding three trails back to the state in which wind, sun, and animals had left them. He knew the design that everything should take. If on brush there were signs that small animals passed there, then he had to bend the brush so that it made a tunnel. No small animal, vulnerable to things on wing or foot, would move into unguarded light. Once he had to redraw with his fingers the horse-broken passage of a snake. He plucked horsehair where he found it and placed it in a piece of cloth torn from his clout.

(106–7)

We all know who is following Blanco, the white boy raised as an Apache. He may think it is the cavalry, but it is the Deerslayer, Natty Bumppo. And we know who is following the writer. It is James Fenimore Cooper's *Leatherstocking Tales* that Forrest—and we—hear behind us on the back trail.

. . . .

. . . . . Experienced Reality

Travis McGee has located a witness, in John D. MacDonald's *Cinnamon Skin*, and has stopped at her house trailer to talk to her. There is a large, four-wheel-drive Bronco parked in the yard, and Travis and his friend must park in the road. Most of us give more of our time to Hawthorne and Blake and Spenser than we do to MacDonald, but where in their books, or in any others written before our century, could we find this scene?

I parked beyond her mailbox and we got out and stood there, stunned by the profusion of junk that filled the yard from fence to fence. Car parts, refrigerators, cargo trailers without wheels, stove-wood, rolls of roofing paper, bed frames, broken rocking chairs, broken deck furniture, piles of cinder block, piles of roof tiles, a stack of full sheets of plywood, moldering away. Glass bottles, plastic bottles, cans, fenders, old washing machines, fencing wire, window frames, 55-gallon drums rust red, an old horse-drawn sleigh, crates of empty soft drink bottles, and many other bulky objects which did not seem to have had any useful purpose ever. The scene stunned the mind. It was impossible to take it all in at once. In a strange way it had an almost artistic impact, a new art form devised in three dimensions to show the collapse of western civilization. It made me think of an object I had seen in New York when a woman persuaded me to go with her to an exhibition at the Museum of Modern Art. That object was a realistic-looking plastic hamburger on a bun with an ooze of mustard, pickle, and catsup. It was ten feet in diameter and stood five feet high. This scene had that same total familiarity plus unreality. (48–49)

The scene is familiar—it is part of the image of reality we create from the data of raw experience—and while we do find analogues in Dickens (though not earlier, I think), it is the intricacy of "quotation" that intrigues us, as it did MacDonald. The yard quotes randomly from our culture (the sleigh, the car parts, the refrigerator), and MacDonald joins in by quoting—as low culture never did before—from high culture, from our own Museum of Modern Art. It is a scene from our times perceived as our times perceives. Almost against our will we find ourselves giving it an inverted reading. Like hundreds of other paragraphs, it seems to comment on pulp fiction itself, which also quotes from the full range of our culture. Renaissance theorists would have said that John D. MacDonald is holding up one of our mirrors—the genre of the thriller—to our life and reflecting also in that mirror another mirror—a pop art object. It is a commonplace that the best novels of our time help us see our lives more clearly. If our paperbacks were not doing that also, we would not be finding pleasure in them.

We have space for one more example of this reflection of our own reality. This is an instance of what the Russian formalists called "defamiliarization," of making the familiar visible by making it strange.

Consider the superhighway. The limited-access, divided-lane highway first appeared in the early 1940s in Germany and in America. (The Pennsylvania Turnpike and the Merritt Parkway were completed in 1941, the Reichsautobahnen in 1942.) Our ancestors knew all about roads and even highways; but they did not know automobiles and superhighways. We know them so well we can no longer see them freshly and have to have them reinvented for us in books. Because no era but our own has known what it is to drive on a superhighway, no time but our own could have produced Roger Zelazny's *Road Marks*. It gives us a superhighway, but it is more than that. Zelazny's superhighway is simultaneously a science-fiction conceit, a joke, and an interpretation. "Red Dorakeen was on a quiet section of the Road, straight and still as death and faintly sparkling. A pair of futuristic vehicles had passed him several hours earlier, moving at fantastic speeds, and he had later overtaken a coach-and-four and then a solitary horseman. He kept his blue Dodge pickup in the right-hand lane and maintained a steady 65 mph. He chewed his cigar and hummed" (4). It is apparently a road through, or outside, time—we are not certain: " 'I do not know whether there are parallel futures, but I do know that there are many pasts leading up to that time from which I have come. Not all of them are accessible. The sideroads have a way of reverting to wilderness when there are none to travel them. Do you not know that Time is a super-highway with many exits and entrances, main routes and secondary roads, that the maps keep changing, that only a few know how to find the access ramps?'" (45). Perhaps some of us have driven across or under it without recognizing it. Perhaps we have just never turned at the right moment. "The Road," Red explains, "is an organic thing"; and the creatures who made it find it funny to watch "the few who have noted it as they scramble along from probability to probability" (131).

This is science fiction amusing itself with an idle play on the familiar, but the Road is not so very different from our own superhighways. Reading about the Road, we abruptly recognize that we do time jumps, too. We can leave the highway in Iowa and find ourselves in a town straight out of the 1930s or in Arkansas and find ourselves in the 1920s. The distinction between clock time and mind time is unmistakable, and Zelazny has caught that nicely. Nothing has been quite like this in our past: not canal-boat travel, not steamboat travel, not railroad travel, and certainly not travel by horse on the mud-or-dust roads of the nineteenth century.

A heavier-handed writer would have frozen the road into a metaphor for Time or for Life or for who knows what; but Zelazny does not lose control. Whatever it looks like to the dragons that made it as part of the games they play sleepily with one another, for its travelers and for us it is a road, and we are prepared, too, to recognize that if our kinds of people came upon this road some of them would take professional advantage of it, as Red discovers when he meets in ancient Ur a research archaeologist from the 1980s who claims he is between jobs. We cannot guess why; he would certainly not lose in the tenure battles.

"What are you doing in Ur?"

"I'm from these parts originally, and I'm between jobs just now. Thought I'd come back and visit the folks and set up some more work for myself."

He nodded toward the corner, where several burlap sacks leaned against the wall.

"What sort of work?" Red asked, lowering his crock and wiping his mouth.

"Oh, about sixty C's up the Road I'm an archaeologist. Every now and then I come back to bury a few things. Then I go forward and dig

them up again. I've already written the paper on this batch, actually.
It's a pretty interesting piece on cultural diffusion. I've got some
really nice artifacts from Mohenjo-Daro this time around."   (184)

We know that archaeologist is lying. If he were from Ur, he'd be bringing aspirin back for his family, or cheap, machine-made perfections to
trade. His mind, like ours and Zelazny's, was created in the context of
twentieth-century research activity. Even the people of the nineteenth
century, who transformed research into a profession and were just as dishonest as we are, would not have understood his easiness with his own
dishonesty. For better or worse: our kind of road, our kind of people.

Human Reality

Readers and writers agree—too quickly, I think—that the
people in paperback fiction are simply drawn. Jacques Barzun and Wendell Hertig Taylor face the charge directly in their excellent *Catalogue of
Crime:* "Some readers report that the reason the genre fails to hold their
interest is its 'lack of reality.' They mean by this: truth of character and
depth of motive" (7). Barzun and Taylor are treating this familiar complaint with more respect than it deserves. Readers' interest in fictional
characters does not depend upon their complexity. (We find little evidence
of an interest in complex characterization in Aristotle or in Horace or in
Longinus or in the critics of the Renaissance, for instance. An explicit
interest in "well rounded" characters does not begin to appear until the
Romantics begin writing about poetry and drama and fiction.) It seems to
be the construction of complexity which, in some queer way, is at issue.
Some readers are committed so strongly to one image of the human character that they reject an alternate image. The novel and the tale differ in
the manner in which they create characters, as becomes evident when we
place stories from two different traditions side by side. Almost any two
roughly similar stories will do. I shall examine two spy stories: Joseph
Conrad's *Secret Agent* and John Le Carré's *Tinker, Tailor, Soldier, Spy.*

Conrad's Mr. Verloc is a spy, and so is Le Carré's George Smiley.
George Smiley is as fallibly human as Conrad's Mr. Verloc: he loves

his compulsively unfaithful wife, he reads German poetry, he has moral commitments often at odds with his work. If anything, he is more complex than Conrad's Mr. Verloc, yet we do not think of him as coming from the tradition of the novel.

Bill Russell of the Boston Celtics used to insist that he was not a basketball player, that he was a man who played basketball. George Smiley is a spy; Conrad's Mr. Verloc is a man who works as a spy. Mr. Verloc would not be greatly different if he left spying for another job. We easily imagine his doing so, for he seems more at home selling pornographic miscellanea than as a foreign agent. George Smiley, however, is a spy first and foremost: what makes him more interesting than other paperback spies is the fact that he happens also to be a man like the rest of us. He is human, then; we grant him that, but we cannot imagine George Smiley as anything but a spy. We can imagine him as a teacher, but only as an unemployed spy who needed temporary money. We can even imagine him spying against England, but we cannot imagine him separately from spying. Mr. Verloc is a man whose job ends his domestic happiness and costs him his life; he is destroyed by his job. George Smiley is a man whose domestic life interferes with his work; he is first and always a professional.

Having said that Mr. Verloc is larger than his role as spy, have we said that there is less truth of character in George Smiley? Probably not. Most of our connections with one another are by virtue of our roles: teacher-student, doctor-patient, lawyer-client, writer-reader, colleague-colleague, and so forth. Always, our relationships transcend our temporary role identities, and we trust that not one of us can be defined as nothing more than the assemblage of all the roles that individual plays; but role identities are fundamental social realities for urban humanity. Almost everything we say and do to one another is strictly or loosely governed by role responsibilities. Almost all conversations occur because a role relationship has emerged. How many people would any of us speak with if it were not that some bit of business—a role relationship—has to be conducted? The tale—paperback fiction—begins with this truth and creates characters from role identities to give us the spy humanized (as in Graham Greene's *Human Factor*), the sheriff with arthritis (John M. Cunningham's "Tin Star"), and the burglar who studied Spinoza (Block).

And, of course, it begins with the recognition of just the roles that we, its contemporaries, identify. That is why we find in George Smiley his own, though different, truth of character.

And while the tale in its purest form does deal in simple characters, writers of tales rarely are satisfied with that. They include complex characters. Such a character is the Lord Gro. E. R. Eddison's *Worm Ouroboros* is in the tradition of the tale, a story of high heroism competing with high villainy. Caught in all this stylish action and thought on both sides is the Lord Gro, a man who puzzles both the heroes and the villians. Gro is to villainy what Huckleberry Finn was to Tom Sawyer's stylish schemes. He is an ally of the villains, the Witches (the reader of this tale needs a certain patience with Eddison's elaborately archaic diction), but the Witches do not know what to make of him. When one of them asks how they might triumph over the well-fortified Demons, Gro offers a characteristically nasty scheme. " 'Bid Juss to a parley. Offer him conditions: it skills not what. Bribe them out into the open. . . . Shall the King blame us though we sign away Demonland, ay and the wide world besides, to Juss to lure him forth? Unless indeed we were so neglectful of our interest as suffer him, once forth, to elude our clutches' " (175). But the villain he is advising is appalled. There is an ethic even in villainy, and he scorns the tactic. Gro's suggestions are so treacherously efficient that we are surprised, in spite of some earlier hints, when he switches from the side of the villains to the side of the heroes precisely at the moment when villainy seems sure to triumph. He explains himself. " 'It hath been present to my heart how great an advantage we held against the Demons, and the glory of their defence, so little a strength against us so many and the great glory of their flinging of us back, these things were a splendour to my soul beholding them. Such glamour hath ever shone to me all my life's days when I behold great men battling still beneath the bludgeonings of adverse fortune that, however they be mine enemies, it lieth not in my virtue to withhold from admiration of them and well nigh love' " (187–88). Now fighting with the Demons, the heroes, against his former allies and friends, he kills one of the Witches, and a former villain-friend protests.

Corund, when he saw it, heaved up his axe, but changed his intention in the manage, saying, "O landskip of iniquity, shalt thou

. . . .

kill beside me the men of mine household? But my friendship sitteth
not on a weather vane. Live, and be a traitor."

But Gro, being mightily moved with these words, and staring at
great Corund wide-eyed like a man roused from a dream, answered,
"Have I done amiss? 'Tis easy remedied." Therewith he turned about
and slew a man of Demonland.   (471)

A Demon runs him through on the instant, and he dies, leaving behind
him the name of traitor to both sides. But he had earlier spoken his
own epitaph, and it is in this way that we readers remember him. " 'And
who dares call me turncoat, who do but follow now as I have followed
this rare wisdom all my days: to love the sunrise and the sundown and
the morning and the evening star? since there only abideth the soul of
nobility, true love, and wonder, and the glory of hope and fear' " (366).
Lord Gro is not unusual. An experienced reader could list a hundred
characters equally vivid and humanly strange. Here is Anthony Boucher
on Margaret Millar's *Beast in View:* "It is a pure terror-suspense-mystery
story, complete with murder, detective and surprise twist. But it is also
so detailedly convincing a study in abnormal psychology, so admirably
written with such complete realization of every character, that the most
bitter antagonist of mystery fiction may be forced to acknowledge it as
a work of art" (qtd. in Bargainnier 224). Gro appears in a tale, a story
which works with role figures, with types; but Gro himself is not simple.

Nor, I think, is he a man of, and for, the ages. Earlier readers would not
have understood him, but we do because he is all around us. We disapprove of trickiness and treachery among human beings, but they are the
pure technician's chief weapons when he sets out to outwit Mother Nature
for us, which is why we have airplanes, microscopes, and computers.
And Gro manifests the pure technician's utter bafflement at the strange
ways of other human beings. Who does not know someone like Gro?

Still, we would agree, I think, that the paperback traditions are loved
not least precisely because they are so marvelously inventive in the creation of the sharply etched character. In "Literature and Psychology,"
Jung says that the characters are modern versions of ancient gods and
heroes. Here is a character from the mind of Ross Macdonald whom Jung
would have recognized.

The houseman came up close to me and smiled. His smile was
wild and raw like a dog's grin, and meaningless except that it meant
trouble.

He invited violence as certain other people invite friendship.

(Margolies 79)

In Neolithic caves, our ancestors were meeting these people.

Our epoch—like every other epoch—gives its own nuance to these ancient shapes, however. Nineteenth-century moralists worried about books
and the moral fiber of women. Heroines were not allowed to guess that
their wicked Uncle Jack had a private library. Presumably, if they had
found the library their fates would have been sealed: death by spontaneous
combustion. Our heroines are a bit more complex.

In Ross Thomas's *Eighth Dwarf*, Minor Jackson has been making investigations for a properly brought-up young Jewish woman, Leah Oppenheimer, still a virgin, who writes and speaks in clichés drawn from early-
twentieth-century romantic fiction. Jackson finds her prose tiring, but he
is too nice a person to say anything. It is 1946, and while searching in
Berlin for her lost brother, the two go out for what Jackson thinks of as
merely a dinner but what the young woman excitedly calls her first date.
We are not surprised that in a story written in 1979 they should end
the evening in bed. But then Jackson is surprised: she is a remarkable
performer. She asks if she was clumsy.

"You weren't clumsy at all. You were very—inventive."
That also pleased her. "You're sure? You're not just saying so?"
"I'm sure. That thing you did with the ribbon."
"You didn't like it."
"No, it was fine. Quite a sensation. Somebody once told me it
was the specialty of a Mexican whorehouse he'd once spent a little
time in."
"Was I like a whore? I tried so hard to be."

While he is waiting until his breath quiets enough so he can light a
cigarette, he asks how she learned these intricacies. She explains that
she learned from books.

"My father rented this villa from a man, and it had a library. There was one glass case that was kept locked. I found the key. The books were all written in English, but they had been written a long time ago —in the 1890's, I think, because everybody went about in hansom cabs. They were mostly stories about what men and women do to each other. I read them aloud to myself sometimes because I thought it would be good for my English. Some of them were very exciting. Occasionally, when they would do something really interesting to each other, I would make a note about it in my diary."

"For future reference."

She nodded solemnly. "I thought if I were ever to get married, it would please my husband. Of course, we did not do all that I read about."

"We didn't?"

"No, there are many other things. Some of them, I think, are very strange. Do you like strange things?"

"Sometimes."

"Do you want to do this with me again?"

"Very much."

"I was not sure. You will be going to Bonn, of course—you and Mr. Ploscaru."

"Tomorrow."

She frowned—a puzzled, earnest sort of frown. "Do you think they have little whips in Bonn?"

"I have no idea," Jackson said.   (207–9)

We remember that the story of Lancelot brought Dante's Francesca into adulterous union with Paolo—"That day we read no further"—and both of them, ultimately, into the second circle of hell. Our own Leah Oppenheimer's reading brought a blush to her maidenly cheek, but she used the occasion for self-improvement. What would William Dean Howells have said? And Anthony Comstock: all his worst fears confirmed. His body cannot be easy in its still-honored grave.

Philip K. Dick and Roger Zelazny have a scene in their science-fiction novel, *Deus Irae*, that is about being a writer, surely; but it is about being alive at any passing moment in history, too.

He thought then of a thought which had buffeted him for years. A picture of a creature, some kind of fairly small furred animal. The animal, silently and alone, at its burrow, would build gay and complex oddities, which eventually, when there were enough, it at last carried to a nearby road. There it would set up shop, spreading out on each side of it the things it had made. It sat there in silence all day, waiting for someone to come along and buy one of the things it had made. Time would pass; afternoon would disappear into evening; the world would darken. But the creature had not sold any of its creations. At last, in the glooming, it would wordlessly, meekly, gather up its oddities and go off with them, defeated, but voicing no complaint. Yet its defeat was total, despite the fact that the defeat came slowly, amid silence.   (141–42)

The scene is an image, also, of our epoch: our forms of criminal ingenuity, our quarrels with our literary canon, our genre dialogues, our superhighways, our technicians, our conscientious virgins. They are the inventions of and for this time only; our grandchildren will hardly acknowledge in them an antique charm. Paperback fiction recognizes these bits of our reality, and in recognizing them recognizes us. That is one of our reasons for turning to it in the tired hours of the day.

Why, then, since we do enjoy paperback and other popular fiction, since we do feel comfortable with it, since we do like it and like its liking us—why do we speak of it so depreciatively? Why do men feel that women who enjoy romances are weak of mind? Why do women feel that men who enjoy thrillers must be intellectually immature? Why do many of the women who enjoy the romances and many of the men who enjoy thrillers feel ashamed that they enjoy them? It is an ancient puzzle.

on low

taste

· · · · · · · · · · ·

*There is no one of critical ability who has not experienced
intense and profound pleasure from something simultaneously
with a low critical valuation of what produced it.*
—*Northrop Frye*, Anatomy of Criticism

Traditionally, we have divided readers of the novel into three
types. There are the discriminating few—the *serious readers*, who include
the reading of certain novels among the most important experiences in
their lives; there are the many—the *plain readers*, who seem to read only
what everyone else is reading; and there are the millions—the *paperback
readers*, who sometimes seem to be browsing on novels rather than reading
them. None of these readers feels anyone really understands him, but
none would object to the labels we are using.

We all see that this division is inexact; for one thing, the three bookscapes in which the serious, plain, and paperback readers are supposed
to be leading separate reading lives overlap. Still, the division is everywhere accepted, and readers do seem to identify themselves as principally
one or another of these three types. Some of the differences we recognize
are shown in the table. (I have taken some of the observations on the serious reader from C. S. Lewis's *Experiment in Criticism*, 1–5, and some of
those on the plain reader from the chapter on the best-selling social melodrama in John G. Cawelti's *Adventure, Mystery, and Romance*, 260–95.)

	Serious Reader	Plain Reader	Paperback Reader
Orientation	Reads by author	Reads by book	Reads by genre
Paradigmatic work	*Ulysses*	*The Godfather*	*I, the Jury*
Favored form	Experimental novel	Social melodrama	Thriller
Admired author	Italo Calvino	Sidney Sheldon	John D. MacDonald
Socializing	Writes about books	Chats about books	Reads alone
Expectations	Originality	Information	Gratification
Stimulus to read	A good review	Book club	Titles, covers
Writers' rewards	Fame	Money	Love

Some of the difficulties we encounter when making charts of this type—
however useful they may be—are evident in the item "Writers' rewards."
All writers want fame, money, and love, of course; but the serious writer
usually has to settle for fame alone; the plain writer, for money alone;
and the writer of junk fiction, for love alone. (The large financial rewards
come only to writers who are successful with plain readers.) The standard objection to this sort of charting of differences is that it is difficult to
locate any person who is purely and only either a serious reader or a plain
reader or a paperback reader, however. We certainly do find people talking as though they were one of these types, however, and as though they
were implacably opposed to every other. Here, for instance, is Benjamin
Walker writing in a cold rage about the sorts of degenerates who swell
the ranks of the readers of serious fiction. "There is also the higher class
of degenerate. Young men and women of this category win scholarships
and fill the universities. The chief faculty of the higher degenerate is
the excessive development of the speech centres in the cerebral cortex
that gives them an extraordinary facility with words. But though remarkably articulate they seldom have anything original to say"(57). Walker
is apparently so mistrustful of these higher degenerates that he would
be equally mistrustful of the sorts of stories they prefer: he would not,
perhaps, be patient enough to learn how to read them.

We cannot always be certain that people who condemn other reading
types mean everything they seem to be implying. Here, for example, is
Anthony Burgess writing of the inadequacies of science-fiction writers
and, by implication, their readers: "Certainly, in respect of the techniques
and insights of modernism, they cherish a peculiar blindness: there is not

one SF writer whom we would read for freshness or originality of his style" ("Apocalypse" 256). Burgess goes on to insist that "fiction is not about what happens to the world but what happens to a select group of human souls, with crisis or catastrophe as the mere pretext for an exquisitely painful probing, as in James, of personal agonies and elations." We infer from this essay that Burgess disapproves sharply of paperback fiction; but a year later (1984) we find him putting together his own selection of the best novels of the modern era and confessing that he does not confine his reading to serious fiction. He reads best-sellers and paperback fiction, too. "When I say that I have read a great number of novels for sheer pleasure, as opposed to cold-eyed professional assessment, I have to admit that some of these novels never stood a chance of being placed on my list. I am an avid reader of Irving Wallace, Arthur Hailey, Frederick Forsyth, Ken Follett and other practitioners of well-wrought sensational fiction" ("Modern Novels"). Burgess's distinction between his reading "for sheer pleasure" and his reading with "cold-eyed professional assessment" is curious. Presumably, the sentence was hastily struck off; it certainly encourages the inference that we do not read the best novels for pleasure —a suggestion that serious readers (and Burgess himself) would dismiss immediately.

In Burgess's personal acceptance of both a body of serious fiction and a body of popular fiction, we see a familiar incoherence in operational aesthetics: although we believe we know which is the better, we nevertheless choose what we believe is the worse. The people who read one of the three strands of fiction but refuse to read either of the others are intriguing in their own right, and we shall look at this sort of reading allergy in a later chapter. The people who feel one of these strands is better than the others but still do read the others are more interesting. The fact that readers as sophisticated as Burgess also read paperback fiction is a continuing warning against the oversimple explanation of its appeal.

Taste Incoherence

It is 1775, and Sheridan's Lydia Languish in *The Rivals* is preparing to entertain certain sharp-eyed visitors.

LYDIA. Here, my dear Lucy, hide these books. Quick, quick! Fling *Peregrine Pickle* under the toilet—throw *Roderick Random* into the closet—put *The Innocent Adultery* into *The Whole Duty of Man* —thrust *Lord Aimworth* under the sofa—cram *Ovid* behind the bolster—there—put *The Man of Feeling* into your pocket—so, so— now lay *Mrs. Chapone* in sight, and leave *Fordyce's Sermons* open on the table.

LUCY. O burn it, Ma'am! the hair-dresser has torn away as far as *Proper Pride.*

LYDIA. Never mind—open at *Sobriety.* Fling me *Lord Chesterfield's Letters.* Now for 'em.

Lydia, alas, had low taste: she read novels. Or, at least, her contemporaries felt she had low taste. Sometimes low taste successfully redefines itself as good taste over time; twentieth-century Lydia Languishes are more likely to hide *Fordyce's Sermons* and put *Roderick Random* on display. They would certainly rather be caught reading Smollett's novel than, say, a romance by Barbara Cartland.

It is tiresome for us always to be returning to the Greeks when we begin asking ourselves fundamental questions about good and bad, high and low taste; but they formulated our kinds of questions with a directness that allows us to see the problem clearly. Plato turned his mind to the question of differences in response in book 2 of his *Laws.* He asked himself the question we still have not answered, "Are beautiful things not the same to us all, or are they the same in themselves, but not in our opinion of them?" He spoke about his contemporaries' different responses to the dance. "Choric movements are imitations of manners, and the performers range over all the various actions and changes of life with characterization and mimicry; and those to whom the words, or songs, or dances are suited either by nature or habit or both, cannot help feeling pleasure in them and applauding them, and calling them beautiful. But those whose natures or ways, or habits are unsuited to them, cannot delight in them or applaud them, and they call them base." We cannot prevent ourselves taking pleasure in some dances (or books) and so we applaud them; we cannot find a way to take pleasure in others and so we dismiss them. Whether it is nurture, nature, or both that have made us what we are, these responses are unselfconscious, immediate. "There are others, again, whose natures are right and their habits wrong, or whose habits are right and their natures wrong, and they praise one thing, but are pleased at another. For they say that all these imitations are pleasant, but not good. And in the presence of those whom they think wise, they are ashamed of dancing and singing in the baser manner, in a way which would indicate deliberate approval; and yet, they have a secret pleasure in them" (220–21). Well, we recognize those others. They are the aesthetic pretenders. They secretly like one thing but praise something that gives them no pleasure. And they know better: they are embarrassed when those they think wise find them enjoying themselves in the baser manner.

We are not shocked when we see others praising one kind of book and taking secret pleasure in another, for we are all experienced in the observation of hypocrisy. We do become confused when we uncover it in ourselves, when we hear ourselves giving public approval to books in which we have little interest and public disapproval to books that please us greatly, or when we find ourselves reaching past the book we know is good for the book we know is poorer. We will all generously admit to being complex; we deny we are hypocritical. Are we hypocritical if we allow others to suppose we enjoy reading Milton when the truth is that we prefer reading Ian Fleming's James Bond stories? Are we aesthetically confused if we do thoroughly enjoy Milton but enjoy the westerns of Louis L'Amour also?

How unusual is the serious reader who deeply enjoys pulp fiction as well? Whenever and wherever there has been a division recognized between serious and popular culture, the serious reader has probably always participated quietly but deeply in popular culture.

We misread Sir Philip Sidney's *Defense of Poesie* of 1594, from two centuries before Sheridan, if we suppose that the author was stoutly declaring his loyalty to England's traditional balladry when he said he loved the ballad *Chevy Chase:* "Certainly (I must confess my own barbarousness) I never heard the old song of Percy and Douglas that I found not my heart moved more than with a trumpet, and yet is it sung by some blind crowder with no rougher voice than rude style" (29). It was not for two hundred years that *Chevy Chase* would come to be venerated. Sidney— very much the serious, intellectual poet of his day—was confessing that he loved popular poetry.

The Middle Ages was familiar with the duality of serious/unserious taste to which Anthony Burgess confessed. In *Popular Culture in Early Modern Europe*, Peter Burke shows that medieval participants in the learned traditions also participated in the unlearned traditions.

> There were two cultural traditions in early modern Europe, but they did not correspond symmetrically to the two main social groups, the elite and the common people. The elite participated in the little tradition, but the common people did not participate in the great tradition. This asymmetry came about because the two traditions were transmitted in different ways. The great tradition was transmitted formally at grammar schools and at universities. It was a closed tradition in the sense that people who had not attended these institutions, which were not open to all, were excluded. In a quite literal sense, they did not speak the language. The little tradition, on the other hand, was transmitted informally. It was open to all, like the church, the tavern and the market-place, where so many of the performances occurred.
>
> Thus the crucial cultural difference in early modern Europe (I want to argue) was that between the majority, for whom popular culture was the only culture, and the minority, who had access to the great tradition but participated in the little tradition as a second culture. They were amphibious, bi-cultural, and also bilingual. Where the majority of people spoke their regional dialect and nothing else, the elite spoke or wrote Latin or a literary form of the vernacular, while remaining able to speak in dialect as a second or third language. (28)

We are perhaps not so very different. There are traditions we learn in the schools and others we learn informally, by word of mouth, by example. (We would want to be a bit cautious about using the words *little* and *great*, though. American jazz in the early twentieth century was transmitted informally, but it was not in any diminishing sense a "little" tradition.) We still find the learned participating in the unlearned traditions. At Christmas festivities, at the great national horse race (the Grand National, the Kentucky Derby), at the World Cup or World Series, at the Indianapolis 500, the learned are not always smallest of voice and dimmest of eye.

The awareness of popular culture appears incidentally in serious reflection. Here is Clive James in the *New York Review of Books* on the editors of a fine scholarly study of the photographer Eugene Atget: "Together, they have performed prodigies of research, but one expects no less. Less predictable was the way Szarkowski, while diving around among all this visual wealth like Scrooge McDuck in Money Barn No. 64, has managed to keep his critical balance, something that a man with his capacity for enthusiasm does not always find easy." James's reference to Carl Barks's delightful *Donald Duck* comic books gives precisely the simile needed, suggesting the visual arts, hoarded treasure, an apparently methodless porpoising—and with just enough humor in that slant analogy to save the reviewer's own enthusiasm from lapsing into uncritical awe. And here is Michael Roaf, Research Fellow at Wolfson College, Oxford, commenting in the *Times Literary Supplement* on a report of archaeological excavation: "The illusion of being in the realm of science fiction is increased by the melodramatic names of the places that Helms has coined—the Black Desert, *bilad ash-shaytan* (the country of the devil), the Road of the Rising Sun—and by the occasional Arabic words and place-names which bring Frank Herbert's *Dune* to mind." Neither reviewer felt their serious readers required a gloss on their references to popular fiction.

Of course! we say. Who makes any fuss today about the distinctions between high culture and low culture? Some do still keep what they no doubt perceive as the Faith. Not all publishers are ready to submit their authors—even the dead ones—to the humiliation of having their work mentioned by purveyors of pulp fiction. A science-fiction story written by Dean McLaughlin for the magazine *Analog* included a quotation from Hemingway's "Snows of Kilimanjaro" as an epigraph. McLaughlin requested permission from Hemingway's publishers, Charles Scribner's Sons, to use the passage. In a letter to *Locus* in March 1981, McLaughlin says that the editor of *Analog* announced that "Scribner's rights department had phoned him to assert that they did not want a quotation from

Hemingway to appear 'in a science fiction magazine.' " Apparently, while McLaughlin reads Hemingway, the people entrusted with Hemingway's fragile reputation do not read science fiction.

· · · · · · · **Paperbacks for the Learned**

Apparently the guardians of Hemingway's reputation do not reject with equal fervor all the forces that would corrupt. His work has appeared in *Ellery Queen's Mystery Magazine*, at least. And, according to a list that Dilys Winn quotes in her delightful *Murder Ink*, he is only one of the Nobel Laureates whose stories have been printed in that sturdy survivor from the tradition of the pulp magazines. Others are Heinrich Böll, Pearl Buck, T. S. Eliot, William Faulkner, John Galsworthy, Rudyard Kipling, Sinclair Lewis, Bertrand Russell, George Bernard Shaw, and William Butler Yeats (36). She also identifies some twenty-four winners of the Pulitzer Prize whose work appeared in the magazine.

There is little doubt that the writers of serious fiction and their readers do have an interest in some paperback fiction. This has not always been welcomed. T. J. Binyon, in a review of John M. Reilly's *Twentieth-Century Crime and Mystery Writers*, claims that the involvement of academics in the detective story is extensive. Plainly, he does not approve.

> There has always been a close link (much deprecated by observers such as Raymond Chandler) between the academic world and crime —especially detective—fiction. . . . University libraries are collecting the manuscripts of crime writers with the reckless abandon of drunken sailors. Princeton clutches to its bosom Helen MacInnes, Jack Iams, and S. S. Van Dine; the University of Wyoming at Cheyenne walks tall with the Nabokovian and dapperly Jamesian Ray Russell in its possession. Should it not be a cause for national concern that Michael Gilbert's manuscripts are at the University of California at Berkeley, and those of Julian Symons in the Humanities Research Center of the University of Texas? Mecca for future researchers, however, will be Boston, where the Mugar Memorial

Library houses the original manuscripts of no less than ten per cent of the writers included in [Reilly].

We associate that kind of disapproval with the gate guardians of literature, but Binyon reads and reviews detective stories himself. Apparently he is expressing the distress that some enthusiasts for paperback fiction feel when academics begin to move into their territory: pulp fiction has its gate guardians, too. This disapproval is worth special notice, for the serious readers who also read paperbacks must in some genres read against a sort of outward pressure that tells them they are not welcome.

There is nothing new about the serious writer's and the serious reader's interest in certain strands of pulp fiction. At the turn of the century, Arnold Bennett was writing both the serious novel and the "entertainment": *Anna of the Five Towns* and *The Old Wives' Tale* for himself and for other serious readers, and *The Card* and *The Loot of Cities* for himself and for other readers of light fiction. C. S. Lewis was successful both with the scholarly study (*The Allegory of Love*) and with science fantasy (*Out of the Silent Planet*). Paul Linebarger wrote academic papers in political history and a standard military text (*Psychological Warfare*), but he also wrote science fiction as Cordwainer Smith (*Norstrilia*). Robert B. Parker has a doctorate in English and writes novels (*Promised Land, Looking for Rachel Wallace*) about his highly literate detective Spenser, who tells his clients his name is spelled like the poet's and who may originally have been modeled on the Red Crosse Knight.

Some of the paperbacks seem to have been written primarily for serious readers, and it is not just the tale of detection that is addressing itself to readers who are comfortable with canonical and serious fiction. It is easy to misread Peter Beagle's *Last Unicorn*. Indeed, a brief summary of its fable might keep adults from reading it at all. A unicorn who has been living in a grove becomes lonely, discovers that all the other unicorns are gone, and sets out to find them. This sort of fantasy finds its most enthusiastic response among the kinds of readers who have read Tolkien's *Lord of the Rings* half a dozen times or more: adolescents especially, in my experience. That is, when we pick the book up we think we know who it is that might like that kind of story, but *The Last Unicorn* is not imitation Tolkien.

The unicorn meets a butterfly as soon as she sets off on her quest.

"Do you know what I am, butterfly?" the unicorn asked hopefully, and he replied, "Excellent well, you're a fishmonger. You're my everything, you are my sunshine, you are old and gray and full of sleep, you're my pickle-face, consumptive Mary Jane."

And the unicorn comments ruefully to herself:

You know better than to expect a butterfly to know your name. All they know are songs and poetry, and anything else they hear. They mean well, but they can't keep things straight. And why should they? They die so soon.

The butterfly swaggered before her eyes, singing, "One, two, three o'lairy," as he whirled; chanting, "Not, I'll not, carrion comfort, look down that lonesome road. For, oh, what damned minutes tell he o'er who dotes, yet doubts. Hasten, Mirth, and bring with thee a host of furious fancies whereof I am commander, which will be on sale for three days only at bargain summer prices. I love, I love you, oh, the horror, the horror, and aroint thee, indeed and truly you've chosen a bad place to be lame in, willow, willow, willow."   (10–11)

This exchange sets the thematic conflict dramatized by the action. The writer assumes his reader will recognize that a melange of Shakespeare, Milton, Yeats, and contemporary advertising prose has come together higgledy-piggledy in the mind of a creature who lives in the same stew of the trivial and the significant that all time-bound creatures know. The unicorn is timeless, of course.

In *The Last Unicorn*, Peter Beagle dramatizes a conflict that all humans know but that only serious writers and readers discuss directly. (Yeats's "Sailing to Byzantium" is the best-known brief treatment in modern English poetry.) This is that tension in our lives between the love of Beauty and the love of beauty, between Heroism and heroism, and so on. The conflict is not exclusively the concern of the educated. It is the conflict between a man's being in love with a Marilyn Monroe, say, and also being in love with his wife. His wife is getting older and putting on weight and is sometimes shrill and does *not* have a cunning way with sauces, but he is no longer quite sure whether she is his right arm or he is her right arm. For him, no woman can be more beautiful than Marilyn Monroe—but his wife is more beautiful. Meanwhile, his wife is having no trouble distinguishing between her husband and Robert Redford: her husband is the one without the vulgarity of good looks, intelligence, culture, talent, wealth, and charm; but she thinks she will probably stay around for a while. Popular songs tell us about our puzzlement at our own love for the less than ideal: "He's just my Bill," and so on. They do not explore the problem. Like Yeats, Beagle does, but solidly within the tradition of popular fantasy.

We do not have to infer an interest in the conflict between the ideal and the real from the action in *The Last Unicorn.* The characters themselves talk about the differences between the real and the ideal, and they compare themselves with the terrifying or grand images of the ideal that they evoke in others. A band of cold, dirty, hungry, discouraged forest outlaws (whose captain's chief ambition is to meet Francis J. Child, editor of *English and Scottish Popular Ballads*) is suddenly given a vision of Robin Hood and the Merry Outlaws of Sherwood Forest—in fact, the image they themselves will evoke in later generations—and the men cry out in anguish because they cannot be members of that idealized band. The half-comic magician, Schmendrick, concludes that though absolute Beauty is more beautiful than mortal beauty, only mortal beauty can be fully satisfying to mortals; he is content to be left with the slatternly Molly Grue rather than with the blindingly beautiful unicorn.

In *Einstein Intersection,* Samuel R. Delaney discusses the relations between Einstein's and Gödel's theories. This perhaps should not surprise us in a work of science fiction, though people allergic to that genre seem to suppose its interest in science is far simpler. Readers who come to it from the humanist tradition may be surprised when the book opens with epigraphs from Joyce's *Finnegans Wake* and Erasmus's *In Praise of Folly.* Delaney offers us an intriguing dramatic situation. We learn that the strange, shape-changing Earth creatures we follow are not human, that they are creatures who came to Earth after we left it and found that Earth is still governed by the patterns of human myth and that their bodies and personalities are being shaped by those myths even more decisively than by the laws of the physical universe. It is appropriate to add that the story was far from being regarded as an eccentricity: the Science Fiction Writers of America voted it the best novel of the year.

No one will attempt to equate the paperback genres with stories like that paperback fantasy *The Last Unicorn*, or that paperback science-fiction story *The Einstein Intersection*. If it were all that simple, we should have no difficulty at all explaining why so many readers of literature and of serious fiction do light reading as well.

The problem of the appeal of paperbacks to serious readers is seen best in works such as Peter O'Donnell's *Modesty Blaise*. This story—which apparently began as a comic strip—is in the tradition of John Buchan's *Thirty-Nine Steps* and the thrillers of E. Phillips Oppenheim. Stories like theirs feature high adventure, bizarre villains, international political crime, inventions that will freeze every drop of oil in England, and desperate gambles against all odds; and *Modesty Blaise* is squarely and unembarrassingly in that silly, sturdy tradition. It is very much of our time, though, for Modesty Blaise has the fighting skills normally reserved in this sort of story for men. Her lieutenant, Willie Garvin, admires her with the devotion of a courtier; he is not her lover. It is the only (or at least the first) successful presentation of a woman out-thinking and out-fighting her male underlings that does not make us feel that the men are thereby diminished.

We all know who reads that sort of thing, and we all know what that sort of person wants; a brisk opening, for instance. Here is the attention-compelling opening of *Modesty Blaise*.

> Fraser adjusted his spectacles to the angle which he knew would produce the effect of prim stupidity he favoured most. Running a finger down his nose, he stared obtusely at the open dossier in his hands.
>
> "I would suppose, sir," he said cautiously, "that Modesty Blaise might be a person awfully difficult for us—er—actually to get." He blinked towards the big grey-haired man who stood by the window, looking down at the night traffic hurrying along Whitehall.
>
> "For a moment," Tarrant said, turning from the window, "I hoped you might split that infinitive, Fraser."

"I'm sorry, Sir Gerald." Fraser registered contrition. "Another
time, perhaps."   (7)

What sort of novel begins with a man's narrow escape from a split in-
finitive? In this case, a novel about high adventure with bizarre villains.
That opening is an invitation directed to readers who enjoy stories about
attempts to steal shipments of diamonds worth ten million pounds and who
also enjoy stories in which infinitives are scrupulously protected: the kind
of people who are not put off by a science-fiction novel that opens with
a sentence from *Finnegans Wake* or by the traditional tale of detection
or by a paperback fantasy that insists upon brooding about the ideal and
the real.

The Badness of the Writing

One explanation for the serious reader's interest in this or
that strain of pulp fiction suggests itself: that the ultimate preoccupations
of paperbacks are indistinguishable from the ultimate preoccupations of
canonical and serious fiction.

Here are the five themes that the MLA (Modern Language Association)
identified in 1984 in its "Trends of Scholarly Publishing" as the themes
on which scholars who specialize in canonical literature are most often
writing. I attach the names of paperback genres that the themes bring
to mind.

death	the detective story
nature	the western.
religion	fantasy
love	the romance
time	science fiction

Such matchings are sometimes useful. The western is more resonant to
the theme of man in nature than is the detective story; science fiction,
more resonant to speculations on time than is the romance; and so on. A
western that concerns itself with love (Wister's *Virginian* has a love story)
is an antinomy, however welcome. So—the argument would continue—

the paperbacks attract serious readers because their thematic burdens are those that have always attracted thoughtful people. This claim cannot satisfy us, however, for people do not have to turn to the paperbacks for these themes: best-sellers and serious fiction concern themselves with those five major themes, too.

If we choose our books carefully (or luckily), a second answer will suggest itself. As stories like *The Last Unicorn* and *The Einstein Intersection* demonstrate, paperback fiction is much, much better than we have supposed it is. Some of the stories equal the best that serious writers give us. This claim is made by each genre's enthusiasts and especially by those passionate few who read in that genre exclusively. This second defense is very attractive, but it is based on an error—a subtle and dangerous error. It is predicated on a false assumption about the reading focus of a genre's followers—a matter I shall go into in a later chapter. The claim that the stories are excellent is also denied by the readers we are considering at the moment. The people who read both serious fiction and popular fiction say that the stories that come from the popular tradition are poorer.

And the writers of those books have a poorer opinion of those readers. As Binyon's impatience with the academic reader of the tale of detection suggests, some paperback writers lash out at serious and academic readers before the latter have a chance to be rude to them—preemptive insults, as it were. The writers of paperbacks are confident that serious readers despise them: as we saw in our brief consideration of "Ghost Writer," the story about a future in which some men and women are recovering the lost works of Swift and Shakespeare by sending their psyches backward in time, popular writers find it easy to suppose that originality can bring upon them the wrath of the critical establishment. The detective story—or at least the kind that calls itself the tale of detection—likes academics; but most paperback fiction mistrusts them and anyone else who reads serious fiction. For serious readers, to read in these traditions is rather like maintaining a cordial relationship with people who are always making it plain that they dislike you.

The stories really do not measure up to the standards that serious readers set for the other fiction they read. People who do not read in the paperback genres sometimes wonder whether readers who are faithful to them see how badly written the stories in these genres are. They do, of course. Paperback readers love to compare their inadvertently gathered collections of clumsiness and staleness of invention in their favorite genres. There is so much that serious readers find unintentionally funny and it is so much a part of reading these stories—and not just for the more sophisticated readers—that we shall be looking into the matter of clownish writing in the next chapter. Here, in anticipation, is John Sladek's long inventory of science-fiction clichés from Peter Nichols's *Science Fiction Encyclopedia*.

Sf cliché plots and plot devices are so numerous that any list must be incomplete. We have the feeble old nightwatchman left to guard the smouldering meteorite crater overnight ("Ill be all right, yessirree"); the doomed society of lotus-eaters; civilization's future depending upon the outcome of a chess game, the answer to a riddle, or the discovery of a simple formula ("a one-in-a-million chance, but so crazy, it just might work!"); the shape-shifting aliens ("One of us aboard this ship is not human"); invincible aliens ("the billion-megaton blast had no more effect than the bite of a Sirian flea"); alien invaders finally stopped by ordinary water (as in the films of both *The Day of the Triffids* and *The Wizard of Oz*); the android spouse who cuts a finger and bleeds machine oil; the spouse possessed or hypnotized by aliens ("Darling, you've been acting so strangely since your trip to Ganymede"); disguised alien sniffed out by "his" pet dog, who never acted this way before; destruction of giant computer brain by a simple paradox ("When is a door not a door?"); robot rebellion ("Yes, 'Master' "); a *Doppelgänger* in the corridors of time ("It was—himself!"); Montagues and Capulets living in parallel universes; the evil Master of the World stops to smirk before killing hero; everyone is controlled by alien mind-rays *except one man;* Oedipus kills great-great-grandad; world is saved by instant technology ("It may have looked like just a hunk of breadboard, a few widgets and wires —but wow!"); a youth-elixir—but at what terrible price?; thick-headed scientist tampers unwittingly with elemental forces better left in the hands of the Deity; immortality tempts Nature to a terrible revenge; monster destroys its creator; dying alien race must breed with earthling models and actresses; superior aliens step in to save

mankind from self-destruction (through H-bombs, pollution, fluori-
dation, decadence); Dr. X's laboratory (island, planet) goes up in
flames. . . .

Pulp can always be recycled.   (124)

(A small but excellent collection of inept and clichéd sentences from the
detective story appears in Barzun and Taylor's *Catalogue of Crime:* see
pages 450, 622, 700, and 722.) People who fiercely dislike any of the
popular genres find in a catalog of the genre's clownishness definitive
confirmation of their worst imaginings and may suppose that the compilers
of those catalogs share their feelings about that genre. We saw Sladek
himself end his list of clichés with a dismissive remark: "Pulp can always
be recycled." That genre's followers are not angry, however. They know
that none of us is born with the knowledge of what is and what is not a
cliché: we earn that knowledge. They know that no one can parody a genre
so well as one of its devoted followers, that a good catalog of clichés is
the precipitate of dozens, scores, hundreds, of stories. Anyone who puts
together a useful list of clichés has been reading steadily in that genre.
They may be wincing at every cliché, but they are reading onward, ever
onward, nevertheless.

Clichéd stories are merely silly, and we feel no worse than foolish when
we catch ourselves reading them. Sometimes the materials in paperbacks
are offensive. What else is one to say about E. C. Bentley's anti-Semitism
in the much-reverenced *Trent's Last Case?* Trent, Bentley's detective, is
talking as he enters his favorite restaurant: " 'This is the house of fulfill-
ment of craving, this is the bower with the roses around it. I see there are
three bookmakers eating pork at my favorite table. We will have that one
in the opposite corner' " (209). Readers—or at least some readers—recognized the snobbery, xenophobia, and smugness of the British detective
story even as it was in full flower. Colin Watson's *Snobbery with Violence*
shows how deep it was.

American traditions have their own ugliness. Lionel Derrick's *Death
Ray Terror* (The Penetrator series, No. 34) has immanent within it a moral
logic that guarantees that men, be they ever so evil, will die either with
tidy little bullet holes in their foreheads or in spectacular explosions. The
women, be they ever so good (and they are never *very* good), meet death

by slow torture. We are always helpfully told how those deaths came
to them.

> He understood why Dr. Bill Dessel had been shocked into uncon-
> sciousness. The girl lay on her back—one breast had been cut off
> her chest and lay beside her. Her stomach had been deeply slashed
> with crisscrossing marks, and all had bled profusely. Her right hand
> had been amputated at the wrist and lay on her throat. Both legs
> were sliced with deep gouges, and one eyeball hung obscenely on
> her cheek. From all appearances, the girl had bled to death. She
> had been alive when she was slashed, so there had been a maximum
> amount of pain and blood.   (123)

This is so grim and so pathetic that we are more likely to feel pity for
those who seek such stories out than to take the time to feel superior.
Mickey Spillane is more aware of what he is doing when he writes violent
scenes (none so blunt as this, I think) and much more likely to share with
his readers an amused savoring of outrage—not, however, a savoring of
the outrages inflicted upon the characters in the stories he writes but a
savoring of the outrages he is inflicting upon certain overly familiar pieties
inside the thriller tradition. Still, the description of this young victim
is only some few steps further along a continuum of violence in which
paperback fiction has always indulged.

Ugliness is not unique to pulp fiction. If it were argued that we need
instances of ugliness now and then to help us see the beauty of high art
and that paperback fiction does at least provide that service, every experienced reader would instantly protest that anyone who knows anything
about books could easily put together a shelf of serious stories (Céline's
Death on the Installment Plan, Réage's *Story of O*, and many others) that
provide scenes of cruelty, violence, and bigotry more difficult to forget
than even that bloody scene from The Penetrator series. Serious readers
can find enough intellectual and moral roughage within the learned traditions to satisfy all their hungers, no matter how bizarre.

The people who read both serious fiction and pulp fiction are reading
materials that sometimes do not like them, materials that usually do not
meet the standards they hold up for other stories they read, materials that

may even offend them. Many of the easy explanations we offer for the appeal of paperback fiction do not fit these readers, at least.

Some readers will protest that this elaborate interest in the attention that a small and perhaps idiosyncratic group—sophisticated readers—shows in pulp fiction is a waste of time; but there is method in it. We shall keep these readers always in mind, even when it is not this group but another group entirely that interests us. The loyalty that readers of serious fiction feel for this or that kind of pulp fiction—whether it be the fantasy novel, a daily comic strip, or a television series—is a paradox, a puzzle. Bertrand Russell defended his own interest in the lowly puzzle: "A logical theory may be tested by its capacity for dealing with puzzles, and it is a wholesome plan, in thinking about logic, to stock the mind with as many puzzles as possible, since these serve much the same purpose as is served by experiments in physical science" (305). Anomalies of reading preferences—puzzles of another kind—serve a parallel purpose: theories of reading may be tested by their capacity for dealing with reading anomalies. Any theory that purports to explain the appeal of pulp fiction but cannot account plausibly for the time that sophisticated readers give to it is unstable.

The interest that cultured readers manifest in what they themselves think of as throwaway materials denies us certain conveniently belittling explanations: that, say, paperbacks appeal only to the unintelligent or only to those who do not know of better books or only to the young or the neurotic. Pulp fiction appeals to readers of whom none of these claims is true. It appeals to intelligent, educated, and well-informed readers who are mature and who are as healthy as those of us who find their behavior interesting. If some of its readers are unintelligent or uneducated or young or neurotic, the fact that cultivated people are reading shoulder to shoulder with them is a continuing reminder that inexperience, distress, and the like is irrelevant.

The kinds of readers we have been considering in this chapter are reading poorer stories when they have better stories available. That is the anomaly, the puzzle, in its simplest form, but no sentence that talks about books and uses words like *better* and *poorer* (or *good* and *bad*, *high* and *low*) is simple, and especially not now, when none of us is quite certain how anyone else is using the words. Here, though, there should be no difficulty. Questions of absolute and relative literary value are not at issue, for we are not concerned with whether one novel is, or can be, intrinsically superior to another. What interests us, rather, is that readers who do feel that some novels are better than others do continue to read those others. When they have finished Calvino's *Invisible Cities* or Jane Austen's *Emma*, they confess that they admire those novels more highly than they do Mickey Spillane's *I, the Jury* or Louis L'Amour's *Heller with a Gun* but go on to read more Spillane and L'Amour anyway—even when there are Austen and Calvino novels yet to read.

These are the people Plato described. They praise one thing but are also pleased by another; they agree that while many stories are pleasant, only some of them are good; in the presence of the wise they are ashamed of their reading but find in it a secret pleasure. Not all are ashamed, of course, nor even most of them, perhaps; but they all know that there are others who think they should be ashamed. Betty Rosenberg's *Genre-flecting*, a bibliography of paperback fiction, begins with characteristic bravado: "This book is the fruit of a blissfully squandered reading life" (15). Anyone can translate that sentence: "I refuse to be ashamed of the behavior that I think is shameful."

How many of the learned follow fictions inside the world of pulp culture? An intriguing question, one not easily answered. It is not always easy to find out about others. It is not always easy to be sure about oneself.

For his now-classic study of the interaction of social structure and speech pattern, *The Social Stratification of English in New York City*, William Labov found a way to expose the linguistic insecurity of New Yorkers. When Labov had his subjects pronounce a word and then afterward asked them how they had pronounced it, he uncovered "a systematic tendency to report their own speech inaccurately. Most of the respondents seemed to perceive their own speech in terms of the norms at which they were aiming rather than the sound actually produced" (479–80). Apparently, it is not what we have done but what we think we should—and therefore must—have done that distinguishes us.

In his *Sociology of Literature*, the French scholar Robert Escarpit comments on a difficulty facing people investigating the kinds of reading habits that interest us here.

. . . .

While the confession of one's sexual peculiarities may flatter a latent exhibitionist, the avowal of literary or antiliterary tastes (whether too undiscriminating or too refined) which lower one's position in society can only be painful. Most people find great difficulty in confessing to themselves the nature of their taste.

The comparison of data obtained by direct and systematic observation of the cultural comportment of one person with data which he himself supplies, even in good faith, enables one to understand the extreme difficulty of using subjective information. He who cites Stendhal or Malraux as customary reading and who confides that he sometimes reads a detective novel or two to relax, will hardly admit that the time he devotes to detective novels is several times greater than the time he gives his "bedside" books. If he mentions newspapers, he will forget the few minutes he spends looking at the comic strips which, accumulated, represent an appreciable period of time. Similarly, the reading one does in waiting rooms or the reading of books borrowed from children's libraries goes by unnoticed. Who will ever be able to completely appreciate the enormous importance of such a book as the *Sapeur Cammembert* or *Tintin* in the reading of a cultivated French adult?   (16–17)

We all do seem to have the capacity to disregard the facts when they threaten to cloud those deeper truths about ourselves that we prefer.

When the matter of pulp fiction and its consumers comes up, we seem to map ourselves and our tastes against a usably simple grid we have inherited from the past. Two groups read pulp fiction, we say. The people in its primary readership may be brilliant in business, in politics, or in some other realm, but when they turn to books it is always and only to pulp fiction that they turn. It is this primary readership that publishers, editors, and writers have in mind when they market their wares. We have been taught to say that these people may have other qualities any of us might envy, but they do have low taste. Pulp fiction does find other readers as well, for it has long been recognized that a secondary readership comes to it occasionally from the study of literature and reads alongside that primary readership now and then. These people have good taste—for they take unselfconscious pleasure in literature—but they also have low taste. If they did not have a taste for the low, they would not be taking unselfconscious pleasure from the Mickey Spillanes and Louis L'Amours and Adam Halls of the paperback bookscape.

This is the question with which we began: how many of the people who are at home in those learned bookscapes also make regular visits to pulp fiction? I suggest that all of them do.

It may be that there are readers who have only low taste, but there are no readers who have only good taste. Even the most sensitive readers of literature enjoyably read, watch, or listen to some form of vernacular fiction as well. Today, pulp materials are coming at us from every direction within our culture and at every moment (Roberts, "Fiction Outside Literature"). If the taste of our most cultivated sensibilities were too refined for them to find something rewarding in some form of pulp fiction —some television, some movies, some paperbacks, some jokes, some comic monologues—they would not be able to remain in contact with the rest of us. If only in self-defense, our psyches find ways of turning what seems dross to gold. If our psyches cannot do that, we withdraw from the human conversation.

book types and
book antitypes

•   •   •   •   •   •   •   •   •   •   •   •   •   •   •   •

Richard Geis, the editor of that delightfully idiosyncratic fan-zine *Science Fiction Review*, once stopped dispiritedly in mid-review of a translation of one of the novels of Boris and Arkadi Strugatski to remark that "there is in each reader what I'd call a subliteracy toleration threshold, a point of verbal ineptitude below which he just shuts off" (74). I shall refer to it as the *aversion* threshold: it marks the division between the books we can and will read and the books we can but will not read. I propose three additional thresholds: a veneration threshold, an excellence threshold, and an inversion threshold. These boundaries delimit five classes of serious books that lie above, below, and between those

Thresholds, Types, and Antitypes

The Secular Sacred	vs.	The Chthonic
	The Veneration Threshold	
The Classic	vs.	The Pretentious
		The Manipulative
	The Excellence Threshold	
The Readable	vs.	The Inexcusably Unintelligible
	The Aversion Threshold	
The Unsuccessful	vs.	The Illiterate
	The Inversion Threshold	
Clowning	vs.	The Clownish

thresholds: sacred books, classic books, readable books, unsuccessful books, and clowning books. Nothing unusual in all this, but I want to warn my readers in advance that neither these thresholds nor the five classes they mark off will be so important to us as their antitypes, the categories listed in the right-hand column in the chart titled "Thresholds, Types, and Antitypes." What do paperback stories look like to readers who come to them from the scriptures? Since paperbacks are not sacred, they must be the Other: what, for readers of the sacred, *is* the Other? What do paperbacks look like to people who spend most of their time with the classics? What for classics readers is the Other?

The Sacred

I am less interested in the shadow cast over paperbacks by the class of the scriptural than in the indirect effects of the modern recognition of a special class of the secular sacred. Here is Coleridge's declaration of the sacredness of the Shakespearean oeuvre.

> Assuredly that criticism of Shakespeare will alone be genial which is reverential. The Englishman, who, without reverence, a proud and affectionate reverence, can utter the name of William Shakespeare, stands disqualified for the office of critic. . . . [I]t has been, and still remains, my object, to prove that in all points from the most important to the most minute, the judgment of Shakespeare is commensurate with his genius—nay, that his genius reveals itself in his judgment, as in its most exalted form. And the more gladly do I recur to this subject from the clear conviction, that to judge aright, and with distinct consciousness of the grounds of our judgment, concerning the works of Shakespeare, implies the power and the means of judging rightly of all other works of intellect, those of abstract science alone excepted. (430–31)

The class of the excellent includes both the sacred books and the classics, with that veneration threshold separating them. Both the sacred and the classic are privileged in being beyond human rejection, but only the sacred is also beyond faultfinding. We would of course feel that texts with extrahuman origins, the Gospels, the Talmud, the Koran, are beyond our poor mortal powers of criticism; but even some texts admitted to have human origins, the works of Shakespeare, Goethe, Dante, and Cervantes, in different language communities, for instance, have that privilege of the sacred. If one of us should feel that the Gospel of Matthew or a scene in *King Lear* or a speech in *Faust* is dull or obtuse or mistaken, say, those for whom reading these texts is an act of reverence demand that we blame ourselves, that we recognize that it is we who are dull or ignorant or slow. When a book is sacred, the dissatisfied reader is always wrong. In religion (the world's many different scriptures), in politics (the Declaration of Independence), in law (the Constitution), and in the humanities, texts can win these privileges. Not all students in any of those disciplines share in the sense that there are texts that exist above that special, veneration threshold, but there are enough who do so that the class of the sacred does cast a long, dark shadow.

The antitype of the sacred—the shadow cast by it—is the class of the *chthonic*. Readers fiercely devoted to one of the scriptures take books seriously, none more so: the chthonic in print—for some, all fiction, for all fiction is lying—can ruin us utterly. Scripture-mad readers make little distinction between serious and popular fiction.

Those who reverence only a secular sacred are less fearful of the chthonic and even claim that the notion is absurd, but the dislike of vernacular fiction is sometimes so fierce and so undiscriminating that we can explain it only on the assumption that behind this hatred there lies an unadmitted identification of the stories as chthonic. The detestation in which some readers hold professional writers (the people who say, "I write for money"), especially the men and women who openly declare themselves fiction factories, can be traced back to an unconscious, perhaps even an unwanted, sense of art as sacred.

The Classics

We do not expect to find readers claiming that any paperback story is sacred, but sometimes they come very close to that. Brian Aldiss in his history of science fiction, *Billion Year Spree*, talked about English teachers and Olaf Stapledon's *Star Maker:* "How it is that the funeral masons and morticians who work their preserving process on Eng. Lit. have rejected Stapledon entirely from their critical incantations is a matter before which speculation falls fainting away. His prose is as lucid as his imagination is huge and frightening. *Star Maker* is really the one great grey holy book of science fiction—perhaps after all there is something appropriate in its wonderful obscurity and neglect!" (208). But of course Aldiss is not in any sense claiming that *Star Maker* is sacred. He is insisting that it and the same writer's *Last and First Men* belong in the company of James Joyce's *Ulysses* and T. S. Eliot's *Waste Land*—that is, that Stapledon's novels are classics.

A sacred book is not satisfied that we should read it; it demands nothing less than our devotion—or so we are assured. A classic is not satisfied that we should read it, either. We cannot expect to begin to appreciate it on a single reading. We are told that classics are not read, they are reread, but, really, there is more to it than that: books in the class to which we shall be turning next, the readable, are read and then sometimes reread. What makes the classics different is that they win from us that odd kind of reading-rereading we call studying. And what Aldiss was claiming for *Star Maker* was not that it deserves our devotion, or that it can be read more than once, but that it would reward the kinds of study we have been giving canonical literature, the kinds of study that permit faultfinding, of course, as a part of a larger, serious effort to reach full appreciation of Stapledon's flawed and magnificent achievement.

The idea of the classic has thrown several shadows, of which the most interesting is a sort of echo. This is the category of the *genre classic*. We usually are content to claim no more than that these subclassics, classics within their traditions, are only taller hills among smaller hills; but we should add that enthusiasts, when speaking to other enthusiasts, are not always so dispassionate as they would have outsiders think them. We see this tendency, for instance, in the waspish conclusion to a brief, laudatory review of a collection of essays on the Sherlock Holmes stories, a review that appeared in Jacques Barzun and Wendell Hertig Taylor's column "A Catalogue of Crime" in the fanzine *The Armchair Detective:* "Many other items make [Philip A. Schreffler's *Baker Street Reader*] worth a place on the Sherlockian's shelf, but it is absurd to label it, as Greenwood does, a contribution to the study of popular culture. There's popular and popular, and Sherlock Holmes isn't Nick Carter" (221).

One street-corner test of reading competence in any vernacular genre is to ask the people talking about a genre how they liked the genre's classics. When readers of Westerns do not know Owen Wister's *Virginian*, Zane Grey's *Riders of the Purple Sage*, the stories of Eugene Manlove Rhodes, and the works of a dozen writers like Max Brand, Ernest Haycox, and Clarence Mulford, those readers are just learning their way around the tradition.

For the reader of paperbacks the Other of the classic is the genre classic; but for those who are most at home with the classics and now are looking into the paperbacks, the Other seems to have at least two shapes. For these readers, paperbacks are either *pretentious* or *manipulative*, both terms suggesting the ersatz.

If we are newly come to a vernacular genre from the classics, it is the genre classics that we dismiss as mere pretenders to excellence, and that, I think, is because so few of them invite the activity of study, the great pleasure of the reader of classics. If it is only loved, never respected, we brush to one side the notion that a story—an Edgar Rice Burroughs's *Tarzan of the Apes*, say, or an E. Phillips Oppenheim's *Great Impersonation*—might in some sense be a classic. We do not become angry about the continuing interest shown in genre classics, however. We seem to feel that their writers and their admirers are harmlessly deluding themselves that the books are excellent but that they are not likely to lead anyone astray.

We are not so tolerant of the other paperback stories, the ones for which no one claims greatness. If people do not buy the stories, we think of them as trash perceived as trash. If they are bought, if people are reading them with pleasure, we are puzzled, frustrated. We cannot see the differences between the stories in that genre that its readers like and the stories they do not like. (Sometimes, in a genre new to us, the stories we like are the stories the others do not like.) Since we are experienced with fiction—or we would never have taken an interest in the reading of others—we are reluctant to admit that we do not understand a tradition that even some very young people find intelligible. Inevitably, perhaps, we label the stories *manipulations* and invent for ourselves an image of an industry characterized by a kind of low cunning, a conspiracy of writers, editors, and book distributors that has somehow guessed its way to the secret emotional pressure points in the minds of the mob and is cynically churning out counterfeit books with huge profits for all. The whole image is magnificently absurd, of course, but it is easier for us to live with than the image of ourselves as ignorant. That conspiracy theory of vernacular fiction collapses the moment we look into it, and any student of popular fiction who subscribes to it is not to be trusted. Two facts alone demolish it. The first is that those publishers, editors, book distributors, and writers of popular books who are supposed to have discovered how to appeal to the baser passions of the mob often fail—fail in the primitive sense that the publishers go bankrupt, that no readers can be found for the books, and that writers can find no publishers for their output. The second fact— or at least apparent fact—is that the more cynical that writers are about the stories they are telling, the more likely that they will fail. The most successful writers of popular fiction are conscious craftsmen, of course, and know their readership, but those writers, too, enjoy the kinds of stories they are writing. There is no less—but no more—manipulation in the writing and sales of popular fiction than in the production of serious fiction.

The Readable

We seem to identify books as readable more or less by default. Neither expert readers nor the texts themselves insist that we feel that *readable* stories are excellent, say; but, then, neither are the stories unintelligible, or illiterate, or offensive. They give us *the good read;* and while the sacred and the classic texts give more, many stories give less. What enthusiasts recognize as genre classics—the Father Brown detective stories of G. K. Chesterton, the horrific fantasy of H. P. Lovecraft, and the like—are probably for less enthusiastic readers of the genre only the *readable,* stories whose antiquity makes them no less vulnerable to rejection than the stories published last month. They are more likely to be labeled unreadable eventually than to be touted as true classics.

When critics of the last generation tried to distinguish between serious and paperback fiction, they would sometimes claim that the paperbacks give us only quick, cheap, passing pleasures, that we exhaust them on our first reading. We are less likely to say that sort of thing today. As I remarked in connection with the classics, when we are genre users we often reread our favorite paperbacks—even if we adamantly refuse to study them. Some paperbacks—most notably, tales of detection— simulate an invitation to study, and perhaps we respond with a simulated form of study, but we do not give even these more than a careful reading. We do not take notes, we do not review earlier evidence, we do not talk the problem over with friends. We read alertly, we even reread alertly, but we do not study. I suppose that when we do begin to study a paperback, we have already unconsciously accepted it as a classic.

The Others, the antitypes, of the readable are the *unreadable*, the books we do not want to read, and the *unintelligible*, the books we cannot read. We shall be turning to the unreadable books in a moment; here we shall briefly consider the unintelligible.

The pages of any journal in mathematics are unintelligible to most of us, of course, but those journals are excusably unintelligible. It is the *inexcusably unintelligible* that interferes with our minds in our forays into strange genres of fiction. Sometimes we impatiently lump unintelligible stories in with the unreadably subliterate, say, when it is merely that they are so deeply embedded in their tradition or in a specialized subculture that they temporarily baffle us.

Robert A. Heinlein's *Stranger in a Strange Land* provides a convenient example of the sort of allusive demands a paperback can make on its readers. His central woman character, Jill, is wondering about the nature of comedy and so she runs a catalog of jokes through her mind, each identified by its punch line. That is all we are ever given: the punch lines. For instance, one of those lines is, "Neither one, you idiot—*instead!*" Here is the version I once heard of the joke that ends with that line.

> A man tells his friend that he has found the perfect contraceptive.
> "What is it?" says his friend.
> "Orange juice," is the reply.
> "Do you take it before sex or after?" the friend asks.
> "Neither one, you idiot—*instead!*"

Heinlein puts eleven jokes into Jill's mind.

> Doubtfully but earnestly Jill started digging into her memory for jokes that had struck her as irresistibly funny, ones which had jerked a laugh out of her:
>
> "—her entire bridge club." . . . "Should I bow?" . . . "Neither one, you idiot—*instead!*" . . . "—the Chinaman objects." . . . "—broke her leg." . . . "—make trouble for *me!*" . . . "—but it'll spoil the ride for me." . . . "—and his mother-in-law fainted." . . . "Stop you? I bet three to one you could do it!" . . . "—something has happened to Ole." . . . "—and so are you, you clumsy ox!"   (300)

I recognize only four of the eleven jokes, and I suppose the average reader does only a little better than that. That one allusive paragraph, at least, is less intelligible to some readers than Milton's (acceptably) allusive *Paradise Lost:*

> . . . though all the giant brood
> Of Phlegra with th'heroic race were joined
> That fought at Thebes and Ilium, on each side
> Mixed with auxiliar gods; and what resounds
> In fable or romance of Uther's son,
> Begirt with British and Armoric knights;
> And all who since, baptized or infidel,
> Jousted in Aspramont, or Moltalban,
> Damasco, or Marocco, or Trebisond;
> Or whom Biserta sent from Afric shore
> When Charlemagne with all his peerage fell
> By Fontarabbia.
>
> (book I: lines 576–86)

The classic is felt to have the right to demand whatever learning it wishes of us. By contrast, a book whose writer seems to be asking for it no more than the status of the readable is wrong when it becomes unintelligible. So it is that the difference between Heinlein's and Milton's allusions for many readers lies in that they are prepared to confess their ignorance while reading *Paradise Lost* but not while reading *Stranger in a Strange Land.*

So long as we recognize that passages like Heinlein's review of punch lines are only unintelligible and not subliterate (because, say, those jokes that come from an oral culture are therefore "low"), we are not likely to blunder badly. We shall of course want to remind ourselves that every vernacular genre does produce stories that are slightly or deeply unintelligible to the newcomer, that just as there is a skill and lore required to read literature, there is for each genre a genre competency.

On its simplest level, genre competency includes a familiarity with genre-specific vocabularies. Graham Greene's *Human Factor* is a spy story. It refers without explanation to "microdots" and "scramblers" and "drops"; genre-competent readers in that tradition do not need to have them explained. Theodore V. Olsen's *Stalking Moon* has its protagonist trailed by a vengeful Apache. Olsen does not explain who the Apaches were or where they lived or how they differed, as menaces, from the Nez Percé and the Crow; genre-competent readers of westerns would have found those explanations insulting. Readers of popular fantasy do not need to be told in Robert Bloch's "That Hell-Bound Train" that men who make an agreement with the devil will later face a reckoning.

None of us needs to be assured that if we are sometimes uncertain of the meanings of the words used in books that were written "for the uneducated masses," there may be other, deeper matters in those stories that are confusing us. We say that we do not need to be reminded of this; but, judging by what is still being printed about paperbacks, it is easy to forget two blatant facts about popular fiction: that each vernacular genre has its taproot in at least one specialized subculture—police work, astronomy, psychology, history—and that every story in every popular genre is referring deliberately or unconsciously to every other story in that genre. Most of what seems inexcusably unintelligible in popular fiction is crystal clear to the people who have learned how to read it.

The Unreadable

We considered the veneration threshold, separating the sacred from the classic. Then we looked at the excellence threshold, separating the classic from the readable. And now we have reached the aversion threshold, separating the readable from the unreadable.

Each of us has a personal dead-letter office, a place to which we assign the stories we would like to stamp RETURN TO SENDER or UNDELIV-ERABLE or to label, in *New Yorker* style, "Stories We Never Finished Reading." When serious books are unreadable, their readers label them *unsuccessful,* but they label unreadable paperbacks *illiterate.* The class of the unreadable, under either name, does not cast shadows in quite the same ways that the sacred, the classic, and the readable do, but it, too, is a source of confusion.

Speaking for people who cannot read mysteries, Edmund Wilson described an encounter with the unreadable in an essay of the 1940s, "Why Do People Read Detective Stories?" Wilson reported that he had to force himself to finish reading Agatha Christie's *Death Comes as the End:* "Her writing is of a mawkishness and banality which seem to me literally impossible to read. You cannot *read* such a book, you run through it to see the problem worked out; and you cannot become interested in the characters, because they never can be allowed an existence of their own even in a flat two dimensions but have always to be contrived so that they can seem either reliable or sinister, depending on which quarter, at the moment, is to be baited for the reader's suspicion" (234). And he said that he had to give up trying to read Rex Stout's Nero Wolfe mysteries: "I finally got to feel that I had to unpack large crates by swallowing the excelsior in order to find at the bottom a few bent and rusty nails" (233).

Geis's subliteracy threshold marked off verbal ineptitude, but most unreadable stories today are unreadable not because of solecisms (editors now filter out most barbarisms in usage) but because their writers are inept at building stories: their sentences are correct but flabby; they cannot invent interesting people, challenging problems, or dramatic events; their observations on the world—a world we share and observe with them—are no more original than our own.

Trapped in a waiting room or a bus in which there is nothing to read but the unreadable, any of us can be overcome with an antipaperback hysteria, a temporary rage at one of those vernacular genres, and then we wonder whether there is any limit to the tolerance of that genre's followers, whether there is anything at all they will not read. But, of course, all paperback readers have aversion thresholds that keep whole traditions at a distance, and they all have aversion thresholds even within the genres they most favor. In science-fiction circles, there is a formulation so well known that reviewers allude to it simply as Sturgeon's Law. When newcomers to the genre ask about Sturgeon's Law, they are told, "Ninety per cent of science fiction is crap!"—and, immediately afterward—"but, then, ninety per cent of *everything* is crap!"

Perhaps the unreadable seems the least interesting of the five types of books and that "aversion threshold" only another sad instance of labeling gone melodramatic. Not so. The aversion threshold is important.

I do not suppose anyone would quarrel with the proposition that we all do have our private aversion thresholds. I know that I do. Here are two examples of prose from reviews that appeared in the London *Times Literary Supplement*. For me, the following description creates an image of one kind of book I have no interest in reading. "The themes of loneliness, betrayal, sexual maladjustment and the untethered mind, which provide Jonathan Gathorne-Hardy with the material for his collection of stories, are familiar enough in contemporary fiction; so too is the ironic reserve with which tragedy is kept politely at bay. Assured and fluently written, the stories, despite their often considerable satirical edge, leave behind, for the most part, a dampening sense of melancholy and defeat" (J. K. L. Walker 327). I should add that Walker is not dismissing *The Centre of the Universe Is 18 Baedkerstrasse;* he is recommending it.

Victoria Glendinning is not so sympathetic in her review of *My Sister and Myself: The Diaries of J. R. Ackerley,* an account of the life of the man who for twenty-five years was editor of a respected British journal, *The Listener.* Glendinning describes Ackerley as "author, dog-lover, boy-lover, poet, literary talent-spotter, editor, diarist—not necessarily in that order" and tells us that Ackerley had an Alsatian bitch that all his friends hated: "Well, not quite all his friends. On November 1, 1948, Ackerley recorded a visit from his East End friend Freddie, the former Guardsman (the 'Johnnie' of *We Think the World of You*). Freddie made the dog happy before he turned his attention to her master. 'He began to tickle her tits and the base of her little vulva. . . .' Queenie liked this, and all that followed, very much indeed; and then, 'after Queenie's turn, it was mine'" (478). All readers have their limitations, and one of my limitations surfaces at moments like these. It is not the pornographic element in the entry that disturbs me; stories about sexual contacts between humans and dogs do exist in the vernacular traditions of pornography, and if others enjoy that sort of story I cannot feel that it is much of my business. What I find disturbing is the self-hating giggle in Ackerley's account—and, of course, the fact that it will be some time before the phrase *dog-lover* means to me what it once did.

I do not knowingly choose to read books like *My Sister and Myself: The Diaries of J. R. Ackerley* and Jonathan Gathorne-Hardy's *Centre of the Universe Is 18 Baedkerstrasse*, and when I find that I am reading them, I put them aside and pick up something else—which, I suppose, is what Edmund Wilson did whenever he found that he had inadvertently picked up a mystery. And because Wilson could not read weakly written mysteries, he never learned how to take what that one genre has to offer.

The reading of paperbacks is bulk reading. We read them by the half dozen, by the dozen, by the score. We read them almost without noticing who wrote them or caring what else that writer might have published. Sometimes we continue reading after discovering, a few pages into the first chapter, that we have already read the story and cannot remember exactly what happens to the characters. (All of this is of course anathema to the cult of the great author and the great book. I would merely remind us all that some of the people who sincerely profess the cult of great authorship are also bulk readers of paperbacks.)

As I shall be suggesting later, the reading of genre fiction is one of the kinds of reading that are text superior. The reader is reading not the text but the genre by means of the text. The reader is following the interplay among the texts, the changes in what is newly permitted, what is worth exploring, what can be abandoned. We can follow this byplay only if we are able to read a very large number of stories, which means that we must have a very high tolerance for inept writing. A high tolerance is possible only when we have low standards, that is, a low aversion threshold.

A group's aversion threshold, therefore, is more important than its excellence or inversion thresholds as predictors of its reading. Readers with different genre interests—different tastes—disagree less than we might expect as to which stories in the various genres are the best the genres have produced. It is not in their admirations that they differ but in their aversions.

Before turning to the inversion threshold and the clownishness that lies beyond it, we ought to look once again at Sturgeon's Law, a "law" that enthusiasts for many other genres might also endorse. I shall merely suggest that it does not mean quite what it seems to say. Though enthusiasts for science fiction may speak calmly of the validity of Sturgeon's Law, we can be confident that they do not really believe that 90 percent of science fiction is crap. If they did feel that they have only one chance in ten of finding a readable story in science fiction, they would not be reading in that genre. What they mean, surely, is that only one story in ten is "recommendable," that 90 percent of all science fiction can be enjoyed —if at all—only by that genre's enthusiasts, readers distinguished from all other readers by very low aversion thresholds in this one genre. The occasional reader can enjoy only that one story in ten, but that is not to say the other nine are all bad. Some of them are no worse than excusably unintelligible to the inexperienced reader.

The Clownish

Finally, far beyond that aversion threshold lies the last and strangest boundary, the inversion threshold, the line between the books so bad they are unreadable and the books so bad they are good. Where good is bad and bad is good, everything is inverted. Instead of a category in serious writing creating an antitype, the clownish, it is the category of the clownish that has inspired an antiantitype, as it were: the clowning, or parody. Where the clownish does not exist or is overlooked, writers create a simulacrum of the clownish for our pleasure. But it is the clownish that interests us.

In a collection of earlier reviews, *In Search of Wonder*, Damon Knight devotes one chapter, "Chuckleheads," to badness in fantasy and science fiction. Those pages constitute one hands-on definition of the clownish. Here are some paragraphs from his remarks on Austin Hall, coauthor with Homer Eon Flint of a 1920s novel, *The Blind Spot*, still occasionally mentioned by bibliographers.

[Hall] was style-deaf. Sample, from the prologue:

> For years he had been battering down the skepticism that had bulwarked itself in the material.

Another:

> . . . he had backtracked on his previous acts so as to side in with the facts. . . .

He was totally innocent of grammar. This is not an exaggeration; Hall could not tell a noun from an adjective, or a verb from either. Two samples:

> She is fire and flesh and carnal . . . at whose feet fools and wise men would slavishly frolic and folly.

He was so little at home in the English language that he could not lay hands on the commonest idiom without mangling it. Three samples, out of dozens:

> It was a stagger for both young men.

> There was a resemblance to Rhamda Avec that ran almost to counterpart.

> It was a long hark back to our childhood.

He was credulous without limit. The myths solemnly subscribed to in this book—none of them having anything to do with the plot —include the intuition of women, the character-judgment of dogs, "animal magnetism," "psychic vibrations" and the influence of intelligence on the color of the eyes.

> He had no power of observation.

> The men about him purchased cigars and cigarettes, and, as is the habit of all smokers, strolled off with delighted relish.

He had no empathy, and, I might add, no sense of humor. This is his notion of writing like a woman:

> I am but a girl: . . . I should be jealous and I should hate her: It is the way of woman. . . . I am a girl and I like attention; all girls do. . . . I had all of a girl's wild fears and fancies. I am a girl, of course. . . .

His knowledge of science, if he had any, is not discoverable in these pages. He used "ether," "force" and "vibration" synonymously. On page 85, a chemist refers to a stone's thermal properties as "magnetism." "Magnetic"—like "sequence," "almost," "intrin-

sic," "incandescense" (sic) and "iridescense" (sic)—is a word Hall
kept tossing in at random, hoping to hit something with it eventually.
For example:

> She [a dog named Queen] caught him by the trouser-leg and
> drew him back: She crowded us away from the curtains. It was
> almost magnetic.   (22–23)

The clownish offers the inexperienced reader difficulties, the most
obvious of which is our occasional failure to distinguish successfully between the parody (a clowning) and clownishness itself. Betty Rosenberg's
Genreflecting is wise on the dangers of starting into a genre—perhaps
inadvertently—with one of its parodies. She lists several for each tradition: for the Western, Alan LeMay's *Useless Cowboy*; for the detective
story, Leo Bruce's *Case for Three Detectives*; for science fiction, *Venus
on the Half Shell*, by Kilgore Trout (Philip José Farmer), and Douglas
Adams's *Hitchhiker's Guide to the Galaxy*; for the modern romance, Margaret Atwood's *Lady Oracle*. What anyone would think of the genre and
its readers whose first, unprepared introduction to them was through one
of those books is hard to guess. Though any of them might seem clownish
to the inexperienced reader, none of these stories is clownish. They are
all—I emphasize—their genres' parodies of itself. Such self-criticism
appears in every twist and turn of every one of the vernacular traditions.

The parodying of a genre is ubiquitous, though only experienced readers will recognize it, and even they do not see its importance. A genre cannot exist until someone has parodied the patterns to which other writers
are beginning to adhere. It is this deliberate clowning, this pseudoclown-
ishness, that makes the rule governance of a tradition explicit and permits
it to face unafraid the criticism of its absurdities, that is, of its conven-
tionalities. And the best parodies, it need hardly be added, are written by
those who most love the genre being parodied. Many of the classic works
in the paperback traditions were or began as parodies—E. C. Bentley's
Trent's Last Case, for instance, which Dorothy Sayers thought one of the
most important novels in the history of its genre, and Stanley G. Weinbaum's "Martian Odyssey," which no less dedicated a group than the
Science Fiction Writers of America voted one of the best science-fiction
stories ever written.

Students of vernacular fiction risk professional suicide if they assume too quickly that the story they have before them, that impossibly clownish story, is not, rather, a clowning, a parody, an expression of the writer's amusement about his own writing or an affectionate poke at the traditions of the genre—in short, self-criticism.

Of course, in the case of Hall and Flint's *Blind Spot* we can be confident that we have a novel that is not mock clownishness; it is clownishness itself. What is to be said about it and all the other clownish stories that appear each year? First, the genre itself recognizes that the stories are clownish, and outsiders should avoid using them as evidence of the reading incompetence of a genre's enthusiasts when those very readers are simultaneously quoting from those books with great, if cruel, hilarity.

I think readers should be cautious, also, about labeling a story clownish too quickly. When we are impatient and especially when earlier experiences have made us mistrustful of a genre, the first cliché we encounter can trigger in us a catastrophic sense of impending boredom that, in Geis's phrase, shuts our minds off. This is not the place for an extended discussion of the role of the cliché in vernacular fiction. We can note, however, that Edmund Wilson, who disliked contemporary detective stories, did later discover in himself a love of the Sherlock Holmes stories. He could not overlook the clichéd elements in Conan Doyle's stories, and in his essay " 'Mr. Holmes, They Were the Footprints of a Gigantic Hound!' " Wilson is displaying the tolerance for clichés that he cannot excuse when he finds it in the admirers of Agatha Christie and Rex Stout. "The writing, of course, is full of clichés," he says, "but these clichés are dealt out with a ring which gives them a kind of value, while the author makes speed and saves space so effectively that we are rarely in danger of getting bogged down in anything boring. And the clichés of situation and character are somehow made to function, too, for the success of the general effect" (271).

Finally, I should like to suggest that there is something to value in any tradition—popular or serious—that permits the clownish to appear in all its naked truth. Canonical literature has its fictional clowns (Chaucer's Sir Thopas, Shakespeare's Pistol, Dickens's Mr. Micawber), and it has its clowning writers: Laurence Sterne parodying the autobiographical novel with his *Tristram Shandy*, Henry Fielding parodying Richardson's

Pamela with his *Shamela*. Canonical literature, at least by its guardians' intention, includes only the best that has ever been written, however, and so it cannot include the clownish writer, that is, the natural fool, the true incompetent.

Contemporary writing—and I would emphasize that the serious and the popular share this, at least—does have the clownish writer, and I think we are the better for meeting that writer's works now and then. An old definition of the circus clown identifies him as a subhuman who is trying —who is always trying and who is always failing—to be human. It points out that when the clown appears we join the mob in its roar of laughter but that in each of our laughing faces there is a sadness—a combination mirrored, often, in the clown's makeup. Perhaps the clown lets us see in ourselves a something, perhaps a several-sided something, we do not see at any other moment.

Clownish writers make the same odd appeal. They are not just bad writers; they are subwriters trying—always trying, always failing—to be writers. Damon Knight quotes from another novel, Lee Correy's *Starship through Space*. The novel had a clever idea behind it, Knight says, and he admits that Correy managed to make his own kind of engineering sound fresh and exciting. Correy was not a poet, however, and it was unwise of him to have one of his central characters write a lyric and then have the other characters express their awe for his talent. This is the stanza that Damon Knight quotes:

> We who have tasted alien stream
> And done what others only dream;
> We who with earth-dirt on our shoes
> Have walked the paths the sunbeams use;
> We will trod the Milky Way.
>
> (32)

This is not classic poetry. This is not bad but readable poetry. This is not even very, very bad and unreadable poetry. This is subpoetry. Is it bad enough to have broken the inversion barrier? Yes—as a simple test will show: any improvement we make in those lines makes the verse *less* interesting. We are in that zone in which the good is bad and only the bad is good. And bad as these verses and those sentences from *The Blind Spot* may be, they must be valuable to us in some way, for we will remember them long after we have forgotten much that is better.

These, then, are my four thresholds and five primary reading categories, with the several antitypes they generate. Above the veneration threshold are the books that are beyond rejection and beyond criticism as well, the sacred texts—religious and secular—whose mere existence implies the category of the chthonic. Between the veneration and the excellence thresholds are the classics, open to criticism but secure against rejection. Our image of the classic has created the counterimages of the more limited genre classic (which those hostile to the genre think of as the pretentious) and the class of the manipulative. Below this excellence threshold but above the aversion threshold is the vast library of books of which we say only that they are tolerable as against the antitypes of the books that are inexcusably unintelligible. Below that aversion threshold we find two categories. The first is the unreadable, and we remarked that readers who follow any genre closely differ from those who read less of it chiefly in that the former are more tolerant of writing weaknesses. Finally, beyond that curious inversion threshold we find those books in which bad becomes good: the clownish performances of writers too unskilled even to write an unreadable book, the stories that bring out the latent cruelty in the reader.

We come to every book trailing clouds of expectation; some part of our mind has already stamped a label on any new book before we have started reading the first page. If the books we read are sacred—that is, if we try to read always above the veneration threshold—we think that paperbacks are defiling their readers. If we think of our books as the classics, then paperback stories are to us the ersatz productions of demagogues stealing for themselves the honor earned by the classic authors, the classic texts. If we think of ourselves as serious readers who are most at home reading books written for the happy few, for those who will read nothing less than the excellent, paperbacks are absurd. When they are not inexcusably unintelligible, they and their readers are all clownish, we think, and it is the duty of readers with good taste to help those readers who can be saved to lift themselves from out of the mire and into the light. What we think paperbacks are depends upon what we think *true writing* is: paperbacks are variously the chthonic, the ersatz, the manipulative, the pretentious, the clownish.

We do not understand one another very well; we do not understand ourselves very well. Few of us do not know one strand of popular fiction intimately and know how poorly others understand us, but few of us also do not dismiss impatiently one of the other strands in paperback fiction and the readers who favor it.

Some of us are too ashamed to try to understand ourselves. In " 'Mr. Holmes, They Were the Footprints of a Gigantic Hound!' " Edmund Wilson remarked on an unexpected effect of an earlier essay that had attacked the detective story: "The evangelical note at the end of my piece was intended to have a burlesque flavor, but some of my correspondents seem to have taken it more seriously than it was meant, and write to tell me that, though they have long been addicts, they have made a vow, since reading my article, never to touch another detective story" (266). Even for people with years of experience reading paperbacks, the paperback was dangerous: like Milton's Belial, it had slyly insinuated itself in their good graces, sapped their wills, and rotted their minds.

An interest in paperback fiction is a symptom of bad taste, we are assured. It is perhaps not *quite* hopeless to protest that this application of the notion of bad taste has been generated neither by the books we most admire, whatever those may be, nor by pulp fiction. This application has been generated by earlier categorizing; it is an excrescent shadow that makes popular fiction hard to see as in itself it really is.

a variety
of readers

. . . .

We often speak of readers of popular fiction as though they
were simpler and more predictable than they are. Carelessly, we speak
as though one discrete group of readers always chooses westerns and
nothing but westerns and as though a different group reads only detective
stories, a third only fantasies, and so forth. We would say, I suppose,
that the groups overlap thinly at their edges, but we probably feel that
they remain fundamentally distinct. We would be willing to grant that
individual readers look now and then into the stories other groups admire
and that one genre occasionally does win readers from another genre; for
we would grant that there must be some mechanism that permits readers
to abandon one genre and take up another; but we are not likely to be
much interested in this.

And we seem to be assuming that the relations between a genre and the
people who read in it are equally simple. That is, we think (or at least we
speak as though we think) that even readers who display excellent critical
judgment when reading outside the paperback traditions lose their critical
standards while reading inside one of the popular genres.

Whether we individually credit it or not, it is this image that determines
which questions we shall ask and whether we shall accept the answers
people give us. We ask, what kind of person reads the romance? what kind
reads the western? science fiction? the detective story? And we expect
that the answers to these questions will be different, that the people who
read the romance and the people who read the western will appear on

different pages of a national census of readers and, additionally, that they are different in character and situation and in the rewards they are getting from their genres.

Sometimes we need simple images if we are to get anything done, but this image of discrete readerships, of single-genre loyalties would be difficult to validate. People who read most often in one genre usually follow other traditions too; they dip into still other genres with moderate frequency; they manifest strong though temporary enthusiasms for something they have just discovered; they develop fierce genre antipathies.

Here I set that familiar one-genre/one-readership image aside to look more closely at the relationships readers have with the genres they know. The following, I suggest, is a minimal set of distinctions, the smallest number needed to make sense of the variety of reader-to-genre relationships that we find among readers of the paperbacks: the exclusivists, the users (who include certain odd forms of the reading addict), the fans, the occasional readers, and the allergics.

Exclusivists

Exclusivism is enthusiasm at its highest pitch. For exclusivists, a certain genre is not just the preferred, it is the only acceptable source of fiction. Donald A. Wollheim, the science-fiction editor, spoke of enthusiasms and exclusivisms.

> The phases of being a science-fiction reader can be traced and charted. So many read it for one year, so many for two, so many for life. For instance, reading it exclusively can be as compulsive as a narcotic for a period of an intelligent teenager's life. The length of time as I see it—and I have seen and talked with and corresponded with hundreds and hundreds of such readers in my lifetime —is about four or five years of the most intense reading—usually exclusive, all other literature being shoved aside. After that a falling off, rather rapid (often due to college entry or military life or the hard stuff of getting a job for the first time). There is, I suspect, something like an 80 per cent turnover in the mass of readers of science fiction every five years. (6)

There has been so little interest in the reading of fiction outside litera-ture that I find nothing in print on patterns of exclusivism among adult readers. Wollheim himself may have been a lifelong exclusivist for sci-ence fiction, and most of the romance readers Janice Radway located and studied were still exclusivists. My impression, nevertheless, is that adult genre exclusivists are less common than we suppose, that single-focused reading enthusiasms are short-lived. There are exceptions, but the old rule is sound: the people who read anything read everything.

Exclusivism, which readers themselves think of as a temporary aber-ration, would not be worth our attention if it were not that a certain kind of inquiry into popular fiction is predicated on that default assumption that the typical reader of popular fiction is an exclusivist. The results, too often, are essays and books that bibliographers if they were not so polite would lump together under the label *Thunderings*. The thunderers want to show us how ugly, or how violent, or how mindless modern culture has become; and so they use the comic book or a television series or pornography or the stories of Mickey Spillane to create for us an image of Calibans of both sexes created by and living under the exclusive gov-ernance of these materials. (A better-than-average example of this sort of thing is William Ruehlmann's *Saint with a Gun*, an essay on the origins and significance of private-eye fiction that sets out to demonstrate, with crushing contempt, that Spillane, his characters, and his simple-minded readers are all dangerously psychotic.) The weakness in the thunderers' presentation, as we have seen, is their unlikely assumption that anyone who reads pornography or watches television or reads comic books, or westerns, or science fiction, or detective stories or anything else, reads that and nothing else. To show that a culture is unhealthy by citing the deficiencies of one popular genre or one successful writer is like demon-strating that all America will soon be toothless because one of the popular soft drinks lacks five essential vitamins. The exclusivist reader is a fiction convenient for the thunderers; but while we can find isolated instances of the exclusivist reader and while most of us have at one time or another (sometimes, many times) briefly been exclusivist in our reading, no genre, and certainly no writer, could survive for long if it had to depend wholly on exclusivistic enthusiasm. The exclusivist is not a significant presence for popular fiction. There are only people who also read science fiction or

who also read westerns, and so on. That, of course, is something entirely
different.

Users

To readers outside a genre, users are indistinguishable from
exclusivists, but the two are never in doubt about their differences. If,
as we have seen, an exclusivist's motto is, say, "*X* only!" (that is, "The
romance only!" or "The western only!"), the user's motto is "*X* also." Most
of Wollheim's 20 percent of science fiction's readers who retain a lifelong
interest in the genre are users, not exclusivists. Though users are not so
visible as exclusivists in the many activities that buzz around the various
genres (the publication of fan magazines, the organization of conventions,
and the like) there is evidence enough even in the fan magazines that
readers of any one genre are deeply interested in others as well. In an
article in *The Armchair Detective*, Richard Meyers interrupted a survey
of mysteries on television to write angrily about television's misunderstanding of science fiction. *Locus: The Newspaper of the Science Fiction
Field* regularly surveys its readers, and each year they report that they
are interested in more than science fiction. The 1985 survey shows that
74 percent of them are interested in movies, 44 percent in mysteries, 32
percent in historical fiction, and 23 percent in the comics, for instance
("Locus Survey Results," 26). *Zimri*, an excellent British fanzine of a
few years ago, was not at all atypical in combining an interest in science
fiction with an interest in poetry.

It is its users, not its exclusivists, who keep each vernacular genre
alive, and each of those users has several reading interests. The romance
readers that Janice Radway studied were exclusivists, but we would suppose that the more characteristic romance reader is not exclusivistic, that
she does not read romances only. She may read two or three dozen each
year—an average of three per month, say. Eight or ten weeks may pass
without her having any interest at all in the romance, but she will one
day find herself standing before a shelf of romances in a drugstore, idly
poring over the titles, the cover illustrations, the back-cover blurbs. An
experienced reader, she also studies the title pages, since she knows that

paperback publishers do clever things with titles. (Frank Herbert's first science-fiction novel has appeared as *Under Pressure*, as *Dragon in the Sea*, and as *21st Century Sub*. Forrest Carter's *Outlaw Josey Wales*, a fine western, first appeared as *The Rebel Outlaw: Josey Wales* and was then reprinted as *Gone to Texas*.)

If our romance reader is like many of the rest of us, she may find herself standing outside the store a few minutes later with a sales slip in one hand and books in the other. She may feel that she is afflicted with an innocent form of kleptomania, as though she unconsciously steals books but then unconsciously pays for them. It is of course one of her reading addictions that is governing her.

She will feel momentarily foolish, but she will read those romances—perhaps in one glorious weekend binge. When whatever drew her to those stories in the first place has been satisfied, she will stop reading. She cannot predict when she will stop, but, of course, the better the stories the longer the binge. She will put the romance completely out of her mind. Two weeks later, however, she may find herself standing in front of some shelves in a library, looking through the detective fiction: the start of a new but different binge.

Plainly, we are dealing in cases like this with addictions, no less addictions for being multiple and discontinuous. We readers dislike it when others say we are "compulsive" and "addictive," but these terms do seem to describe some of our behavior. So much has been said about popular fiction being an opiate, however, that we should also insist that these reading dependencies are found not only among readers of paperbacks. That devout Christian who cannot let a day pass without reading a chapter in the Bible is an addicted reader, as are those among us who cannot go for more than a few days without reading in Shakespeare or in Karl Marx or in history.

The taxonomies of readers that we would find most useful in the study of the vernacular genres have yet to be designed. These would identify readers not by reference to their favorite genres alone but by reference to their addiction clusters: that, say, one group that reads westerns also reads eighteenth-century fiction and Proust, but that another group that reads westerns reads nineteenth-century poetry and James Joyce. The mysteries of taste lie hidden in curious, overlapping patterns of superficially contradictory addictions that defy easy explanation. It is an indication of the inadequacy of older explanations that the people who do read in one of the vernacular genres always feel that the explanations describe other readers, not them.

We can lump exclusivists and users together as *enthusiasts*. Most—not all—of the next group are enthusiasts, too.

Fans

In "Paradise Charted," a good history of pulp science fiction, Algis Budrys explains the importance to the genre of its fandom.

> While tens or perhaps hundreds of thousands of "science fiction" readers have never heard of it, everyone who publishes, edits, writes, or illustrates in the field must take its articulations into account. It is the repository of the amorphous oral tradition; almost all professionals who are now adults were imbued with its preconceptions as children.
>
> . . . "Science fiction" has hundreds, perhaps thousands, of amateur publications; at least one convention of some size nearly every weekend, culminating in an annual world convention with attendance approaching five thousand; innumerable subgroups founded on special interests within the special interest, particularly heroic fantasy; art shows; costume balls; its own repertoire of folk ("filk") songs; a well-developed jargon sufficient for good communication without more than passing reference to English.   (15–16)

Its development of its own special vocabulary in its amateur magazines is a sign that fandom is a special world that knows it is a special world. Budrys offers the following sample: " 'I used to look at things in a fiawol way, you know. I was really into crifanac. Then I sent this poctsard to all the smofs about my idea for marketing filksongs. Well, it turned out four of them had gafiated, and three of them were just letterhacks. So, I don't know, man. I feel this fijagh attitude coming on' " (16). The playfulness of the language suggests something of the feelings of the fans about the stories that are at the putative center of interest. The jargon, like most jargons, amounts to a few hundred new nouns, verbs, and adjectives firmly embedded in English syntax: *Crifanac* is "critical fan activity"; a *poctsard* is a postcard about science fiction; *smofs* are the sardonically termed "secret masters of fandom"; to *gafiate* is to "get away from it all"; a *letterhack* is a fan whose only fannish activity is the writing of letters to the *fanzines*, the magazines the fans publish for one another. The acronyms *fiawol* and *fijagh* advance the opposed opinions that "fandom is a way of life" and that "fandom is just a goddamned hobby." The nontechnical *gafiate*, to "get away from it all," that is, to withdraw temporarily from social activity, may eventually find a wider use; but the jargon seems designed chiefly to serve as a barrier between fans and others. It is interesting—significant, I should say—that the jargon seems to have little analytic value for students of the genre. Fandom is a quasi-orgy, an erotics of reading, not a scientific assault on a genre.

While everyday usage names any reader of any genre a fan of that genre, the more careful use of the term identifies fans as those readers of a genre who correspond with one another. Very few of any genre's readers know that a fandom exists, and few who do learn of it have any interest in becoming a part of it. (When Radway questioned romance readers, she learned that as enthusiastic as they were about the stories they were reading they had no interest in keeping in touch with others like themselves.) The modal genre reader, in the statistical sense, is the isolated user.

Genre fans are a tiny minority; but, as Budrys suggests, they are of special importance both to the genre itself and to anyone who is trying to understand it. Fans can easily be located, are very cooperative, and every year are writing thousands of pages of comment on the stories, the genre, its writers, and its readers. Even if their sociability as readers makes them atypical, they are invaluable as sources of information for students and readers of any of the vernacular genres.

It is with the fanzines that we would begin. One definition of the amateur fan magazine is that its editor pays no one for anything he or she prints and that it appears at least four times a year. Its readers contribute most of the text and art; the editor puts it all together and mails it out to his readers. The fanzines come and go so quickly that any list of purely amateur fanzines is quickly out of date, and any attempt at quick characterization is doomed. They come, for instance, in many forms: in 1984, a fanzine calling itself *FSFNET: BITNET Fantasy-Science Fiction Fanzine* began to be sent out from the University of Maine via a computer network (BITNET) to readers at other universities. Some of the fanzines I have enjoyed were Ed Cagle's *Kwalhioqua*, a zany publication that became too popular for its editor's wallet; Harry O. Morris's *Nyctalops*, which dealt intelligently with fantasy; Richard E. Geis's *Science Fiction Review*; Edward C. Connor's *SF Echo*, which came in the shape of a handmade paperback; Dave and Mardee Jenrette's wide-ranging and inimitable *Tabebuian*; Otto Penzler's prozine *The Armchair Detective*; the lighthearted obeisance to sword and sorcery, *Amra*, which came to us from the Terminus, Owlswick and Ft. Mudge Electrick St Railway Gazette. I have been reading Bill Danner's *Stefantasy* with pleasure for years, and I remember with a special regard J. J. Pierce and Paul Walker's argumentative *T.A.D.* (*Tension, Apprehension, and Dissension*), which insisted upon taking science fiction seriously. Some twenty to fifty of the hundred and more fanzines I have read were as interesting as the stories they discussed.

In 1973, Fredric Wertham published his *World of Fanzines: A Special Form of Communication*, which, though hasty and inadequate, at least identified the cultural significance of the fanzine. Through fanzines, any group can create its own network of literary criticism, can give the books that interest it adequate review (they are mostly overlooked elsewhere), can publish its readings of those books, can query its writers (and have them answer), can award prizes, and can publish its own first, shy efforts in the writing of genre fiction.

Students of popular fiction who do not search out and study the fanzines and fandom associated with it put themselves at great disadvantage. The fanzines are easy to locate. Some of them announce themselves in the professional magazines, and their editors read and talk about one another all the time. A single LOC (letter of comment) to one of them puts one's address on display to all, and one is soon receiving issues from strange places. At least in the case of science fiction, readers who write letters of comment to the fanzines can find themselves receiving fifty different magazines within a few months of getting their first. Some fanzines are worth reading in their own right: some of the fanzines devoted to the art of the comic book (*Witzend*, for instance) have been better than most of the comics they discuss.

In the fanzines the readership of a genre becomes conscious, and if the silliest and most naive remarks on any genre are found in its fanzines, there too appear the shrewdest, the best-informed, and the most imaginative criticism.

These users and exclusivists, some of them fans, are a genre's readers. Beyond their number are other readers and nonreaders who contribute to the floating mass of misinformation about any genre that we all accept as a part of general knowledge. Among the nonreaders are people who, though they do not read, are sure they understand the western novel or the detective story, say, because of the films they have seen. I will not look at all the sources of sincere inaccuracy, but I will examine the people who read stories in a genre now and then but not often enough or widely enough to get an intuition into the life of the tradition. I will then complete this minimal survey with a consideration of the people who detest certain genres, who will read anything except the stories that come out of these genres.

Occasional Readers

All readers are users of more than one reading category and only occasionally a reader of many others, by which I mean that we are all willing to read now and then in some area we favor less—in this author, in that genre—but that we never become interested enough to stay with it. That reader who loses control of herself in a bookstore or a library every few weeks is a user of romances and detective stories; we can imagine that she is an occasional reader of spy stories, ready to read Eric Ambler's *Mask of Dimitrios* if strongly urged to and even to enjoy it but won by neither Ambler nor the espionage tradition to read more. Against the exclusivists' "*X* only!" and the users' "*X* also," occasional readers would hoist aloft that mildest of all reading mottoes, "*X* sometimes."

As occasional readers we come in different forms, each producing a characteristic misunderstanding. In some cases we were enthusiastic readers of a genre when younger and are now returning to it as adults, anticipating a misremembered simplicity. We had last read the John Buchan style of spy thriller, something like *The Thirty-Nine Steps*, or the E. E. Smith type of science-fiction novel, *Skylark Three*, say, and now pick up John Le Carré's *Tinker, Tailor, Soldier, Spy*, a story in which our spies are just as bad as theirs, or Ian Watson's *Embedding*, a novel about the human incapacity to accept multiply embedded linguistic structures, and we become annoyed. We were looking for a nice little daydream but are being asked to think. If we are not careful, we may find ourselves speaking of a Golden Age of this or that genre and complaining that a once-delightful tradition has become self-conscious and pretentious. The probable truth is that we had then known only adolescent versions of the genre's stories or had read adult stories with an adolescent eye, quite naturally and properly overlooking those features that would catch our attention later. We certainly had not thought the stories mindless while we were reading them.

There are other varieties of the misinformation-generating occasional reader: for instance, the one-book expert. Every now and then, a popular genre will produce a book that sells hugely, as did A. B. Guthrie's *Big Sky*, a western; Walter Miller's *Canticle for Leibowitz*, a science-fiction novel; Frederick Forsyth's *Day of the Jackal*, a crime thriller; and John Le Carré's *Spy Who Came in from the Cold*. These books are widely read and discussed and they produce a blossoming in us of one-book expertise. Our opinions are the stronger and more powerfully advanced because they have the virtue of extreme simplicity. When we do look into other stories in that tradition, we are disappointed. We had expected a certain characterology, the thematics we find in the reading categories we do use, or at least that solidity of specification that so often distinguishes best-sellers. We do not find any of this, and we feel we have been misled —that, contrary to the implied promise of that book, only a few writers (the kinds of writers who specialize in the genres we favor, of course) can do anything with the tradition. Readers of Aldous Huxley's *Brave New World*, an interesting novel which is from, but not in, the science-fiction tradition (for one thing, it is shot through with Huxley's curiously obsessive hatred of "vulgarity"), typically feel that way when they try to read Robert Heinlein's novels or one of science fiction's short-story anthologies.

We are one step closer to understanding a genre than we were as one-book experts when we become one-writer experts. There are many one-writer experts among us, for it seems to be the case that when we occasional readers visit another genre more than once we go usually to the same writer. Those of us who read no more than two or three detective stories a year may know only the works of Agatha Christie. For us, to read the mystery means little more than reading an Agatha Christie novel; reading the western, reading a novel by Louis L'Amour; reading science fiction, reading something by Isaac Asimov; and reading the spy thriller, reading one of Ian Fleming's stories. The writers of choice differ from one reader to the next, of course, and with each generation; once the best-known writers in their genres would have been Conan Doyle, Zane Grey, Jules Verne, and E. Phillips Oppenheim. Against this identification of the genre with a single writer, the users of that genre protest in vain. We occasional readers are surprised to learn, if we ever do, that none of those names has nearly so high a reputation with the genre's regular readers as we outsiders suppose.

We are occasional readers when we pick up a story in a new genre out of curiosity or while we are still learning how to read a genre that is beginning to interest us. Neither the curious reader nor the novice reader is likely to issue ex cathedra statements about the genre, however. Other occasional readers are not always careful: most notoriously, those angry journalists who read one detective story or horrific fantasy randomly chosen and then bemoan (and in themselves reveal) the death of mind in Western civilization. Academic scholars who assign themselves the task of discovering the appeal of some genre or subgenre they do not read themselves—historical romances, sword and sorcery, the caper novel— and who solemnly read and annotate some six or twenty of the novels are handicapped by the ignorance of the occasional reader, though they cannot afford to allow their readers, or themselves, to recognize this. The misunderstandings they foster do more mischief, for their descriptions are supported with massive citations and are snugly embedded in method.

It would of course be impossible to say at what instant an occasional reader has become a user. The one-book reader who evolves into a two- or three-writer reader may soon be a genre user and no longer an occasional visitor.

When we are genre allergics, of course, no one who listens to us is in any doubt about that.

Allergics

In the course of her research for *Reading the Romance*, Janice Radway discovered that the suburban readers she was studying detest the pornographic romance.

> The reactions of the Smithton women to books they are not enjoy-ing are indicative of the intensity of their need to avoid offensive material and the feelings it typically evokes. Indeed, twenty-three (55 percent) reported that when they find themselves in the middle of a bad book, they put it down immediately and refuse to finish it. Some even make the symbolic gesture of discarding the book in the garbage, particularly if it has offended them seriously. This was the universal fate suffered by Lolah Burford's *Alxy* (1977), a book cited repeatedly as a perfect example of the pornographic trash distributed by publishers under the guise of the romance.   (70)

When we feel like this, we find it difficult to read the stories, as though we were trying to eat spoiled or taboo food. We do not think of ourselves as having an allergic reaction, of course, but as truth seeing: this or that sort of story *is* obscenely violent, or viciously snobbish, or stupid, or grossly ignorant, and those who read it are themselves violent, brutish, stupid. Our reading motto then replaces the words "only," "also," and "sometimes" with "never": "*X?* Never!"—that is, "The detective story? Never!" or "Science fiction? Never!"

Readers of any genre learn to live quietly—if possible, anonymously —with that genre's allergics. As allergics we are just as abrasive, and so fierce and simple in our dislikes that our voices have an influence out of proportion to our numbers. The occasional readers, the nonallergic avoiders, and the inexperienced will always hear our voices of hatred more clearly than the milder approval of the users.

Reading allergies have indirect consequences when not recognized for what they are. Even if we are expert in fiction and in the theory of fiction,

. . . .

when we look into a genre or writer to which we are allergic we will not
be able to read enough of the stories to make sense of them: Mickey
Spillane has suffered grievously from the hit-and-miss reading that is all
that allergics can manage. An allergic historian refuses to acknowledge,
even to see, that a book worth admiring comes from the hated tradition,
as when the science-fiction allergic insists that Hawthorne's "Artist of the
Beautiful" and Twain's *Connecticut Yankee in the Court of King Arthur*
are not science fiction, not even nineteenth-century proto-science fiction,
and when readers allergic to westerns deny that James Fenimore Cooper's
Leatherstocking Tales are westerns. Sometimes it is useful to think of
proposals for censorship of this or that kind of book as the consequence
of unadmitted reading allergies.

No one has taken the trouble to study reading allergies, though they
are interesting in their own right. Walker Gibson offered one (partial)
explanation for our dislike of some reading materials. He suggested that
each book elicits from its readers a personality appropriate to it. A story
that is intelligent, or nasty, or comic creates in its real human reader a
mock reader who is intelligent, or nasty, or amused. Mark Twain asks
us to be one person; Henry James, another. When we find that a story
is making us into someone we do not want to be, Gibson continued, we
throw it down and say it is a bad story (265).

I am not persuaded that this alone accounts for the Smithton rejection of
pornographic romances, but it does help us understand some of our more
passionate dislikes. Readers who pass up the British, country-house tale
of detection, as I do, are perhaps suffering from a mild allergic reaction.
Those of us with other social origins and loyalties feel that the British
style of detective story asks us to give full approval to the preoccupations
of the middle class—to its love of gossip, for instance. In the course of the
inquiries, the detective uncovers precisely the kinds of secret about each
of the suspects that would send delighted shivers through a middle-class
dinner party: this woman has been having an affair with her husband's
brother, that man has embezzled, a third proved a coward while serving
in Northern India, that woman has had an illegitimate child, that man
has gone broke. Only one of these people is a murderer, but the gossip-
hunting season is declared open on anyone unlucky enough to be named
a suspect. It all seems definitively "tribal," and some of us are not sure

we want to join the dance of social excommunication. Other readers, some of them our friends, feel a similar reluctance to participate in the ceremonies shadowed forth by the genres we favor.

The people who read paperbacks are not the simple souls their critics make them out to be. They read across genre boundaries. They manifest intricate patterns of reading addictions, reading preferences, reading avoidances, and reading allergies.

They are not easy to understand even when they are speaking about a single, favored genre. Few of the enthusiasts can even agree as to what is and what is not science fiction, say, or what is and what is not a detective story. They politely overlook their differences when they meet, but the differences are not trivial.

Suppose that we want to know what a detective story is to its admirers and so turn to Barzun and Taylor's *Catalogue of Crime*, which is described on its dust jacket as a "Reader's Guide to the Literature of Mystery, Detection, and Related Genres." This is a fine collection of notes on hundreds of stories, and when we have learned to compensate for its biases it makes an excellent guide and companion to our reading. Barzun and Taylor tell us about (*a*) tales of detection and (*b*) ghost stories, but they do not tell us about (*c*) spy stories. That is one ostensive definition of *the detective story*.

We might turn instead, and with equal assurance, to Julian Symon's *Mortal Consequences: A History—From the Detective Story to the Crime Novel*. This is not a reading companion; as its title tells us, it is a history of *the detective story*, but it will also serve as an excellent reading guide. Symon's history does not cover (*b*) ghost stories, however, but *does* cover (*c*) spy stories. For people who are interested in the two volumes only for their help in finding a good read, these differences are only mildly amusing. When we are trying to understand what *the detective story* is to the people who read it, however, they are unsettling. Ghost stories and spy stories are not at all alike. What is the detective story to its readers, we ask, if some of them think of it as the tale of detection plus the ghost story and others think of it as the tale of detection plus the spy story?

There are other differences, differences in topography between the two genrescapes these readers map for us. The tale of detection—the sort of story that Conan Doyle made famous with his tales of Sherlock Holmes —looms large in Barzun and Taylor's *Catalogue of Crime*. For them, the later "crime novel"—the study that focuses on motivation rather than detection—is a decline from the Olympian heights of an earlier, golden age of the detective story. In the genrescape that Julian Symons describes in *Mortal Consequences*, however, the tale of detection that Barzun and Taylor love is snobbish, silly, adolescent—merely a stage the tradition had to go through if it was to mature into the crime novel. What is the detective story to its readers if some of them think that we shall find its center in those tales of detection and others think we shall find it in the contemporary crime novel? Nor are these the only images of that detective story we encounter when we listen to its readers. Neither of those two volumes is greatly impressed with the American style of detective story that descended from the *Black Mask* school of writers and included such honored names as Dashiell Hammett and Raymond Chandler—a school of writing that other, equally expert readers value above all others. "What *can* readers be finding in the detective story?" its critics ask. Which readers? we ask. Which detective story? "What can readers be finding in the romance?" Which readers? Which romance?

It would be difficult enough to identify the "typical reader" and the "typical science-fiction story" if we had only exclusivists to consider— people who read nothing but science fiction or the detective story or the romance. Few readers are so simple of focus, and most of those who are will be shifting to something else later.

Within every reader there lies an intricate pattern of addictions, preferences, random interests, avoidances, and allergies which is never quite the same as the pattern in any other reader. We can easily imagine two friends who exchange detective stories. One of them, though comfortable with that genre, is uncomfortable with the ghost story, is only occasionally a reader of a western, is indifferent to science fiction, violently allergic to romances. The other, also a user of the detective story, enjoys ghost stories too, however, but is allergic to westerns, uncomfortable with science fiction, and merely indifferent to the romance. What, other than the detective story, do these two readers have in common? As often as not, the reader of paperbacks is a user of many genres who becomes exclusivist only briefly. It is easier to study the long-term exclusivists; they have an attractive, laboratory-like purity about them; surely we will not be satisfied until we understand the multigenre users, however. It is the exclusivists who are atypical.

There are some other standards we can set for ourselves in our slow progress toward a better understanding of some very subtle matters: for instance, that when we set out to investigate any of the genres we first determine our own relationships to that genre—that is, whether we ourselves are exclusivists, users, fans, or occasional readers—and that when we start giving explanations, we decide whether we are addressing our remarks to users, to occasional readers, or to nonreaders. While it is not always easy to know whether we are still operating under the handicaps of the occasional reader or have through some creative leap of reading insight grasped the logic and potentiality of a genre, we should be able to tell when we are allergic, at least, or when our information about a genre comes from stories in the same tradition but in another medium—from television programs or from feature films, for instance.

We shall also want to be wary when we read the explanations that others give. We should not entirely trust either praise from exclusivists or blame from allergics, of course. We should recognize that the observations of occasional readers, though well meant, are astigmatic: occasional readers just do not know enough. A still unexploited resource, as we have seen, is the body of readers who have become fans. The men and women who write for such fanzines as *The Armchair Detective* and *The Science Fiction Review* know more about those two genres than do academic sociologists, ethnologists, and literary scholars. Further, they are intelligent, and they too want to know whether, how, and why they are different from others.

Their explanations, too, are governed by tradition, however, and we can be confident that some of them will enthusiastically assure us that reading thrillers or romances or science fiction is "fun" and that it provides "escape" and that the writers are providing them with "surrogate daydreams." One of these explanations is worth looking into, but the other two should have been thrown out long ago.

5

of fun,
of escape,
and of
daydreaming

. . . .

Many paperback readers are highly sophisticated by any measurement we choose. Their reading is value-intensive; they love and hate
writers passionately, and they distinguish between classics and genre
classics, between the good and the tolerable, between the clowning of the
talented and the clownishness of the incompetent. Further, there is no
single reader type for any genre. Each genre has its exclusivists, but they
are outnumbered by the users (regular readers who are regular readers in
other genres, too) and by the occasional readers (who do not read regularly
in the genre but do often visit it). Nor should we ignore the fans (some of
them exclusivists, some not) who play decisive roles in these genres: they
make direct contact with the writers and through their strongly expressed
likes and dislikes shape the writing of the stories.

When we look into a genre we cannot bring ourselves to enjoy, we
sometimes become rude, and then we get what we deserve, which will
take the form of a reply one of the characters in John D. MacDonald's
Scarlet Ruse gives to Travis McGee.

"You like futzing around with postage stamps?"

She gave me a blank, frowning look. "What do you futz around
with huh? Hitting an innocent little white ball with a long stick?

Soldering wires together and playing four-track stereo? Slamming some dumb little car around corners, upshifting and downshifting? Are you a gun futz or a muscle futz?"

"I think I know where you're going with that."

"Where I'm going is that there's no list to tell you where you rate on some kind of scale of permanent values and find out how unimportant you are. But I can tell you what nobody ought to be doing."

"What's that?"

"Nobody ought to be sneering at anybody else's way of life." (44)

Most readers of the paperbacks do not feel strongly enough about the stories to protest, however, and simply agree with one or another of the three most popular explanations for their interest. It is easier to do that than face certain anger.

We shall look at these three well-worn explanations: that it is fun to read paperbacks, that they provide people with an escape, and that they provide a surrogate form of daydreaming. The explanations, everywhere accepted, are not very good; but our review permits us to look closely at the endings of the stories, at the uses of different virtual realities, and at those larger-than-life heroes and heroines we associate with popular fiction.

We shall be testing these explanations against our own, common experiences with popular fiction. If an explanation fails to account for our own leisure-time experiences, we have good reason to be skeptical about its relevance to others.

Having Fun

The explanation that we read popular fiction because it provides *fun* (or *pleasure*, or *entertainment*, or *amusement*) both explains and does not explain why we are doing what we are doing.

Every naming of a type implies an antitype, every term implies a contrasting other: if we say that paperback novels are fun to read, we imply that other novels—serious and classic novels—are not. That division—paperbacks are fun, classics are dull—might seem about right to those who read only paperbacks but certainly not to the people who read

Chaucer and Dickens and Sterne. If paperback fiction does provide fun, it is not thereby distinctive: so do *The Canterbury Tales* and *The Pickwick Papers* and *Tristram Shandy*.

That is one reason why we become disenchanted with that useful word *fun*. A second is that when we use that word as our primary term, we all too quickly find ourselves engaging in deformations of its normal senses. The word *fun* suggests a state of euphoria. When, while reading, do we experience that special kind of happiness? Those euphoric experiences are bright and memorable, but they come on only four occasions. (1) The word *fun* describes our feelings very well when we are talking about good-humored books: James Thurber's *My Life and Hard Times*, H. Allen Smith's *Low Man on a Totem Pole*, and P. G. Wodehouse's *Meet Mr. Mulliner*, for example; (2) it is the right word to use when we are reading parodies: Joyce Porter's *Dover One*, Harry Harrison's *Bill, the Galactic Hero*; (3) it is also suitable when we are reading clownish writers, when we are cruelly finding fun where we were intended to find fear and love and beauty and truth.

Those three types of books provide fun: humorous books, parodies, incompetent books. Finally—(4)—there are comic chapters in books whose other chapters are exciting or tense or sorrowful: those parts of books are fun, too. That completes the inventory, though, and we have already reached the point at which we are recognizing that some books might have bits of fun in them but are not, as wholes, providing us with the kinds of euphoria that have us using that word *fun* elsewhere. The books that provide *fun* in the word's primary sense make up only a small fraction of paperback fiction. There are many occasions when *fun* is wildly inappropriate.

It fails to account for the experiences we have when reading thrillers such as Brian Garfield's *Recoil*, for instance. *Recoil* tells us about a lawyer who testifies against a mobster and is then relocated by the government in a new occupation and with a new name. When the mobster is released from prison, he hunts the lawyer down and tries to kill his family. The witness retaliates with an ingenious scheme that shows the mobster that he and his own family are just as vulnerable to that witness as the witness is to him. Garfield is a skillful storyteller, and no one—witness, mobster, or reader—finds any of it *fun* in any of the usual senses of the word.

Algys Budrys caught the design of this sort of novel very neatly in a series of columns about writing that appeared in the science-fiction fanzine *Locus*. Paperback fiction always tells a story, he says. But what, he then asks, is a story?

> There is a thing which readers will recognize as a story every time. It has seven parts:
> (1) a protagonist with a
> (2) problem in a
> (3) context in which his
> (4) efforts to solve the problem are a succession of
>   revelatory failures which lead up to a
> (5) precipitating event which makes inevitable a
> (6) solution followed by a
> (7) reward.
> Stories with villainous protagonists go as follows: (1) A protagonist with a (2) problem in a (3) context in which his (4) efforts to solve the problem are a series of revelatory increasing successes which lead up to a (5) precipitating event which makes inevitable a (6) failure followed by (7) punishment. Clearly, these are the same thing. (12)

Garfield's *Recoil*, with its sympathetic hero, follows the first of those patterns. Books with villain-heroes, such as W. R. Burnett's well-known *Little Caesar*, follow the second pattern; the gangster Rico rises inexorably in the ranks of criminals only to fall from power at the end and die in a hail of bullets. Frederick Forsyth's *Day of the Jackal* is probably the most successful thriller we have had in the past thirty years; it is far better known than any story by a contemporary humorist (that is, fun-provider)—and so, presumably, more representative of the kinds of reading experience we ask paperbacks to provide. In *The Day of the Jackal* we are following two people. One is an assassin hired to kill de Gaulle; the other is the detective who has the job of stopping the assassin. Forsyth alternates a series of revelatory successes for the assassin with a series of revelatory failures for the detective. A precipitating event then awards sudden success to the detective and sudden failure to the assassin. Forsyth has used both of the patterns simultaneously.

We find all three stories stressful until we reach those precipitating

events, when the sympathetic characters suddenly succeed and the unsympathetic characters suddenly fail. Strictly speaking, it is only while
reading the last couple of chapters of those novels that we experience
euphoria, for until we reach that end we are being frustrated with descriptions of successes and failures we do not want.

Perhaps it is the endings that are creating illusions? Perhaps we look
back at the books we have read and see them through the arches of
their happy endings. We do that sort of revaluation when we fondly recall
one of our own experiences in school or in a game or in a career, when
prolonged stress or even embarrassment is suddenly rewarded with victory
(as though God were writing O. Henry short stories with our lives) and
we forget the minutes or hours or days of tension that preceded the few
moments of triumph, looking back at the stress through the golden haze
of that brief happiness, deciding that all of it was great fun.

We might develop an argument based on the recognition of two kinds of
displaced fun: retrospective fun and anticipatory fun. Paperbacks do not
really provide fun, but they create an illusion of fun. We look back on the
reading we have done, and those happy endings fool us into supposing
that what we experienced before reaching those endings was euphoric.
In addition, our knowledge that the ending of the story we are currently
reading will be happy modifies our tension even in the case of the thriller.
We know that the Jackal will not kill de Gaulle (because we know that
no assassin did kill de Gaulle and because we know the rules for writing
thrillers), and so we enjoy the tension as a source of fun. What paperbacks
provide, then, is that retrospective fun and that anticipatory fun.

That is the best argument I can make for the continued use of the word
fun in the discussion of the paperbacks. It is not entirely convincing. The
problem lies in the endings of paperback stories.

Of the forty-two women Janice A. Radway studied, twenty-two selected
a happy ending as "the essential ingredient in romance fiction out of a
list of eleven choices, while a total of thirty-two listed it in first, second,
or third place" (65–66). Such figures confirm the widespread belief that
readers of paperbacks want happy endings. Certainly, readers of tales of
detection want to be assured that the stories end happily for the detective
in each case: the detective must solve the mystery or it is not a tale of
detection. Still, we do note that of those forty-two readers of romances,

ten did not feel a happy ending important enough to be ranked even third out of eleven.

How often are the endings of paperback stories happy? Less often than we remember. Indeed, in one sense, not very often at all.

No one would identify Richard Jessup's *Cincinnati Kid* as serious fiction or pause to wonder whether it will be assigned in courses in the novel fifty years from now. It tells of a five-card-stud player who challenges the old master, Lancey. In the novel, the Kid is a sympathetic character: more attractive than the character played by Steve McQueen in Norman Jewison's film version. The Cincinnati Kid loses his climactic match with Lancey, and at the end of the novel (though not the film) he goes on a long drunk, recovers, and challenges Lancey again. And the Kid loses again, and now knows that he always will lose. He is very good, but when it comes to five-card stud he will always be Number Two to Lancey's Number One. We like the Kid; we want him to win; but he loses. We feel that the ending is a good one—that is, we are pleased with that ending—but we certainly do not think of it as *happy* in any of the simpler senses of the word. This is not an isolated instance.

No one would think that paperbacks invariably end happily who knew the twenty-nine thrillers that Jim Thompson wrote, for instance. The world he offered his readers in novels like *The Getaway* and *Pop. 1280* has a uniquely bitter flavor—though the characters in that world are unable to imagine a better universe and are not themselves bitter. Sam Peckinpah's film of *The Getaway* has a happy ending, but Thompson's novel ends differently. In the book, the bank robber and his wife have escaped to a professionally run hideaway in Mexico, but they are now running out of money. They recognize that they love one another deeply but that it does not matter. One of them, they know, will succeed in murdering the other and will probably end up eating that person's body. The universe of *Pop. 1280* is so bleak, so grim, that the story of the psychopathic sheriff in a small Texas town who kills half a dozen people is a comedy. The only universe that sheriff knows is an emptiness.

> There were the helpless little girls, cryin' when their own daddies crawled into bed with 'em. There were the men beating their wives, the women screamin' for mercy. There were the kids wettin' in

the beds from fear and nervousness, and their mothers dosin' 'em with red pepper for punishment. There were the haggard faces, drained white from hookworm and blotched with scurvy. There was the near-starvation, the never-bein'-full, the debts that always out-run the credits. There was the how-we-gonna-eat, how-we-gonna-sleep, how-we-gonna-cover-our-poor-bare-asses thinkin'. The kind of thinkin' that when you ain't doing nothing else but that, why you're better off dead. Because that's the emptiness thinkin' and you're already dead inside.   (482)

The sheriff's own murderousness seems almost a divine deliverance. Thompson manages to give us a story with comic overtones set in a land-scape that is not funny at all. This story does not end happily, either. The sheriff, who is telling us the story, is about to be killed himself.

It is not only the thrillers that have unhappy endings. Carr and Green-berg's *Treasury of Modern Fantasy* is a collection of thirty-three stories drawn directly from the lower depths of the pulp magazine, from the likes of *Weird Tales*, *Stirring Science Stories*, *Thrilling Wonder Stories*, and *Star-tling Stories*. Fully one-third of the stories (eleven of the thirty-three) end unhappily for the people in whom we invest our sympathies.

The unhappy ending is always a possibility, as the experienced reader knows. These stories deny us that "precipitating event which makes inevi-table a solution followed by a reward." The endings of paperback stories, when they are as well written as *The Cincinnati Kid* and *The Getaway*, often please us, but they do not give us fun; and since we know that there is as much as one chance in three that the ending will be unhappy, any anticipatory fun is diminished. Happy endings are easy to find, but they are probably outnumbered by the combination of unhappy and ambiva-lent endings. Even in detective stories, we are never confident that the detective will not identify as the murderer someone we have come to like.

There is a second and more decisive objection to the claim that their happy endings generate euphoric feelings in readers of paperbacks: the happy ending is not always a *satisfactory* ending. As it happens, *The Day of the Jackal* is a story with a satisfactorily happy ending, and *The Cincinnati Kid* is a story with a satisfactorily unhappy ending: in the latter case, the reader is pleased, though the central fictional characters are not.

However, the unsatisfactory ending—whether it be happy, ambivalent, or unhappy—is far more common than the satisfactory ending. Indeed, we could not read for long in the paperbacks if we insisted upon satisfactory endings.

We find a more typical paperback ending—in this instance, happy— in Jeffrey Archer's *Not a Penny More, Not a Penny Less*. This novel was well reviewed, won a prize in its genre, and seems always to be in print. It is one of those novels about amateur crooks that the British seem to love. An American stock manipulator swindles four Englishmen out of money they can ill afford to lose. They join forces and resolve to swindle him out of the money he swindled from them. Three of the four have special expertise, in the worlds of art, of medicine, and of the university. The fourth, a likeable but inexperienced gentleman, has no special skills or knowledge. One after another, the first three put their intricate confidence tricks successfully into operation. Meanwhile, the young gentleman is worrying about devising a scheme that will enable him to recover his money and win him the respect of his new friends. Everything in the novel and in the tradition that spawned it assures us that the scheme of this nice young man will triumphantly prove to be most ingenious of all. Abruptly, he does develop an elaborate financial swindle and begins to rehearse the others in their parts; but, even more abruptly (within the last half-dozen pages), the writer marries the gentleman off to the swindler's daughter and gets him his money back that way. We never do learn what the scheme was; the gentleman never does get to show his friends and his girl that he too can take care of himself. The ending is happy—four fictional characters are smiling who were not smiling earlier—but it is unsatisfactory for us.

This failing is typical of pulp fiction. The writers lack the time, patience, or ingenuity to fashion a satisfactory ending—happy or unhappy; and the slapdash happy or ambivalent or unhappy ending is so common that we can only suppose that readers do not care much about the endings, anyway.

The stories are more often tense than good-humored, and so it cannot be that we are feeling euphoric while reading them. And if we try, as I did earlier, to reason that the stories' happy endings make them seem to have provided fun, we discover that a significant portion of them end unhappily and that only a small portion of those stories that do end happily persuade us that their endings are tailored to their beginnings and middles. It is here, in the realities of paperback endings, that that argument for a hypothetical retrospective fun and a hypothetical anticipatory fun founders. The endings rarely produce closure, that tying up of all the threads of the action that can be so satisfying. Normally, the ending of a paperback novel is not an ending for the narrative that the novel brings us. It serves a different function: it is a signal the writer is sending directly to the reader's central nervous system.

The ending of a paperback story is a conventionalized indication that the writer is abandoning the story. The ending does not interfere with readers' caring about the characters in the story: we all continue to care for and about Hamlet and Mr. Pickwick and Simon Legree and all heroes, victims, and villains in fiction after we have closed the books. We continue to love them, to grieve for them, to hate them, and—as two centuries of literary criticism prove—to ponder them. The ending does end whatever worrying we have been engaged in, however. That is, the ending tells us that it is no longer appropriate to hope that Uncle Tom will escape from slavery or that Hercule Poirot will solve that case that has the local police scratching their heads and speaking in dialect. Uncle Tom is dead, and Hercule Poirot has been triumphant again. We do not believe the unsuccessful endings, but we know that the writer has stopped worrying about the characters and that we may as well, too.

Paperback fiction does sometimes provide fun—in comic novels, in a scene here or there, in its self-parodies, in the uncommon happy ending that is also convincing—but not often enough for us to explain with that one limited word all the reading that we do. It is far more accurate to say that paperbacks provide tension. Men and women leading lives of quiet desperation during the day are turning in the evenings to stories that tell them about fictional characters who are leading lives of quiet— well, sometimes very noisy—desperation. When we insist upon using the word *fun* or one of its synonyms, we seem to be conveying little more than our own passion for reading the stories, to be declaring that we have read them, that we are reading them, and that we will continue to read them.

When we protest that we shall continue to read these stories but that the word *fun* is misleading, others immediately assure us that we are using those stories as an *escape*. But what does this mean?

Reading as an Escape

Escape has always been a word nonreaders use to make readers defensive. The physician who is reading Virginia Woolf, the teacher of literature who is reading a Max Brand western, the lawyer who is reading a rare copy of *Action Comics,* and the engineer who is reading Henry James are all alike to the people who do not read: they are all escaping from a reality they do not have the fortitude to confront. We readers should have learned by now that the word *escape* is safe to use only when we are using it about ourselves. It is dangerous when we use it to explain the reading preferences of other people.

The word dazzles us. Our minds seem to work in approximately this way: we look at the stories whose appeal we are trying to understand— romances, say, or horrific fantasy—and we find that they do not interest us, that reading them is a chore. Since the materials fail by the only test we can fully trust—their impact upon our own reading selves—we assume that those who do read them go to them not because of what they offer but, as it were, because of what they do not demand: intelligence, perhaps, or alertness or education. Readers of these stories, we decide, are running away from something else, not running toward stories they think of as valuable in their own right. And, our minds assure us, if those readers can take pleasure in materials as uninteresting as these, then their lives must indeed be monotonous and dreary. That is, when we read stories that find us dull, we use them as evidence of the dullness of the minds of others and of the irredeemable dullness of their lives. It is circular reasoning, of course, but it is none the less persuasive for that. When we use that word *escape* about the reading of others, then, we always mean "avoidance" and "flight." But when people read paperbacks, they do not feel as though they were running from something else.

What those other readers feel is what we are feeling when we use the word *escape* about our own discretionary reading. C. S. Lewis talked about reading and escaping: "Now there is a clear sense in which all reading whatever is an escape. It involves a temporary transference of the mind from our actual surroundings to things merely imagined or conceived. This happens when we read history or science no less than when we read fictions. All such escape is *from* the same thing: immediate, concrete actuality. The important question is what we escape *to*" (*An Experiment in Criticism* 68). When we turn to our favorite leisure-time reading materials, it does not feel at all like Odysseus's escaping from the Cyclops, or Satan's escaping from Milton's hell, or Melville's Bartleby escaping inside himself from the numbing monotony of office chores. The analogy that seems most apt is Edmund Dantes' departure from the Chateau d'If for the riches of Monte Cristo. The phrase *escape reading* for us (and for all other readers) implies "treasure hunting," not "running" or "avoiding."

The old metaphor has it that different writers, books, and genres create different virtual realities, that to leave the virtual reality of one genre is to enter another virtual reality. These are bounded infinities, like the set of all even numbers, which is limitless in extent (we cannot count to the end of them) and yet will never contain a member of the equally limitless, equally bounded set of all odd numbers. No one could read all the books on the law, much less trace out all the implications of all the laws and all the decisions and commentaries in those books. Yet, however extensive that law-book infinity is, no matter how long we remain in it, we shall never meet Dashiell Hammett's Continental Op, Dickens's Ebenezer Scrooge, or the tragicomic Martian invaders Olaf Stapledon gives us in *Last and First Men.* We may very well hear about those people and creatures in an allusion, a paraphrase, or a quotation, but we must go outside that virtual reality to meet them.

Thackeray and Dickens were countrymen and contemporaries. They used many of the same proper nouns (London, France, England), and they saw some of the same oppositions (old-young, men-women, rich-poor), but the universes of *David Copperfield* and *Henry Esmond* have different textures. Thackeray's virtual reality could never give birth to a David Copperfield; Dickens's could never create a Henry Esmond. We know that we shall never exhaust the world of Shakespeare but we know also that we shall never meet in Shakespeare's world the people we meet in our own paperback fiction: that self-taught virgin, that counterspy Quiller, that butterfly who mixes high and low degree.

What nonreaders think of as an escape-from seems to the rest of us an escape-to. It is a journey that begins with a turning away from chemistry, or Milton, or the law, or medicine—or the detective story—and ends with an adventuring into the alternate worlds created in our minds by other genres, other writers. It is not the from-ness, it is the to-ness that we treasure.

There is an old story about Henry Ford, whose early cars were always black. When reminded that he gave his customers no choice, he replied, unanswerably, that he did give those who wanted black anyway all the choice they required. Reading exclusivists are like those customers: they have all the choice they want. They cannot understand how important it is to the rest of us to be able to shift temporarily among different virtual realities. They have been so shaped—by nature or by habit or by both, as Plato put it—that the world they have found offers all the world they want. Dashiell Hammett's detective in "The Gutting of Couffignal" spoke for all exclusivists of all times and all places when a criminal asked him to let her go and he replied that he could not do that because he was a detective and he liked being a detective: "I don't know anything else, don't enjoy anything else, don't want to know or enjoy anything else. . . . It's the only kind of sport I know anything about, and I can't imagine a pleasanter future than twenty-some years more of it" (201). The exclusivist-as-reader is no different. Readers whose interest in word play, mythic resonance, satiric sketch, character type, and thematic focus precisely coincides with that of James Joyce have no reason ever to leave the works of Joyce. They do not know anything else, do not enjoy anything else, do not want to know or enjoy anything else, and they cannot imagine a pleasanter future than twenty-some years more of it. Readers who are science-fiction or detective-story exclusivists have an equal capacity for finding all they will ever want in the worlds they have so fortunately discovered.

The users among us do disappoint the exclusivists. We lack the capacity for unflagging resonance to the creative playfulness of that splendid writer, this endlessly fascinating genre. However much we may admire the writer or genre, we become weary; that admittedly unique world be-comes slightly claustrophobic; we begin to remember, dimly, the unique possibilities in other fictional worlds; and we turn our backs on these worlds to visit other worlds.

We often misjudge one another. If an academic woman reads Chaucer by day and the romance novel by night, the rest of us—the men, espe-cially—may suppose that it is at night that her ultimate, character-defining taste is revealed, that if she turns in her free time to the Harlequin romance, her interest in Chaucer is mercenary or pretentious.

Brusquely impatient with readers who perversely insist upon enjoying the books we detest, we punish them by simplifying them beyond all that we know about ourselves, for we know that no one could accurately infer our own taste from his knowledge of any single strand of reading activity in our busy days. We are none of us so simple.

We all have intricately interconnected preference patterns—preference hierarchies. We do not simply like poetry or baseball; we like poetry four or five times a year; the western three or four times a month; the detective story as a break from the western; the film a couple of times a month; baseball only at playoff time. We enjoy many kinds of books, but we always enjoy some more than others. When we change from one kind of book to another, the experience is parallel to our moving back and forth at dinner between our steak and our potatoes. That is, while reading we are moving within our personal preference hierarchy—down in our hierarchy, or up, or across. To pass accurate judgment on any reader's taste, we need to know the scope and the structure of his or her preference hierarchy. The Chaucerians who spend their evenings reading romances and westerns are only moving from one of their higher ranks to one of their lower ranks. They never read outside their taste. Those lawyers and philosophers and physicists who are exuberant when they turn to the spy story in the evening are even more exuberant when they return to their first preference on the morning after; then it is the law, or philosophy, or physics that is the escape from the spy story. Which is the escape activity? They all are. Each kind of book is an enrichment for every other kind of book.

The word *escape* is a very useful word in everyday apologetics. Like the word *fun*, our critics find it meaningful and justifying. If the two words explain very little—confuse the issue, rather—and if they do not persuade anyone, they at least have the merit of signaling that argument is useless. That is not what we need, but it is something.

Daydreaming

The association of paperback fiction with daydreams is potentially interesting, but it has not been seriously pursued. The best book on daydreaming is Jerome Singer's *Inner World of Daydreaming*, which describes Singer's own elaborate daydreams and what little has been learned about this activity through research. Singer's study is disappointing for the student of paperback fiction, however, for the parallels between reading and daydreaming, though mentioned, are not explored. Nor does Singer provide an operational definition of daydreaming; after closing the book we are as unclear as when we opened it as to how daydreaming differs from such activities as remembering, anticipating, thinking, and meditating. Singer does show us that people create many different kinds of daydream, though, and that is helpful, for most of us associate daydreaming exclusively with the sorts of reveries James Thurber described in "The Secret Life of Walter Mitty," a story about a man with a nagging wife, a man who borrows situations from popular fiction (from radio drama of the 1930s, apparently) for daydreams in which he casts himself as the heroic central character. So strong is that image of us wrapping our inner wounds with daydreams that in the United States the only association of reading with daydreaming is what we might call the Argument from Walter Mitty.

If we put the Argument from Walter Mitty in its baldest form, it would go something like this: life bruises some of us, and when it does we resort to the kinds of daydreams Walter Mitty created for himself. (In an essay on the notion of escape, D. W. Harding refers to this as the *analgesic* or *prophylactic* appeal of some entertainment [26].) Alternatively—and especially if our wounds are deep enough, our capacity for inventing our own daydreams dim enough—we turn to popular fiction, whose stories, like so many daydreams, serve as psychic bandages. We especially seek out stories with strong heroes and heroines, for then we can slip inside their personalities and live, vicariously, the successful lives they are leading.

Put so bluntly, it is not a convincing explanation. For one thing, it completely overlooks those unhappy endings we just examined. One more piece of evidence in this matter of happy versus unhappy endings: Robert Silverberg's *Science Fiction Hall of Fame* gives us twenty-six stories from the pulp magazines of 1934–64, a period we now refer to as an age of naive optimism in the genre; sixteen of those stories—60 percent— end unhappily. Many other paperback stories do not have heroes with whom we can identify—humorous stories, for instance; and some have so many heroes that we cannot fix on any single one—the stories with group heroes, teams, whole precinct stations as their central characters.

Perhaps the most disappointing feature of the argument is that it asks us to believe the incredible. It asks us to believe that all readers suffer, at least marginally, from that pathology of multiple personality which has so fascinated filmmakers over the past couple of decades (e.g., Nunnally Johnson's *Three Faces of Eve*, Daniel Petrie's *Sybil*). It asks us to believe that some remarkably aware men and women—T. S. Eliot, Jacques Barzun, Ludwig Wittgenstein, for example—get so confused that they think they are Christie's Miss Marple one day, Dashiell Hammett's Sam Spade the next, and James Joyce's Stephen Dedalus in between. One can only protest, hollowly, that it seems rather unlikely. By smuggling in the assumption that people who read popular fiction are not only deeply uncertain of their own identities but remarkably stupid, it begs the question it purports to answer.

There are more instructive analogies than the one suggested by Thurber's sketch of Walter Mitty—in sports stadiums, for instance. There we see a cerebral extension of that odd human proclivity we call *body English*, which takes the form of a close "identification" of the team's supporters with that team's best players. We would especially remark that the first consideration in sports fans' identifications with athletes is the uniform those players are wearing: it is not the players' abilities and commitments to the good—their "heroism"—that win the fans' loyalties; it is a matter of the players' wearing white hats or black hats, our uniform or the uniform of the Other: it is uniform first, character second. Nowhere is the cult of the hero more evident than in sports, and yet even here we can see that the fans' identification with their heroes is more subtle than the Argument from Walter Mitty recognizes.

Are there uniforms in popular fiction? The uniforms are different, but they are just as important to us, and in the same ways. Here are two descriptions from Raymond Chandler's "Nevada Gas." Is there any doubt that one of these characters is on our team and that one is not?

> George Dial was tall, dark, handsome, Hollywoodish. He was brown and lean, and had a hard, outdoor look. Everything about him was hard except his full, soft lips and his large, cowlike eyes. (266)

> Johnny De Ruse was tall, lean, quiet, dressed in dark clothes dashingly cut. His cool gray eyes had fine laughter wrinkles at the corners. His thin mouth was delicate but not soft, and his long chin had a cleft in it. (271)

The time has not yet come when the word "Hollywoodish" will be an honorific in fiction, but even without that giveaway we know that George Dial is on the enemy team: he has soft lips and cowlike eyes. And he is opposed by Johnny De Ruse, who has fine laughter wrinkles at the corners of his eyes. We do not know when writers first started giving out fine laughter wrinkles to their characters, but we know that writers have never given fine laughter wrinkles to the corners of the eyes of people we are expected to dislike.

In "The Guilty Vicarage," W. H. Auden caught the gamelike tensions of popular fiction neatly when he said, "The interest in the thriller is the ethical and eristic conflict between good and evil, between Us and Them" (302). In popular fiction, as in sports, *good* means only a little more than "us" and *bad* means only a little more than "them." That elicits from us some strange allegiances and some curious confusions.

We praise tales of detection as celebrations of intelligence, but which kind of intelligence do they celebrate? In "The Function of Criticism at the Present Time," Matthew Arnold rehearsed a traditional distinction between the creative and the critical intelligence, admiring both but giving precedence to the former, as do we all. A central irony of the tale of detection is that in it creative intelligence is embodied in the murderers, who invent bizarre methods of killing, who devise brilliant alibis, and who, having just committed murder, have the magnificent self-control to act calmly innocent. True, most of us do not want our best minds giving their energies to killing—unless it be to the killing of weeds, predatory insects, and viruses—but we acknowledge the powers of those minds even when we disapprove of them. In the tale of detection, a murder is an elaborately original production—so elaborate, so original, so difficult to bring off that we cannot imagine us doing anything so grand ourselves. The detective, who searches relentlessly for small fractures, flaws, and inconsistencies in this performance, is playing the role of critical intelligence. (Goethe would have said that the tale of detection presents the creative Faust as a murderer and the unimaginative Wagner as a detective.) In short, the detective is pedantry personified; but so skillfully do writers introduce these pedants into our reference groups that we, who give all praise to creative intelligence everywhere else, find ourselves cheering for pedantry: it is dressed in our team's uniforms. This, an Argument from Sports, has one advantage over the Argument from Walter Mitty: it recognizes that the weaknesses of the heroes and heroines are functional necessities.

Paperback stories that feature heroic characters give them three kinds of attributes. The first, already mentioned, includes those attributes that we identify as uniforms telling us whether the characters are on our team or not. The second, a source of much amusement to outsiders, includes those attributes that make us identify the characters as heroic: their intelligence, or their skills, or their poise, or their beauty, or their courage. The third kind of attribute is the weakness. Critics of paperback fiction sometimes suppose that writers do not notice the defects in their fictional characters, but those weaknesses are fundamental to the relationship that readers establish with the characters. Readers have no interest in characters, however heroic, who do not have vulnerabilities the readers do not have. We see this in the most outrageously conceived of all the heroes in popular fiction, Superman. Superman has two weaknesses: his love for the curiously dim-witted Lois Lane and his vulnerability to krypton. We set the first of these aside (for who among us does not have that kind of flaw?) and look at that laughable weakness to krypton. It can stand in for all the defects in all the other characters in popular fiction.

Of course Superman must have some weaknesses or the stories would have no conflict, but Superman's vulnerability to krypton plays another role. He is usually in his heroic mode and out on the playing field representing his readers' reference group, but when krypton has weakened him Superman is not up to representing the group in its struggles with the Other. At these moments, even the youngest children feel that they are more than his admirers, they are teammates of Superman. Even when he is at superhero strength, the child can conceive of situations in which he or she might have to go out on the field and rescue Superman. As we would put it nowadays, Superman's weakness creates an empty position within the semiotic field that the stories project into our imaginations, a position—a sort of seat on the players' bench—into which the reader settles as one who belongs.

In *Genreflecting*, her celebration of paperback fiction, Betty Rosenberg muddies the waters in a way other readers of these materials have before her. She candidly (but I think inaccurately) confesses the truth of the Argument from Walter Mitty: "All genre fiction readers are Walter Mittys, their rich fantasy lives coexisting cosily with humdrum daily living—the parallel worlds of fantasy are their natural habitat" (15). She has those heroes and heroines in mind, of course. The simplest definition of the kind of hero Walter Mitty wanted was given by an actor who played that sort of person. Ben Johnson, who appeared in many of John Ford's best films, said in a filmed interview that he thought his job as an actor had not been difficult: he was supposed to pretend to be the kind of man the men in the audiences would like to be and he was to pretend to do the sorts of things they would like to do. His definition is so elegant that it almost persuades us all by itself that we read paperbacks as Walter Mittys. And then we recall all those unhappy endings and those stories without heroes: George V. Higgins's *Friends of Eddie Coyle* is about a dangerous, doomed group of thieves and killers and provides no hero into which a Walter Mitty might project himself. Part of the success of Patricia Highsmith's *Talented Mr. Ripley* rests upon the fact that it is a story about a murderer whom we very much dislike but who gets away with his crime. Even if we do concentrate on the single-hero stories, we find that during most of the time we spend with the book we are either not reading about the heroes or (more commonly) not giving them our primary attention: it is what the heroes and heroines are seeing that interests us.

As I indicated earlier, the association of reading with daydreaming is potentially interesting: it is only the limiting definition of daydreaming as exclusively a bandaging of psychic injuries that needs to be rejected. Singer, for instance, writes about his own daydreaming and we can see that he engages in daydreaming just when some of the rest of us turn to paperbacks in moments of threatened boredom, when we are tired, to tune out music we do not like, to read ourselves to sleep (21). Singer goes on to teach us that daydreaming is far more varied than the Argument from Walter Mitty recognizes (67–72). Some people are apparently too anxious to daydream. Some people use daydreams to give expression to strong self-doubts and self-questionings. Still others use them to solve problems and to make plans. Some daydreams, Singer continues, are expressions of fear, or of failure, or of guilt, or of hostility. Some daydreams are past-oriented; some, future-oriented. In this larger sense of the daydream, there lie suggestions and possibilities for understanding reading which have not been pursued.

The words *fun* and *escape* and *daydreaming* are useful civilities. Perhaps you follow a genre that I find uninteresting, and perhaps my taste in books occasionally gives you doubts about my soundness, but we do like and respect one another and so we each say that we read for escape, or for fun, or for the Walter Mittyish-ness of it all. We are claiming nothing more for the stories than we might claim for an afternoon's doze, a cup of coffee, or a moment's pause to enjoy a vista. We are not insisting that our friends like what we like.

Even readers who come from the learned disciplines would rather not get into debates about their leisure-time reading. They do not shrink from fierce professional disagreement, and they are not averse to thought; but they find it more comfortable to say, to suppose, and even to insist that their experiences with paperbacks are simple. They would rather that others did not analyze the paperbacks they read, either. We probably will not go too far wrong if we think of the paperbacks as the intellectuals' Las Vegas.

Visitors to Las Vegas like feeling that they are rubbing shoulders with gamblers, whores, and gangsters; and when the learned turn to a thriller or a romance they are—or feel they are—rubbing shoulders with people of simpler and rawer sensibilities. That sort of cross-cultural and cross-class experience has its own rewards.

A second part of the appeal of a Las Vegas is that it offers visitors the opportunity to relax their self-governance in eating and in spending and in conscientiously observing all the other secular pieties. In Las Vegas, tourists experience something like the unselfconscious life; and that is one of the appeals of the paperbacks for some readers. In the daytime, the learned must remain intellectually alert and professionally responsible. In the evening, they are not required to respect the writers or the books or other readers or even themselves. The paperbacks are a haven from consciousness, and they would prefer to keep it that way. Words like *fun* and *escape* and *daydreaming* may not be accurate but they suggest the flavor of the experience.

Like everyone else, the learned like to feel that there is a place where they can go to be bad. If the Sunday School Society of America bought and ran all the gambling casinos, Las Vegas just would not seem like Las Vegas, somehow; perhaps the learned dislike analysis of their favorite paperbacks, the comic strips they read, and the movies they watch, not because it might be shown that they are being wicked when they spend time on them, but because it might be shown that they are not being wicked at all.

textures,

designs

• • • • • • • • •

Some of our confusion about the enthusiasms readers feel
about stories that seem undistinguished to the rest of us disappears when
we recognize an old distinction between a story's value as an object and
its value as a function.

A story has value as a function if it is valuable when seen as a part
of a system of texts. This is most easily illustrated with the parody. The
Harvard Lampoon's *Bored of the Rings* is not contemptible as a piece of
writing, but it is most effective with readers who can bring Tolkien's *Lord
of the Rings* to mind as they read that parody. They are reading two texts
at the same time, one with their eyes, the other with their memories.
What pleases them is a certain harmonic dissonance—one text playing
Don Quixote, the other Sancho Panza. Any story that is a reply to an
earlier story takes some of its strength from the set of texts it intentionally
invokes, as do David Wyss's *Swiss Family Robinson* and Jules Verne's
Mysterious Island when they come into the hands of a reader who already
knows Defoe's *Robinson Crusoe*.

A story has value as an object when it is satisfying even when readers
do not know the systems in which it participates. The people who love
Lord of the Rings did not have to wait to read *Bored of the Rings* in order
to enjoy Tolkien's original. We do not have to prepare for Dostoevski's
Notes from the Underground by reading N. G. Chernyshevsky's *What Is
to Be Done?*—the book it was answering.

One major difference between the novels taught in the schools and the novels purchased in drugstores is that the former give satisfaction as objects while the latter give their satisfaction chiefly as functions inside traditions. We understand the logic of pulp fiction better when we have come to understand that it is offering us a literature without texts —which is to say, a literature whose texts are not valuable as objects. The distinction between object and function is useful in other ways, too. As I remarked earlier, it helps us understand differences in response. The more experienced the readers in any genre, the more likely it is that they are taking their satisfaction from the texts as functions rather than as self-sufficient objects. Again, those primary readers of the paperbacks, the people who do all of their reading inside pulp culture, are much more likely to err in their valuations of the stories as objects than are those secondary readers who are reading right alongside them.

This useful simplification is too simple to be allowed to stand unchallenged, however. Anyone who has brushed casually with literary history knows that Charles Dickens was writing stories for the primary readership of pulp fiction in his own day and that those stories (*Bleak House, Great Expectations*) were texts in their own right and did not then—and do not now—require readers familiar with the stories Dickens's rivals were writing.

We have already seen that those plots so familiar to all of us carry materials that define our moment in history. As we saw in Chapter 1, pulp fiction mirrors the one sliver of space and time that we can claim as uniquely our own. The people who write it read the newspapers we read and become excited by just the events that excite us. They honor just those old books that we honor. They record our images of reality: our superhighways, our cars, even our trash. They mirror back to us the images we invent—including the images that allow us to smile at ourselves and the images of the creatures we wish we could also have been. Paperback fiction does not ask much of us—but we do not ask much of it. It does not think much of us—but we do not think much of it. We describe our favorite genres in the way we describe our friends: they see our every fault more clearly than do our enemies—but they like to be with us anyway. There is a friendly sociability in the reading of popular fiction that we overlook when we become too solemn to be serious.

We shall be looking in a later chapter at the sociability of reading, but in this chapter we are examining something entirely different: the formal pleasures the stories provide. Many readers talk about the structures that inform the stories; few talk about the pleasures those structures provide to our intuitions of form. Here is R. A. Lafferty in *Past Master*, that curious science-fiction novel in which Lafferty projects Thomas More out of the past and into a future society modeled too literally on his ironic Utopia. Lafferty is talking about the making of kings, but he might just as well be talking about the making of good paperback stories: "And is it as easy to make a king as all that? Sure it is. It's all in the tune you whistle. It has to be just right, right for its time, and with the special lilt to mark it off. But it's the tune that takes the people. Hit it right, and you can make a king every time" (178). It is these tunes and lilts—or, rather, their prose parallels, textures and designs—that we shall be examining.

Verbal Textures

We forget, sometimes, that stories always come to us in one physical medium or another and that they have different shapes: we read the book differently if we first encounter Jane Austen's *Pride and Prejudice* in a textbook edition, an expensive hardbound edition, or a paperback edition. And of course there are subtleties of physicality and formality that go far beyond this.

In his essay on aesthetics in *The Encyclopedia of Philosophy* John Hospers reminds us of two kinds of formal pleasure that we take from the arts. We take one kind of pleasure from texture ("form-in-the-small") and the other from structure ("form-in-the-large"). We shall look at form-in-the-small and form-in-the-large as they appear in the paperbacks.

In Hospers's terminology, form-in-the-small involves the "sensuous values" of art: "texture, color, tone" (42). Printed fiction does not provide sensuous experience in the direct fashion of painting and music; but, as other aestheticians have remarked, we do experience sensuous values internally as we read. We accept the pages in the way the musician accepts a musical score: as a set of cues to a performance we put on in our minds. We create in our minds a sequence of sounds and syntax to which, in some odd sense, we also listen.

It is not clear why it should be supposed that paperbacks do not have individual voices, that the neutrality of their prose makes the writers stylistically indistinguishable. Since the people who read paperbacks do not say all the writers use the same style, since only hostile critics make this claim, perhaps it is another instance of all Chinese looking alike to Caucasians and all Caucasians looking alike to the Chinese. In nineteenth-century popular fiction, an interest in the prestige, the standard, and the low dialects made itself evident; it is pervasive in the parts of Mark Twain (*Huckleberry Finn, Roughing It*) that we still most enjoy, for instance. The interest that popular fiction has taken in widely different textures of speech has not changed in the past hundred years. Here is Russell Hoban's Punch and Judy showman, Riddley Walker, talking about his life and his art: "If youre a show man then what ever happens is took in to your figgers and your fit up its took in to your show" (206). And here is E. R. Eddison's Lord Gro explaining why he is shifting from the winning side to the losing side: "It hath been present to my heart how great an advantage we held against the Demons" (187). We would certainly not mistake one of those voices for the other. And we hugely enjoy some of the voices we hear in the paperbacks: we read Damon Runyon not for his stories but for his style.

The fact of broad stylistic variation is something that cannot be proved with careful argument. It must be demonstrated—but any who are curious can page through a few randomly chosen volumes and demonstrate it for themselves. Not only do the genres differ from one another in their stylistic preferences, but the writers differ markedly from one another even within a genre. They all manifest a keen interest in speech and writing styles.

Indeed, a collection of old paperbacks is a storehouse of styles once in vogue; there is no style used anywhere that is not mimicked or mocked in vernacular fiction. No one today would misidentify the following, from John Sayles's "I-80 Nebraska M.490–M.205," though—again—it may be that none of our grandchildren will understand it and certainly our grandparents would have been baffled.

"This is that Alabama Rebel, this is that Alabama Rebel, do I have a copy?"
"Ahh, 10-4 on that, Alabama Rebel."

. . . .

"This is that Alabama Rebel westbound on 80, ah, what's your handle, buddy, and where you comin from?"

"This is that, ah, Toby Trucker, eastbound for that big O town, round about the 445 marker."

"I copy you clear, Toby Trucker."   (229)

The story was reprinted in William Kittredge and Steven M. Krauzer's *Great Action Stories*, in which Stan Dryer's "Conquest of the Washington Monument" also appeared. Dryer's mock reportese is nicely managed.

Among technical monument climbers, the ascent of the Washington Monument has always been recognized as the penultimate challenge in purity of execution. . . . I had studied the records of the ill-fated Harkins expedition (see Washington police blotter, May 7, 1971), who were forced to turn back at the 42-foot mark on the north face. Their failure, I felt, was due to their negligence in not disabling the floodlights at the base of the monument to prevent police detection. We would not make this mistake, but other difficulties that I could not anticipate would confront us.   (113)

The weaker writers suppose that the textures that are characteristic of a genre are purely dialectal. Here, for instance, is James Farnsworth's attempt to create a western texture in *Lash of Vengeance*.

"Then whut the hail's yore game, Rangan?"

"Well, I'll tell you, Josiah, since you've asked me so polite an' all. You've took a lot of things from me in the past which was rightfully mine . . . an' now I've got a mind to have 'em back. If you'll sell, I'll pay you for 'em, an' no more said—that'd be the tidy way, an' I do like to keep things tidy, don't you? But if'n you won't sell, why, then, you don't leave me much choice but to take 'em anyways, now do you?"   (51)

The Lash of Vengeance could kill us all with an apostrophe overdose. The novel appeared in 1978, long after *whut* and *yore* and *if'n* went out of fashion in the western. I suppose some might find in the novel a bit of nostalgia for the days when Zane Grey and Clarence Mulford and William

MacLeod Raine were the great names of the western tradition, but they did that sort of thing much better.

Those sentences are unreadable. Worse, they are uninteresting. Steven Overholser does give us interesting western voices in *A Hanging in Sweet-water*, and yet we do not find paragraphs like Farnsworth's. Nothing about the lexicon in the following exchange is unusual (the contractions are standard for informal American English), and yet we know at once we are in a western. We can go so far as to say that the exchange could not be translated into any other tradition. Change the names, change the horse to a car—and we would still know we are reading a western.

> "Smoky won't let me ride him when I've been drinking."
> "What?" Ella said in disbelief.
> "That's right," Buck said. "If Smoky smells whisky on me, he won't let me on."
> Ella laughed. "I've never heard of such a thing."
> "You haven't?" Buck asked. He winked at me. "My grandma was the same way. Damn near drove my grandaddy crazy."

This is in the tall-tale tradition, where the joke lies not in the wild exaggeration (as Easterners sometimes suppose) but in the gullibility of the listener. Mark Twain's "Celebrated Jumping Frog of Calaveras County" made this sort of joke internationally known, but the tall tale remains a trope unique to the western. We recall, too, that we found nothing distinctively western about the lexicon or syntax in that account we looked at earlier of Apaches hiding their trail from the cavalry. There is more to writing a western than using the word *pronto*.

When readers of science fiction want truly awful (that is, clownish) textures, they turn with confidence to the exclamation-mark style of E. E. Smith, a writer of powerful imagination but no great delicacy of ear. Smith was always reaching for adjectives in the superlative form—or, as he would no doubt have put it, *for the finest adjectives in the universe!* The following, from *Spacehounds of IPC*, parts of which were written as early as 1931, would keep a foreign student of American slang happy for hours. " 'How was I to think that a wonder-girl like you could ever love a guy like me? You certainly are the gamest little partner a man ever had. You're the

world's straightest shooter, ace—you're a square brick if there ever was
one. Your sheer nerve in being willing to go the whole route makes me
love you more than ever, if such a thing can be possible, and it certainly
puts a new face on the whole cockeyed Universe for me'" (61). Even
as Doc Smith's contemporaries were reverently stealing his ideas—and
they all did—they were giggling at his earnest attempts to achieve the
Longinian sublime.

This sort of clumsiness occurs now and then in every genre, but the
paperback genres have within them mechanisms for self-correction. Here,
from *Lord of Light*, is Roger Zelazny's amused version of a metaphor-mad
poet. The gods (humans, actually, who have set themselves up as gods
on a distant planet) are gathering for a wedding. We note that Zelazny's
parody comes closer to the sublime than did the eternally youthful prose
of E. E. Smith.

> So they came into the Celestial City. . . . It was said by the
> poet Adasay that they resembled at least six different things (he
> was always lavish with his similes): a migration of birds, bright
> birds, across a waveless ocean of milk; a procession of musical notes
> through the mind of a slightly mad composer; a school of those
> deep-swimming fish whose bodies are whorls and runnels of light,
> circling about some phosphorescent plant within a cold and sea-deep
> pit; the Spiral Nebula, suddenly collapsing upon its center; a story
> [*sic*], each drop of which becomes a feather, songbird or jewel; and
> (perhaps most cogent) a Temple full of terrible and highly decorated
> statues, suddenly animated and singing, suddenly rushing far across
> the world, bright banners playing in the wind, shaking palaces and
> towers, to meet at the center of everything to kindle an enormous
> fire and dance about it, with the ever-present possibility of either
> the fire or the dance going completely out of control.
> They came.   (217)

We do not ask that the voices the writers use be clear, or even intelligible. In some cases it is the rougher textures that please us. That is why
we recognize that Toby Fitton is writing with tongue in cheek when he
suggests that only a few could read the financial thriller: "The financial

thriller has a specialized following, who must have an instinctive knowledge of the rules under which the game is played, be up-to-date in Capital
Transfer Tax regulations and learned in the daily routines of the Tokyo
stock exchange" (354). If not having specialized knowledge stopped us,
we would hardly read at all.

As the writers know, some voices in paperbacks please us because
they sound plausible but are slightly unintelligible, having an odd but
not unattractive texture of their own. Here is an exchange from Donald
Hamilton's thriller *The Mona Intercept*.

> "Main halliard to starboard at the aft end of the deckhouse,"
> Ullman said. "Forestaysail halliard to port. On the mast, that reel
> winch to starboard works the all-wire halliard for the roller-furling
> jib, which has to be set up very taut. It's a bit slack now; you'd better
> take up on it before we break out the sail. You know about those reel
> winches?"
>
> "Sure. They'll take your fucking arm off if you're not careful. I'll
> watch it. You want me to hank on the staysail?"   (422)

Henry James, the least vulgar of American novelists, crossed the Atlantic
in sailing vessels and would have understood this passage perfectly. Put
most of the rest of us on a boat, however, and ask us to point to the
staysail, and we would not know which way to turn. But we keep on
reading.

We especially treasure writers who can give us a simulacrum of the verbal styles of groups we rarely encounter. The list of names Edward Margolies quotes from Dashiell Hammett's "Big Knockover" is more authentic
than most of the voices we hear in the detective stories. The paragraph an-
ticipates the verbal textures of a later underworld that George V. Higgins
was to imitate.

> There was the Dis-and-Dat Kid, who had crushed out of Leaven-
> worth only two months before; Sheeny Holmes; Snohomish Shitey,
> sockless and underwearless as usual, with a thousand-dollar bill
> sewed in each shoulder of his coat; Spider Girrucci, wearing a steel-
> mesh vest under his shirt and a scar from crown to chin where
> his brother had carved him years ago; Old Pete Best, once a con-

. . . .

gressman; Nigger Vojan, who once won $175,000 in a Chicago
crap game—*Abracadabra* tattoed on him in three places; Alphabet
Shorty McCoy; Tom Brooks, Alphabet Shorty's brother-in-law, who
invented the Richmond razzle-dazzle and bought three hotels with
the profits; Red Cudahy, who stuck up a Union Pacific train in 1924;
Denny Burke; Bull McGonickle, still pale from fifteen years in Joliet;
Toby the Lugs, Bull's running-mate, who used to brag about picking
President Wilson's pocket in a Washington vaudeville theater, and
Paddy the Mex.   (Margolies 27)

Hammett's love of these verbal textures is characteristic of the American
crime-story tradition. Here is a paragraph from Damon Runyon's "Hottest
Guy in the World." The voice is unmistakable.

I wish to say I am very nervous indeed when big Jule pops into my
hotel room one afternoon, because anybody will tell you that big Jule
is the hottest guy in the whole world at the time I am speaking about.

In fact, it is really surprising how hot he is. They wish to see him
in Pittsburgh, Pa., about a matter of a mail truck being robbed, and
there is gossip about him in Minneapolis, Minn., where somebody
takes a fifty *G* pay roll off a messenger in cash money, and slugs the
messenger around somewhat for not holding still.   (205)

There is an archness behind Runyon's prose that does not wear well, but
for brief stretches it is delightful.

The hard-boiled detective story got a name for itself—not necessarily a
good name—for its continuing efforts to create a distinctive urban texture
in language. (The writers thought they were producing antipoetry, but
all the good poetry thinks it is antipoetry.) Some of them did this badly,
but writers such as Ross Macdonald used the characteristic metaphors
sparingly and accurately. The following passage, from *The Chill*, may be
the paradigm metaphor: from the streets of the city, the narrator rejects a
nature image.

A moon like a fallen fruit reversing gravity was hoisting itself
above the rooftops. It was huge and slightly squashed.

"Pretty," Jerry said in the parking lot.

"It looks like a rotten orange to me."   (184–85)

Archer, Macdonald's narrator, thinks and sees in one-line poems. Of a dean calling in another dean with sudden news, Archer remarks, "She was pale and grim, like a reluctant executioner" (26). Of an empty college campus, "Diminished by the foothills and by their own long shadows, the buildings resembled a movie lot which had been shut down for the night" (31–32). Of a waitress, "Her name was Stella, and she was so efficient that she threatened to take the place of automation. She said with a flashing smile that this was her aim in life" (66). Of an old policeman, broken by drink and memories, "His fingers were thick and mottled like uncooked breakfast sausages" (128). At his best, Macdonald wrote very good one-line poetry: "She was just an old lady in dirty tennis shoes but her body, indeterminate in a loose blue smock, carried itself with heavy authority, as if it recalled that it had once been powerful or handsome. The architecture of her face had collapsed under the weight of flesh and years. Still her black eyes were alert, like unexpected animal or bird life in the ruins of a building" (19).

The most admired contemporary writer of thieves' speech is George V. Higgins, who gives us underworld voices from contemporary Boston. Here, in *The Digger's Game*, the Greek, a loan shark, has the note for the $18,000 the Digger lost in Las Vegas, but the $600 a week the Greek wants for interest is too high.

> "You think I'm a fuckin' chump, Greek," the Digger said. "I dunno as I go for that. You think you're gonna whack me six on eighteen and I'm gonna sit still for a screwing like that, I'm just gonna fuckin' let you *do* it to me? You know who you're talking to? I'm gonna take your fuckin' *head* off and serve it on a fuckin' *platter* to my fuckin' *dog*, is what I'm gonna do, and I haven't even *got* a fuckin' dog. I'm gonna have to go out and *buy* one, and I will, too, Greek, you know me, you know." (110)

As soon as Higgins's first book, *The Friends of Eddie Coyle*, appeared, even people who do not usually read crime novels started reading him. The voices he gives his characters are unusual and distinctive, but his interest in odd dialects and flavors of speech is solidly within the tradition of his genre. The Digger and the Greek could be the grandsons of those thieves Hammett described: Toby the Lugs, Paddy the Mex, and Alphabet Shorty McCoy.

Other writers give their deepest energies to the creation of scenes. A brilliant realizer of sharply conceived episodes is Chester Himes, whose police stories about Harlem (*For Love of Imabelle, The Big Gold Dream*) parade before us an endless series of bizarre scenes from the life of the night with textures uniquely their own. A newer writer, William Marshall, is giving us police procedurals about Hong Kong (*Yellowthread Street, The Far Away Man*) that distantly remind us of Chester Himes. Marshall is another writer whose gift is for the creation of scenes that at first seem simple but prove to have artfully complex internal music. The best of them are too long to quote; but their structures are hinted at in the following brief scene from the best of his earlier novels, *The Hatchet Man*. An overworked Chinese-American detective, Christopher O'Yee, has not been home for days; but finally he does appear for breakfast:

> Penelope O'Yee, aged five, looked across the breakfast table at her father; Mary O'Yee, aged ten, looked across the breakfast table at her father; Patrick O'Yee, aged seven, looked across the breakfast table at his father; and Emily O'Yee, Christopher Kwan O'Yee's wife, looked across the table.
>
> O'Yee said, "What are you all looking at?"
>
> Penelope O'Yee looked at Patrick O'Yee. Patrick O'Yee looked at his sister, Mary O'Yee looked at both of them. They all looked at their mother.
>
> Penelope O'Yee said, "Mummy, who is this man?"
>
> O'Yee squinted at her evilly. He said, "Don't be funny." He re-filled the child's glass of milk. "I'm your father."
>
> "Father!" Patrick O'Yee said.
>
> "Shut up, you."
>
> "Father!" Mary O'Yee said. She asked her mother. "Is that really him?"
>
> "Yes, dear," Emily O'Yee said. "I think it is." She looked at O'Yee carefully. "You are their father, aren't you? It was you, wasn't it? It's so hard to remember that far back."
>
> "I don't need the Marx Brothers over breakfast. I've been working.

I didn't get in until four in the morning. I slept on the sofa so I wouldn't disturb anyone. I was trying to be nice."

"My father's nice," Penelope O'Yee said. At five, it didn't pay to take the wrong side. In the night when the shadows in your bedroom turned into ghosts and goblins, fathers could be very handy.

(62–63)

The stories invite the attentions of those who do content analysis, who wonder why this group of readers should favor stories in which these kinds of people appear doing these sorts of things. Often, the explanations that sociologists and psychologists give are so powerful that they dazzle us, but they are just as defective as the purely structuralist and formalist explanations. They pass over the values of tone and texture that are so plainly evident to the people who read these stories and that play no small part in the stories' selection of readers.

Design

The pleasures of form-in-the-large are the pleasures that structure provides—"the over-all organization that results from the interrelations of the basic elements of which [a work] is composed" (Hospers 43). Distinctions between textures and structures are often blurry—as we saw when we examined that "textural" breakfast scene with the O'Yee family —but it is worth making that distinction when examining any art form: "We may often wish to distinguish, for example, the work of those composers who are masters of structure and less adept at texture from the work of those composers of whom the opposite is true" (Hospers 43).

The distinction is as meaningful in paperback fiction as it is in music. Readers who prefer fantasy to science fiction, for instance, complain that we never know what things look and sound like while reading science fiction, while readers of science fiction are simultaneously complaining that writers of fantasy tell their stories too simply, in a linear, this-happened-and-then-this-and-then-this fashion. The detective story has always shown a keen interest in textures. As we have seen, writers of the hard-boiled detective story gave their attention to street slang, the sounds and sights of the inner city. Writers of the tale of detection, such as Dorothy Sayers and Agatha Christie, offered bits and pieces from the world of the upper middle class—but they also devised intricate narrative structures. Robert Champigny caught this last neatly in the title of his study of the type, *What Will Have Happened:* we, who are following the story of the detective, are asked to guess another story the writer is withholding from us, the story of the murderer.

We still do not seem to be able to talk effectively about the experience of form in prose. Indeed, in the past three hundred years of literary criticism, no one has improved on John Dryden's salute, in his *Essay of Dramatick Poesie,* to the pleasures of design: " 'If then the parts are managed so regularly, that the beauty of the whole be kept entire, and that the variety become not a perplexed and confused mass of accidents, you will find it infinitely pleasing to be led in a labyrinth of design, where you see some of your way before you, yet discern not the end till you arrive at it' " (49). Dryden was writing about the English drama of 1688. He had certainly never heard of the detective story. Poe was not to write "Murders in the Rue Morgue," the first of his four influential tales of ratiocination, for another 153 years. Yet nothing written about the rewards of stories such as Anthony Berkeley's *Poisoned Chocolates Case* or, say, Charles Williams's tricky little thriller, *The Sailcloth Shroud,* so neatly captures the experience as those two sentences about Restoration drama. When the writer is up to the challenges of the form, it truly is infinitely pleasing even for occasional readers to be led in a labyrinth of design, where we see some of our way before us, yet discern not the end till we arrive at it. The best of the writers are virtuosos who can honor a traditional design and always, somehow, surprise us.

It should not be supposed—as it sometimes is—that every paperback story honors one or another of a tiny number of traditional designs. First, some stories (most of the genre classics, for instance) are decisively untraditional for their genres. Second, the number of traditional designs is not small. There are dozens—perhaps hundreds—of traditional designs for each genre, and often the first problem that we readers must solve is that of determining which one or two or more of these traditional designs we have before us at the moment. At the very least, writers love to crossbreed these designs. John Le Carré's *Tinker, Tailor, Soldier, Spy,* for instance, is the spy story its title proclaims it; but we eventually discover that there lies in it one of the traditional designs of the detective story. Stewart Edward White's "Buried Treasure" manages the unlikely feat of starting off as a western, turning into a sea story about a search for buried pirate treasure, and then turning itself back into a western. Leslie Whitten's *Progeny of the Adder* begins as a detective story but metamorphoses into a horror story. (Apparently writers find it difficult to merge these two genres. Whitten is the only writer I have found who can do this without sacrificing one set of conventions to the other.) Sometimes such experiments end miserably: A. B. Guthrie wrote superb westerns, but his early *Murders at Moon Dance* begins as a western, turns into a detective story—and fails dismally as both.

Often the writers create designs that do not come from genre tradition. Stephen King's *Shining*, like many of his other stories, is structurally fascinating. King played upon public outrage about the mistreatment of children by his ingenious use of the tradition of the haunted Gothic castle. He has the ancient evil that is resident in a hotel attack a child through his father. That is the design of the narrative. The design of the story is also interesting. As we read, we are traveling always in two directions: into the future, where something bloody and horrible threatens; into the past, where the father's own illnesses lie buried. With each chapter, a vista is opening up more and more widely in two opposed directions.

Some writers ingeniously honor a tradition—meeting every expectation —and yet transcend limitations that cripple lesser talents. Maj Sjöwall and Per Wahloo wrote a series of ten detective stories (*Roseanna*, etc.) about Martin Beck, a detective in Sweden. Each story is a well-made police procedural, and each contributes its part to the biography of the series' decent, troubled hero. Behind these two narrative lines there lies an even more interesting third narrative: the persuasive account of a slow ooze of mediocrity and stupidity spreading irresistibly within the Swedish bureaucracy: the vision that the last of the series, *The Terrorists*, leaves in our minds reminds some of us of the final image of *The Dunciad*, Alexander Pope's salute to dullness:

> Lo! thy dread empire, Chaos, is restored;
> Light dies before thy uncreating word;

. . . .

> Thy hand, great Anarch! lets the curtain fall,
> And universal darkness buries all.

We finally decide that the series could aptly have been named either
The Career and Life of Martin Beck or *Murder in Sweden: Ten Cases* or *A
History of Swedish Stupidity* and that our pleasure in it derives in no small
part from the interplay, in each volume, among the three story lines.

We shall examine good design in science fiction, that genre marked if
in no other way by the delight its readers take in intricate patterns of story.
We shall study Ursula K. Le Guin's *The Dispossessed: An Ambiguous
Utopia*, a story in which design, narrative, and theme are all aware of one
another.

Le Guin's novel gives us the story of Shevek, a young man who lives on
a subsistence planet governed by a utopian political system. (There are
hundreds of anti-utopian and dystopian novels in modern science fiction.
As its subtitle indicates, this is a rare instance of a utopian story.) We
see Shevek as an infant, as a gifted child, as a young student of physics
and mathematics, as an influential critic of society, and as the author of
scientific papers that bring him interplanetary fame. We follow his visit
offworld to the planet from which his people had come; and with him
we compare the political system on this Earth-like planet with that of
his home.

The story has two parts. One part is a *Bildungsroman:* the account of
the development of a gifted and responsible young man; if Le Guin had
published it separately, she might have called it *Portrait of the Scientist
as a Young Revolutionary*. The other part is a letters-of-a-Persian-visitor
narrative: the observations on our own political and social systems by
a visitor from a better political system; if she had published that story
separately she might have given it an eighteenth-century title, *A Visitor
from Utopia*.

It would seem that these two stories, however interesting individually,
would not add up to a single novel. Though both narratives are centered
upon Shevek, the book might have ended as the mere butting together
of two long short stories. There is a further difficulty. As it happens,
Shevek's earlier intellectual adventures on his home planet are far more

interesting than his later adventures on the analogue of our own Earth, and a book whose first half is more interesting than its second half is not going to please its readers. Le Guin's solution to these problems is simple and may seem obvious, but it is very elegant. She shuffled the two stories neatly together.

There are thirteen chapters. If Le Guin had numbered them to identify the order in which Shevek lived through the events they describe, the first chapter we read would have been named Episode 7; the second, Episode 1; the third, Episode 8; the fourth, Episode 2; and so on. The sequence, then, is 7, 1, 8, 2, 9, 3, 10, 4, 11, 5, 12, 6, 13.

Looking back at the novel afterward, we can see that the opening and closing chapters were given to Shevek's journeys offplanet and home again; and that episodes 1 through 6 were given to his earlier life; episodes 8 through 12, to his offworld adventures. We do not know the story has this structure when we buy it casually at a newsstand, of course. We bought the book for a quick read, and it takes four chapters, at least, before we have identified the design, the offworld/onworld and later-life/early-life rhythm. Until we have reached that fourth chapter, we are struggling to identify the story design; but then, or shortly thereafter, we relax and do, unconsciously, the necessary sorting of episodes into their calendrical relationships to one another.

This is a simple pattern, but it did solve several problems. The pattern knits two short stories together into a novel. (A shift in two climaxes— a scientific climax and a political climax—further helped to hide the two stories' fundamental disparity.) This pattern also interleaves weaker episodes with stronger episodes, maintaining a steady level of reader interest throughout the story.

Further, the design makes the story itself give testimony to Shevek's scientific and political discoveries. His interplanetary fame as a scientist comes because he develops a General Theory of Time, predicated on a certain Principle of Simultaneity. His homeworld notoriety comes because he is one of the founders of the highly unpopular Syndicate of Initiative, which insists that the revolutionary energies of his society are being lost and which is dedicated to the proposition that in a revolutionary society like theirs every moment should be a moment of revolution, of newness.

Later in the story, all of this comes together—the idea of a Principle of Simultaneity and the idea of a Syndicate of Initiative and the design of the story that keeps both parts of Shevek's life simultaneously present in the readers' minds. It comes together for us as Shevek is watching a protest parade on the planet he is visiting:

> When they sang, both the exhilaration and the fear became a blind exaltation; his eyes filled with tears. It was deep, in the deep streets, softened by open air and by distances, indistinct, overwhelming, that lifting up of thousands of voices in one song. The singing of the front of the march, far away up the street, and of the endless crowds coming on behind, was put out of phase by the distance the sound must travel, so that the melody seemed always to be lagging and catching up with itself, like a canon, and all the parts of the song were being sung at one time, in the same moment, though each singer sang the tune as a line from beginning to end.   (260)

Anyone who has ever watched a patriotic parade has heard several bands playing the same tune. We do not make much of it. Shevek listens differently, however. He is always searching for images of simultaneity and of continuing creation, and so he notices what most of the rest of us overlook: that it is possible for every note in a song to be in the air at the same moment even while each individual is singing the song serially. The image is a verbal icon, "a verbal sign," as W. K. Wimsatt once put it, "which somehow shares the properties of, or resembles, the objects which it denotes" (x). The song so imaged validates both Shevek's achievement and the novel's design.

Before any of this becomes apparent to the reader of science fiction, however, the displacements of the two narratives have already served one overriding purpose. As we remarked earlier, science-fiction readers love stories that challenge them with the kinds of design difficulties this novel provides. (One of their favorite types of story has been the story about intersections of alternate time streams—for example, Philip K. Dick's *Man in the High Castle*—quite possibly because it gives so many opportunities for intricacies of story design.) Le Guin's design is odd enough to quicken her readers' interest but not so intricate that it is distracting.

Most of the prize-winning science-fiction novels of the past two decades have demanded careful attention from their readers; but the valorizing of design intricacy is everywhere in evidence in this genre. We find it in the short stories, too. And we find that anthologists reprinting the best of the magazine fiction pass over the simpler stories in favor of the ones that are design-intensive. James Gunn's selection from Brunner's novel *Stand on Zanzibar* is typical. Brunner's prize-winning story about the year 2010 is a collection of wonderful fragments from the lives of many different people. Since few of these people know one another, it is not until we have moved through a couple of hundred pages that we sense a coherence growing in our image of the action. The novel had begun with ten pages of short fragments, of one or two sentences each, that were almost unintelligible because they were in the slang of 2010 and the book had not yet taught us that slang. After we have completed the novel, we can return to those opening pages and make sense of them; but when we were just starting out, the fragments themselves were only semi-intelligible, and of course the pages were incoherent. Simply put, *Stand on Zanzibar* opens with ten pages of incoherence. Yet it was precisely these ten pages of incoherence that James Gunn chose to help represent science fiction in *From Heinlein to Here*, a paperback anthology sold on the newsstands to people looking for that quick, good read.

Robert Heinlein once reminded other writers of pulp fiction that they were doing nothing more grand than competing with bartenders for people's beer money. That wry allusion to opiates for the masses is characteristically amusing, but the readers of the early Robert Heinlein took him more seriously than he did. They loved the stories he told, but they praised him almost as often for his storytelling skills as for his stories. Heinlein is a particularly interesting writer in this connection, for most of his readers disagreed strongly—sometimes even furiously—with the politics of his novels. They were not reading Heinlein and awarding him prizes because he said the right things but because he said things— usually, they felt, the wrong things—in the right way. It was the tune that made the difference. Heinlein hit it right.

The conventions for talk about the popular arts are more restrictive by far than the conventions for the stories themselves, and those conventions are still encouraging only a sharply limited interest in form.

. . . .

They encourage structuralist studies but not formalist studies. The differences between these two types of study are fundamental.

Dryden was recognizing both structuralist and formalist interests when he remarked that it is " 'infinitely pleasing to be led in a labyrinth of design.' " There lies the distinction: the structuralist identifies the labyrinth of design for us; the formalist anatomizes the pleasure we are taking in that design as we are led through it. We have had some very good structuralist analysis. Janice A. Radway provides a brilliant account of the narrative logic of the stories she reports on in *Reading the Romance* (150), for instance, and Donna Bennett has done much the same sort of thing for the tale of detection. We seem to have trouble going beyond that part of our studies, however.

The conventions governing the discussion of popular culture are not entirely to blame. E. H. Gombrich's *Sense of Order* introduces us to a rich body of inquiry into the nature of the formal pleasures provided by paintings and sculpture, but there is no parallel body of inquiry into the formal pleasures offered by any kind of prose fiction. Students of popular culture, most of whom come from literary studies, have no model for formalist analysis.

Still, structuralist analysis is so much easier to do on popular fiction that we might almost expect that a tradition of structuralist analysis would emerge and be followed by a tradition of formalist analysis in studies of vernacular fiction and from there spread into the study of canonical and serious fiction. This has not happened, and for that we must blame the familiar image of popular fiction as something produced by the fox to gull the geese. If we think of paperback stories as coming from people who do not respect either the stories or their readers and who are writing them to old recipes ("formulas") for a mob too naive, ignorant, and dim to recognize how it is being fooled, we have no interest in the aesthetic experiences those readers are having with the stories. Here and there we find someone looking at the experience of form we have with these materials—as in John G. Cawelti's brief notes on the aesthetics of social melodrama in his *Adventure, Mystery, and Romance* (263–68)—but it is not until we recognize that many of the readers are deeply sophisticated that the potentialities for exploring this aspect of popular fiction seem promising.

Paperback fiction is *form-intensive*. It is as form-intensive as the sonnet, the villanelle, the English ode. So prominent is the interest in verbal textures, in the construction of brightly individual scenes, and in the designs of both the narratives and the stories that bring us those narratives that even its harshest critics will admit that there is strong presumptive evidence of a sharing among writers and readers of intensely formal pleasures. In one sense, reading in a popular tradition is more like listening to music than it is like reading literature. To say that this reading is "musical" might suggest that the stories are empty of intellectual reward, however. They are not. The intellectual content of the stories makes up a surprisingly large part of their appeal even to the highly educated.

7

thinking with
tired brains

• • • • • • • • • • • • •

*Dondragmer spent much of the time on the downstream
trip examining the [differential] hoist. He already knew
its principles of construction well enough to have made one
without help; but he could not quite figure out just why it
worked. Several Earthmen watched him with amusement,
but none was discourteous enough to show the fact—and
none dreamed of spoiling the Mesklinite's chance of solving
the problem by himself.*
—*Hal Clement*, Mission of Gravity

It is a familiar charge that readers turn to the paperbacks as a
refuge from thought, and yet it is an odd one. The mental activity that an
old-fashioned mystery required—at the least, a keen skepticism about
everything we were told—was not trivial; and the intricately fashioned
displacements of the narrative line in some of the traditions could never
have appeared in print if there were not readers who enjoyed being thrown
into initial confusion and working their way out of it. Readers would not
enjoy Hal Clement's *Mission of Gravity* if they did not relish the challenge
the writer posed them of deducing for themselves the shape of a planet
that has eight-minute days and nights and a gravitational pull three times
that of Earth at its equator but several hundred times Earth gravity at
its poles. The challenges of some of the paperback genres are different

from those that serious fiction offers but only because the paperbacks are written for people who will be reading at a different time of the day.

Paperback stories are written for tired brains. T. S. Eliot read thrillers; Ludwig Wittgenstein read pulp detective stories. Robert Sencourt tells us that Eliot read "Conan Doyle, Simenon, Wilkie Collins," and he cites his "taste for Maurice Leblanc's stories of Arsene Lupin, which he shared with Graham Greene" (Sencourt 221). Wittgenstein was quite clear in his loyalties:

> It'll be fine to get detective mags from you. There is a terrible scarcity of them now. My mind feels all underfed.
>
> They are *rich* in mental vitamins and calories. . . .
>
> Your mags are wonderful. How people can read Mind if they could read Street & Smith beats me. If philosophy has anything to do with wisdom there's certainly not a grain of that in Mind, & quite often a grain in the detective stories.   (Malcom 35, 36)

Their minds may have been weary, but the weary minds of T. S. Eliot and Ludwig Wittgenstein were the minds of Eliot and Wittgenstein still. No doubt their weary minds were a bit slower, did not have the same intensity of concentration, did not want to ponder; but they were what they were in their best hours. If the rest of us are not quite Eliots and Wittgensteins, we are at least not less ourselves when we turn to the paperbacks at the end of the day.

The stories are vivid, sometimes outrageous: they must be to keep our attention. Like serious fiction, however, they would not hold us if they did not offer something to feed our minds. Here we shall look at three of the ways in which the stories address our weary but still active minds: first, by bringing us information; second, by parading before us models and countermodels of the exemplary that help us to see ourselves for what we are; third, and most important, by providing a theater that brings our deeper uncertainties into the light so that we ourselves can begin to work on them.

Advice and Information

None of us, I suppose, has ever searched out a science-fiction novel because it has useful information about binary-star systems, but the fact that information of that sort does come our way through science fiction is one of its attractions. That is, we do not turn to the paperbacks *for* the information with which they are bursting. There are quicker, more reliable sources of information about interstellar dust, courtroom tactics, the handling of cattle, ciphers. But we turn to the paperbacks *because* they have that information. We do not always remember how much information and advice there is in the stories.

In *The Grail Tree* Jonathan Gash's disreputable antique dealer, Lovejoy, tells us how to look at a watercolor: "I did my infallible watercolor trick. Always half close your eyes and step back a few inches more than seems necessary. Then do the same from a yard to its right. Then ditto left. Do this and you're halfway to spotting the valuable genuine old master. It works even for painters as late as Braque. You need not know anything about the art itself. Forgeries and modern dross look unbalanced by this trick, full of uneven colors and displeasing lines. It's as simple as that" (62). John D. MacDonald, in *Cinnamon Skin*, has his Travis McGee driving into Houston and telling us, with characteristic impatience, how he drives in rush-hour traffic.

Once you have the concept of the pack making the law, driving the urban interstates is simplified. You maintain just that distance from the vehicle ahead which will give you braking room yet will not invite a car from a neighbor lane to cut in. You pick the center lanes because some of the clowns leaving the big road on the right will start to slow down far too soon. You avoid the left lane when practical because when they have big trouble over there on the other side of the median strip, the jackass who comes bounding over across the strip usually totals somebody in the left lane. When you come up the access strip onto the big road, you make certain that you have reached the average speed of all the traffic before you edge into it. Keep looking way ahead for trouble, and when you see it put on your

flashing lights immediately so that the clown behind you will realize
you are soon going to have to start slowing down.   (48–49)

Sometimes we do not know quite what we are supposed to do with the
information we are given. How is an American reader to use the legal lore
that Cyril Hare provides in his detective story, *When the Wind Blows?*
" 'You may not lawfully marry your divorced wife's sister—and a half
sister, for this purpose, counts as a full one. That is the result of an
Act of Parliament passed in the reign of Henry VIII—a gentleman who
knew quite a bit about divorces. On the other hand, modern legislation
has made it possible to marry a deceased wife's sister' " (237). Primitive
calculation indicates that only divorced Englishmen and Englishwomen
who are contemplating marriage to a living former spouse's siblings would
be made alert. Even for the book's English readership, Hare's information
about remarriage must fall into the category of the odd fact. And why do
law-abiding readers find Frederick Forsyth's remarks about silencers in
"No Comebacks" interesting?

> A silencer on an automatic is never truly quiet, despite the efforts
> of the sound-effects men in television thrillers to pretend it is. Auto-
> matics, unlike revolvers, do not have a closed breech. As the bullet
> leaves the barrel the automatic's jacket is forced backwards to expel
> the spent cartridge and inject a fresh one. That is why they are called
> automatics. But in that split second as the breech opens to expel
> the used shell, half the noise of the explosion comes out through the
> open breech, making a silencer on the end of the barrel only 50 per
> cent effective.   (26)

It may be the reference to television thrillers (there is also a hierarchy
of the lower arts) that is the clue: we accept the information not as what
Kenneth Burke called equipment for living but as equipment for reading
and watching. We will now read and watch other detective stories with a
wicked eye for inaccuracies. Into this group we would put explanations of
specialized vocabularies. Here, from Jake Logan's *Slocum's Debt*, John
Slocum is explaining western dialect to an easterner.

> "There should be a turnoff up the next hollow there," Hayes said.
> "Gulch," Slocum corrected him.

"What say?"

"Gulch. That's what a hollow is called out here. Or canyon if it's deeper. Arroyo if it's cut into flat land. But never a hollow. That's a back-east word."   (86)

If it does nothing else, the exchange will help us read other westerns.

Some of the information might be of practical use, though some of this is grim. One thriller tells us that if we want to do a thorough job of killing ourselves we should fill our mouth with water, put the barrel of a revolver between our lips, and then pull the trigger: the bullet and muzzle blast will shatter our skull. A huge part of the appeal of Forsyth's immensely successful *Day of the Jackal* is the advice it gives in the form of descriptions. From it, we learn how to get a false passport, how to evade customs, how to buy an illegal weapon—some of the trade secrets of the professional assassin.

In principle, there is no explanation that might not appear in a paper-back story, for anything said or printed anywhere else can be quoted. We really cannot be sure what we will find; we can be sure only that we will be given something. We are always given something. Fritz Leiber's "Four Ghosts in Hamlet," in Terry Carr and Martin Harry Greenberg's *Treasury of Modern Fantasy*, stops to tell us something most of us had not known: that there are occasions when an alcoholic actor can be of use to a Shake-spearean company. Apparently, there are parts a drunk plays very well: "King Duncan, for instance, and the Doge in *The Merchant* are easy to play drunk because the actor always has a couple of attendants to either side of him, who can guide his steps if he weaves and even hold him up if necessary—which can turn out to be an effective dramatic touch, registering as the infirmity of extreme age" (396).

All of this is raw information flooding into our minds, and anyone who wanted to take the trouble could compile an encyclopedia of odd and useful knowledge—a good encyclopedia—using only paragraphs and chapters from the paperbacks. (An amateur's intuition into the shapes in which information sloshes around within a culture is available to anyone who will read *The People's Almanac*, exuberantly edited and written by David Wallechinsky and his father, Irving Wallace. This thick volume did not take its materials from paperbacks, but it is an encyclopedia written

in the style of a paperback—and it is none the worse for being that.)
Reviewers recognize readers' interest in the flood of data by welcoming
new writers with explicit identification of the kinds of information embedded in their stories. They hail the new detective series for bringing us
a new city, a new cultural subset—merchant banking, the world of the
New York gypsy, the theater. Raymond Chandler's and Ross Macdonald's
stories give us Los Angeles, Robert B. Parker's stories give us Boston,
Maj Sjöwall and Per Wahloo's Martin Beck stories give us Sweden, James
McClure's stories give us South Africa, Arthur Upfield's stories take us
around Australia. Douglas Johnson captures this feature of the paperback
as well as anyone ever has in his tribute to Georges Simenon's Maigret
stories.

> For many readers, the Maigret novels have the great merit of
> displaying France and the French. With the *commissaire* we dis-
> cover not only the geography of Paris, small provincial towns in all
> their melancholy and the isolated communities that live around har-
> bours, canals and châteaux, but also what exists behind "le visage
> banal" normally presented to outsiders. The *valets de chambre* who
> marry cooks and who come to Paris and take over cafés, the man
> whose Protestant upbringing in Nîmes prevents him from saying *tu*
> to people, the inspectorate which seems to be made up of men from
> the Massif Central, the youth who has "une bonne chaire drue de
> jeune paysan à qui Paris n'avait pas encore pris sa santé," all these
> are part of the display of France.

With appropriate changes we could make that paragraph a tribute to any
paperback writer, though it would be the lore of horse raising, international espionage, or Caribbean voodoo that we would be emphasizing.
And while the paperback is not our most efficient instructor, Johnson's
characterization of Simenon's novels has caught nicely something a nonfiction guide to France (or to anything else) will miss: the effect all the
lore has on people in action. Fiction has always been better than nonfiction at making us see that driving a highway or identifying a counterfeit
watercolor or even traveling between the stars is, or will be, or could be
a human enterprise and not just a set of techniques.

. . . . . Models of Deportment

Writers of paperbacks are always amused by readers who take their characters too seriously. In Dashiell Hammett's *Maltese Falcon*, Sam Spade is challenged by the gunsel, Wilber. Spade is delighted. He sees in Wilber's mind the image of the last of a pulp-magazine Western hero.

> He said to Spade in a voice cramped by passion: "You bastard, get up on your feet and go for your heater!"
>
> Sam smiled at the boy. His smile was not broad, but the amusement in it seemed genuine and unalloyed.
>
> The boy said: "You bastard, get up and shoot it out if you've got the guts. I've taken all the riding from you I'm going to take."
>
> The amusement in Spade's smile deepened. He looked at Gutman and said: "Young Wild West."   (415)

The Young Wild West stories were being printed in the 1920s, and Hammett's earlier fiction was competing with them for the reader's money and time. Wilber is foolish but not because he has taken a model from fiction. We all experiment with that. Ortega y Gasset captures our feelings nicely, though it is Racine and Corneille's characters that he is describing.

> The aristocratic audience enjoys the exemplary and normative character of the tragic happenings. They go to the theater not to be stirred by Athalie's or Phedre's anguish but to feel elated by the model deportment of those great-hearted figures. In the last instance, French theater is ethical contemplation, not vital emotion like the Spanish. What it presents is not a series of ethically neutral incidents but an exemplary type of reaction, a repertory of normative attitudes in the supreme crises of life. The personages are heroes, exalted characters, prototypes of magnanimity.   (64)

Some sharply etched characters elicit our meanings by serving as counter-examples. We may not know who we are, precisely, and what we feel about most of the characters in Harriet Beecher Stowe's *Uncle Tom's Cabin*, but we know we are not like Simon Legree. Some characters strike us as irrelevant: the readers of Sax Rohmer's Fu Manchu stories apparently enjoyed identifying themselves by reference to that wily Oriental, but many of us find those stories boring, even embarrassing. We cannot predict which characters will strike us as relevant and which not. Three pages with S. S. Van Dine's detective, Philo Vance, and I find myself rooting with quiet sincerity for the murderer.

We cannot see versions of ourselves, or of our counterselves, without making internal adjustments—a quiet, but not trivial, form of mental activity. Though the countermodels are as interesting as the models, we shall look at two forms of the hero: the model that reminds us of what we want to be, and the model that reminds us of what we wish we could also be.

Adam Hall's Quiller is a perfect representative of the first type. Like all the others of his kind, he has certain ironies built into him. It may be that, for the moment, we cannot accept grand images of ourselves without a sense of the ludicrous attached.

He is one of those heroes—there are hundreds of them—who can be sent into a dangerous situation to bring an agent out, to identify a saboteur, to ease a crisis that could result in global catastrophe. What we shall notice in him is the fact that his competence is an achieved competence, that it is he who shaped himself into the professional he is. It is a mark of our time that, whatever we were born to, we take pride in having made ourselves into what we are. Even if it is only in changing a tire, or playing bridge, or seeing a film, we like to have our friends think of us as at least no worse than minor-league Quillers. And we find that what is funny in him is also funny in us.

In *The Striker Portfolio* he is standing on a hill in Germany watching the flight of a jet aircraft. The drugged pilot loses control, and the jet puts its nose down and dives straight at Quiller. "The shrilling was so bad now that it was difficult to go on thinking rationally because the primitive brain was telling me to *get up and run somewhere safe* while the modern brain was working out a few figures: the plane was now below half its attainable ceiling and coming on at something like its peak attainable airspeed which put it at a mile every four seconds and that gave me fifteen seconds to get out and there was nowhere to go" (14). That is Quiller. Terrified, he is working out a few figures, and he is also monitoring the signals his primitive brain is sending. He takes scrupulous care of his body: "I ordered liver and carrots because they both have something like four thousand international units of vitamin A and I like seeing as much as possible in the dark" (85). Earlier, two East German agents have trapped him in a car and are about to give him a cautionary beating: "The other ideas [for escape] were worse so I sat there and worked up some anger about what they'd done to Lovett; anger is a prerequisite for action; it turns on the adrenalin" (38). He gets away, but his pursuers do not give up. In the midst of a later chase, he pauses to make sure he is frightened.

> The situation was dangerous and could be mortal but the necessity of working out the mechanics hadn't allowed the onset of normal fear: and a situation becomes more dangerous if there is no fear present to alert the nerves and prepare the body. Blood should be drawn to the internal organs, draining from the digestive and secretory glands and skin by contraction of the arterioles so that the heart, brain, and muscles can be fed. Breathing should quicken so that the muscles can be given an oxygen reserve. The eyes should dilate, admitting more light.   (104)

Achilles did not know about the survival value of fear; it was we who discovered that. We note that Quiller's intense awareness of his body is not matched by equal awareness of his motivation. His controllers manipulate him as cunningly as he does his body.

People in our fiction worry about their bodies' fitness to the task in a way unknown to earlier heroes. Robert B. Parker's detective, Spenser, works out on a Nautilus, punches the heavy bag, and jogs. Cordwainer Smith's "Scanners Live in Vain" is a story about space travelers equipped with neural blocks to protect them from something called the Great Pain of Space—whatever that may be—who read dials on their body to discover how they feel and who can change their emotions: "Martel was angry. He did not even adjust his blood away from anger" (354).

But it is with people from an earlier time that we put Quiller. Here is that eighteenth-century scrutinizer of the soul, the Puritan Cotton Mather: "Every man upon earth may find in himself something that wants mending; and the work of *repentance* is to inquire, not only *what we have done*, but also, *What we have to do?* Frequent SELF-EXAMINATION, is the duty and the prudence, of all that would *know themselves*, or would not *lose themselves*. The great intention of SELF-EXAMINATION is, to find out, the points, wherein we are to *amend our ways*" (35). Cotton Mather trained his soul; we diet, jog, lift weights, and worry about fat. Soul scrutiny versus body scrutiny: the eighteenth-century mind and the twentieth-century mind.

The Quillers of paperback fiction offer us images that simultaneously enhance and deflate us. Many of the heroes and heroines fall into a second, more interesting group. These are the figures who remind us of what we are not but would like also to be.

The type is not unique to our time but the models are. Stowe's Uncle Tom and Charles Dickens's Esther Summerson, in *Bleak House*, are nineteenth-century paradigms of the Christian. No man or woman who read those books was inspired to become an Uncle Tom or an Esther Summerson, but readers honored them. Our century has seen Verdun, the Nazi death camps, the killings in Northern Ireland, the horror of Vietnam, and the reintroduction of torture in police interrogation; and those earlier models are not successful. We credit great-heartedness only in scenes of warlike violence.

Cordwainer Smith's "Dead Lady of Clown Town" is about a revolution that lasted six minutes. The instigator is dead; in fact, she is a recorded personality. Those who break out are underpeople, a sort of coolie-population made from animals. Their leader is a dog-woman, D'Joan, who hears the message the dead offers.

What we are then given is Christianity in the raw, love on a mad cavalry charge against unthinking, unfeeling force—and a cliché if ever a cliché there was. The action is not subtle, but it is powerful in its strange mixture of the ugly and the beautiful. It has its ironies: "The snake-woman wasn't making much progress. She had seized a human man with her more-than-iron hand. Elaine hadn't seen her saying anything, but the man fainted dead away. The snake-woman had him draped over her arm like an empty overcoat and was looking for somebody else to love" (184). In the killing of the rat-woman, we see the fundamental motifs:

> One mother held her children up for the soldier to kill them all.
> She must have been of rat origin, because she had septuplets in closely matching form.

The tape shows us the picture of the soldier getting ready.

The rat-woman greets him with a smile and holds up her seven babies. Little blondes they are, wearing pink or blue bonnets, all of them with glowing cheeks and bright little eyes.

"Put them on the ground," said the soldier. "I'm going to kill you and them too." On the tape, we can hear the nervous peremptory edge of his voice. He added one word, as though he had already begun to think that he had to justify himself to these underpeople. "Orders," he added.

"It doesn't matter if I hold them, soldier. I'm their mother. They'll feel better if they die easily with their mother near. I love you, soldier. I love all people. You are my brother, even though my blood is rat blood and yours is human. Go ahead and kill them, soldier. I can't even hurt you. Can't you understand it? *I love you, soldier.* We share a common speech, common hopes, common fears and a common death. That is what Joan has taught us all. Death is not bad, soldier. It just comes badly, sometimes, but you will remember me after you have killed me and my babies. You will remember that I love you now—"

Smith has shifted his angle of vision. Our interest now is in the effect of this scene on the soldier and on those who viewed the scene on tape in later centuries, their lives changed utterly by this brief protest.

The soldier, we see on the tape, can stand it no longer. He clubs his weapon, knocks the woman down; the babies scatter on the ground. We see his booted heel rise up and crush down against their heads. We hear the wet popping sound of the little heads breaking, the sharp cut-off of the baby wails as they die. We get one last view of the rat-woman herself. She has stood up again by the time the seventh baby is killed. She offers her hand to the soldier to shake. Her face is dirty and bruised, a trickle of blood running down her left cheek. Even now, we know she is a rat, an underperson, a modified animal, a nothing.

The soldier loses control of himself and forgets the power of his "heat remover." He uses it as a club.

His last blow catches her in the face.

She falls back on the pavement. He thrusts his foot, as we can see by the tape, directly on her throat. He leaps forward in an odd little jig, bringing his full weight down on her fragile neck. He swings while stamping downward, and we then see his face, full on in the camera.

It is the face of a weeping child, bewildered by hurt and shocked by the prospect of more hurt to come.

He had started to do his duty, and duty had gone wrong, all wrong. Poor man.   (195–97)

It is easy to be amusing about the scene. One reader said he thought he would wait until our own rats offered the hand of friendship first; a man could lose a finger, he said. And we can sanitize the scene by "placing" it: Joan of Arc lies behind D'Joan; the underpeople were first conceived by H. G. Wells for his *Island of Doctor Moreau*; the image of the slave population whose response to tyranny is the offer of pure love is drawn from legends of Christianity among the Roman slaves. Either response, though legitimate, is an evasion of the grotesque power of the scene itself. The snake-woman and the rat-woman are simple and they are silly, but Christianity in the raw took pride in being simple (i.e., innocent) and silly (i.e., blessed). That was where the power of its vision lay.

The story appeared in 1965, just as the generation of the flower children was becoming aware of the political implications of their lifestyle. They had a profound mistrust of the military and of "the establishment," and they marched behind banners proclaiming PEACE and LOVE. They had found Robert Heinlein's 1961 novel, *Stranger in a Strange Land*, and were weeping at the murder of the innocent Mike, the inadvertent Martian (he was human but had been educated by Martians) who tried to bring love to Earth. "Dead Lady of Clown Town" is a paradigm of the revolt of the loving but powerless against entrenched custom and force. If our grandchildren want to understand how the flower children saw themselves, this story will be invaluable.

Neither *Stranger in a Strange Land* nor "Dead Lady of Clown Town" came from the flower children, however. Robert Heinlein was fifty-four when his novel appeared. He was a graduate of the U.S. Naval Academy, and his *Starship Troopers* of two years earlier had presented the governing image of the professional soldier. "Cordwainer Smith" was Paul Linebarger, a man with impeccable establishment credentials. He was an Episcopalian, a professor of political science at Johns Hopkins University, a member of the American Legion and of the Retired Officers Club, and the author of what was then the standard textbook on its subject, *Psychological Warfare*, still in print in the 1980s.

In the 1960s, it was the soldiers, not the underpeople, who were writing the stories that gave expression to the deepest hopes of the peace movement. Neither Heinlein nor Linebarger joined that movement. Heinlein remained a staunch supporter of the military, and Linebarger continued his academic research.

Mike and the rat-woman were not flower-children images; they were appropriated from establishment images, images that reminded those who did not march for PEACE and LOVE of what it is they honored but could not be; for the establishment, too, has always honored the rat-woman. It sees, however, that her babies died; and in the real world of parents and babies, we do not let the babies die. Even the flower children eventually came to see that and became part of the establishment themselves, grieving quietly that the world is not simple enough to permit them to be Uncle Toms and Esther Summersons. These boldly drawn absurdities are counterimages, too—a different kind of counterimage from the Simon Legrees—that help us define ourselves by mirroring back our lost dreams. Fiction has always done this for us.

. . . . Problems

I am not a faithful reader of the tale of detection, but I agree with Jacques Barzun and Wendell Hertig Taylor when, in their *Catalogue of Crime*, they protest against the cruder forms of rejection of this story: "The fact is that from the outset detection has been written for and by highbrows. The genre has been the preserve of the intellectual and the cultivated, and not so much for relaxation in the ordinary sense as for the stimulation, in a different setting, of the same critical and imaginative powers that these persons display in their vocations. . . . Whatever it is, the detective story is not an idiot's delight" (7). The question that remains is whether the other genres, and other traditions inside that genre, make fewer intellectual demands, offer less challenge to the mind.

Every paperback genre engages its readers in direct intellectual activity in two ways. The first is through the presentation of internal tensions within even the stories that are well crafted, "smooth," apparently reassuring in their solution of the dramatic problems they present, and the second is by means of the problematic story: the book whose chief interest lies not in solving a problem but in defining it. (The stories—and so their readers—also engage in characteristic forms of intrageneric interplay, but we shall be looking at that in the next chapter.)

Dashiell Hammett's *Red Harvest* is an instance of a story that offers a surface satisfaction but has just beneath its surface a boiling of unresolved tensions; Brian Aldiss's science fantasy *The Malacia Tapestry* is an example of a story whose very ambition is to be indeterminate, to present the reader with a clearly defined problem but to withhold a solution.

We think of the detective story as the most reassuring of all the genres. A crime is committed, but the perpetrator, however clever, is identified —in every single story. That is reassuring, but the detection of criminals is not what the detective story is about. That design is as conventional as the sonata form in the nineteenth-century symphony. We accept the pattern without protest, though we have encountered it a hundred times, not because the pattern is in itself satisfying but because it serves so well as a frame for the presentation of certain large questions.

The special concern of this tradition in all its forms (the tale of detection, the private-investigator story, the crime novel, the police procedural) is the conflict between the *lawful* and the *good*. Even at their simplest, the stories are reconsiderations of the institution of the law. Every writer who has followed Conan Doyle and chosen an amateur detective as hero is telling us that the law is an ass: that it is not intelligent enough, not elastic enough, not well-enough informed, not honest enough to do its work. And every writer who has rejected the amateur detective and chosen a professional policeman as hero is telling us that the law, in its own blundering way, can do its job. We (and some of the writers) go from one of these heroes to another, never quite believing, never quite disbelieving, looking at the law now from this side of it, now from that side.

In all cases, the stories are edging us out to a consideration of the *good*. In democracies, where the citizens themselves make the laws, we think of the law as the consequence of our own efforts to define and then to implement the good; and our uncertainties about its clumsiness are inevitable. (When times are hard, the devout bow their heads to their Creator and whisper, "Let thy will be done." When the laws are harsh, it may be that the citizens in a monarchy will bow their heads to their king and whisper, "Thy will be done." When the United States Congress passes a law that its citizens dislike, the people who voted those senators and congressmen into power do not bow their heads and whisper, "Thy will, Congress, not ours, be done." They begin to mutter darkly to one another about liars, thieves, and idiots.) The explicit and the implicit demonstrations in these stories of the inadequacies of the laws, and of the inadequacies of the law as a social institution, permit us to see what it is we feel privately about the good.

Every story leaves us a little dissatisfied with what we had been before reading it. We are a little less smug in our opinions, a little more aware and so a little more thoughtful. The good stories do that to us; the poor stories do that to us. We see this through a brief consideration of one of the best known of the American tough-guy stories, Dashiell Hammett's *Red Harvest*. Having chanced upon the story once, we return to it later because it does such a good job with a familiar problem. It has one of those town-cleaning patterns that both the private-investigator novel and the western turn to so often. An operative for the Continental Detective Agency, the "Continental Op" as Hammett readers call him, comes to the corrupt town of Personville ("Poisonville") and cleans it up. That is reassuring, and yet the story disturbs us. We are troubled, as we so often are with these stories, by the hero the writer gives us.

The problem that this story leaves in our minds is the resolution of a competition of loyalties within us. Shall we feel a closer loyalty to the hero, the Op, or shall we feel it for the criminals who are trying to kill him? Hammett had worked as a private investigator and knew real criminals and so he does not give us pseudocriminals: the cute criminals that the British love or the crooks with hearts of gold that Americans prefer. Hammett's characters are violent. They really are criminals, and we really do feel that Personville will be better off without them. Still, we gradually come to feel that no society could ever develop among people like the Op, who rids Personville of them, but that a functioning society *could* develop among men and women like those criminals. (This can be said of all Hammett's early heroes, including Sam Spade of the much-praised *Maltese Falcon*. None of Hammett's heroes seems quite to understand how the rest of us feel about one another.)

The institution of the law in Personville—the police, the lawyers, the courts—is in the hands of a criminal confederation. The Op recognizes slackness in the police as soon as he arrives: "The first policeman I saw needed a shave. The second had a couple of buttons off his shabby uniform. The third stood in the center of the city's main intersection— Broadway and Union Street—directing traffic, with a cigar in one corner of his mouth. After that I stopped checking them up" (3). We soon learn that the police chief is a part of the gang a mineowner brought in to break a strike and that the gang has now taken over control of the town. "Don't kid yourselves that there's any law in Poisonville," the Op tells the other investigators. "There's no use taking anybody into court, no matter what you've got on them. They own the courts" (79). This, of course, is a familiar fictional situation, and we readers are prepared to sit back and approve of what the detective must now do. Personville would be better off with honest policemen and good judges, and we know that the investigator may have to bend a few laws himself if the town is to be helped. We can accept that. Yet it soon appears that there is something missing from our detective.

We see this in a minor but telling incident shortly after the story opens. The police chief is fighting with one of his associates, the gambler Whisper Thaler, and he sets up an ambush that will kill both Thaler and the investigator. The gambler recognizes that the Op is as much a threat to him as to the police chief, but Thaler helps him escape anyway. Later, he offers the Op a drink and some conversation: "He even gave me what seemed to be a straight tip on the fights—telling me any bet on the main event would be good if its maker remembered that Kid Cooper would probably knock Ike Bush out in the sixth round. He seemed to know what he was talking about, and it didn't seem to be news to the others" (46). Thaler is not trying to bribe the Op or ingratiate himself. It is one of those casual kindnesses strangers become temporarily friends do for one another.

What should the Op do with this tip? He did not ask for it, but that does not release him from responsibility. Of course, it would be a waste of his time, and possibly of his life, for him to tell the police, but he does have other options. He could keep quiet; or he could place a bet on Kid Cooper, though he too would then be stealing other people's money. He could warn other bettors that the fight is fixed, however, and we approve when he visits the workingmen's bars and spreads the news. This is what we expect; the detectives in this tradition have working-class sympathies. He is betraying a trust—all right, an odd, unasked-for trust: a trust nevertheless—but he is doing this to help the gambler's victims.

He does not stop there, however. After spreading the news, he happens to learn something that allows him to blackmail Ike Bush, and he forces the boxer to win the fight with Kid Cooper that the gamblers expect him to lose.

The moral issue—if we can introduce so grand a name into so small an action—has now become tangled. The Op has not turned a fixed fight into an honest fight. He has arranged a fix of his own, and *everybody* who trusted the Op loses. The workingmen, for instance: they had changed their bets because of the Op and lose their money. The Op never reflects on what he has done to them. Then there is the boxer: he is killed because of his hapless double cross. The Op is unmoved. And Whisper Thaler: what has he done to deserve the betrayal? He had saved the Op's life and, though he knew the Op was his enemy, he had even given him a betting tip. Apparently, the fact that Thaler had once been an associate of the police chief who tried to kill the Op was sufficient reason. We ask for a little more than that from someone we accept as representing us. We begin to suspect that the Op betrays the gambler for the simple reason that Whisper Thaler makes his money in an activity that is not illegal in Monte Carlo but is in Personville. Unless we are prepared to say that anything we do is justified so long as it is done to someone who makes his money illegally—even if that person has saved our life—we are going to feel uneasy about the Op's moral crusade to clean up Personville.

He is just getting to work. Within a few pages he has been responsible for the deaths of some twelve people. He knows what he has been doing, and he remarks on his failure to go to the mineowner, who now wants to rid the town of his former allies. A friend tries to comfort him.

> "It's not your fault, darling. You said yourself that there was nothing else you could do. Finish your drink and we'll have another."
>
> "There was plenty else I could do," I contradicted her. . . .
>
> "I could have gone to him this afternoon and showed him that I had them ruined. He'd have listened to reason. He'd have come over to my side, have given me the support I needed to swing the play legally. I could have done that. But it's easier to have them killed off, easier and surer, and, now that I'm feeling this way, more satisfying. I don't know how I'm going to come out with the Agency. The Old Man will boil me in oil if he ever finds out what I've been doing. It's this damned town. Poisonville is right. It's poisoned me." (103–4)

A vivid image: a town become so poisonous that it corrupts everyone who comes into it. But we ask ourselves, Is it the town that has made the Op into a killer, or is this an excuse he is giving himself? It does not seem to have affected even the brutal police chief in the way it affected the Op. After the killings have begun, the chief loses his energies: "I'm getting sick of this killing. It's getting to me—on my nerves, I mean" (95). The criminals are killers, but the Op himself was not pure of heart when he arrived in Personville: "I've arranged a killing or two in my time, when they were necessary" (102). This is the excuse any killer gives, of course: that he only kills when necessary. What especially disturbs us is the fact that the Op will justify his own behavior by reference to the poisonous ambience of Personville but not the behavior of his enemies. He never suggests, for instance, that the gambler is a man more or less like himself who was made dangerous by Poisonville. We cannot quite believe it is the town that is responsible.

The more closely we read this novel, the more we are persuaded that the Op is always true only to himself. We see him betraying his friends, his colleagues, his agency, the citizens in the town. He was attacked, and he set about creating a fire storm of killing and counterkilling that destroys not just the man who tried to kill him but all that man's friends and anyone else who comes too close. He has so little interest in the people of Personville that he leaves them in the power of the very mineowner who brought those criminals to town. Even his agency disapproves of his actions. Why did he do all this? It seems to be a simple case of a dangerously violent man, incapable of making human connections, who flails wildly back at anyone or anything in the world that threatens him.

We can suppose that *Red Harvest* and hundreds of other detective stories are simple but only if we look at them with a very simple eye. The notion that detectives in these stories are heroic forces for the good is patently wrong. In Ted Lewis's *Get Carter* (published in England as *Jack's Return Home*), the detective is a man far worse than the Op. Jack Carter is a vicious criminal (we see him torturing one woman and murdering another). We accept him as Our Sort only because the people the story defines as Their Sort, the criminals Carter destroys, are even worse. And it is not just the antihero who disturbs us. Douglas Johnson finds a self-serving egoism even in Georges Simenon's much-loved Maigret: "*La Première Enquête de Maigret* shows him abandoning the cause of justice and allowing a rich family to go unpunished, accepting in return the successful furtherance of his own career. *Maigret aux assises* shows him allowing the man who has just been acquitted of murder to find and kill the real murderer." If we look closely at these stories—that is, look at them in the way the people who read them regularly do—we find they always leave us disturbed and thoughtful. All of the heroes and heroines are flawed. Rarely is the villain so simply bad as we would like to believe. The world we sense around us, with its imperfect laws and imperfect policemen, with its human victims and equally human villains—that is, the world we leave for the escape from thinking these stories are said to provide—is precisely the world we find when we turn to them. It is hard to imagine why people like T. S. Eliot and Ludwig Wittgenstein would have found the stories interesting when they did turn to them if this had not been the case.

Other paperback stories have no ambition other than to show us the problem. A good example is Brian Aldiss's *Malacia Tapestry*, which will simultaneously serve as an example of the paperback writer's interest in art.

The Malacia Tapestry comes from the genre of popular fantasy. It tells us about Perian de Chirolo, a gifted young actor who lives in the city of

Malacia. Malacia seems to have been modeled on the Rome of 1700, but it is not in our universe. The novel is an alternate time-stream story, a very sophisticated version of the type. It takes us into another cosmos, a Manichean universe created not by God but by Satan. Appropriately, the humans (they seem to be indistinguishable from us physically) are descended not from mammals but from the dinosaurs. God has intruded into Satan's universe, and the two are joined in battle. The issue is still in doubt, and Perian and the others are divided in their allegiances. They know all this, and they also know that it is theoretically possible that there is a universe alternate to their own in which humans are descended from mammals. All of this lies very much in the background of the tale, which is not at all about the battle between God and Satan.

We follow Perian through several adventures of the sort we are familiar with from the literature of roguery. He brawls, makes love, steals his dinner, acts, argues, and wanders through his city. Increasingly, he becomes thoughtful. He does not understand his own art of the theater, and he does not understand the art he finds around him, though everyone else is more or less content. A friend asks him what questions there were in Malacia, the center of the world, which could bother anyone. He replies that there are many matters which puzzle him.

> "Such as why I was moved by Pete's trumpery dolls. They neither imitate nor parody real people; they are just wooden shapes, worked to amuse us. Yet I was concerned. I cheered first for Banker Man and then for Robber Man. A sort of magic was at work. If so, was the artistry the puppeteer's? Or was it mine, in that my imagination stirred despite myself and part of me became Robber Man and Banker Man?
>
> "Why do I weep over characters in a play or book, who have no more flesh and blood than the thirty characters of the printed language?" (169)

Another friend tells him that his difficulty lies in his inability to make proper distinctions "among art and artifice and life" (399). In a world created by Satan, the distinctions are fundamental, but of course they are hardly trivial in our own reality. He discovers that the rich young woman he loves is merely using him and that she is having an affair with his best friend. He had been amused by the banality of a work he is acting in, a story about a young prince desolated by the discovery that his beloved had been sleeping with his best friend, but now he is learning that the story is an image of his own life and that he feels the same desolation the absurd prince feels.

Everywhere he goes in the city, he finds art: plays, puppetry, paintings, dances, costumery, pageantry, glass-engravings, flute music, phonograph music, shadow plays, religious chants, popular songs, ritualistic hunting, frescoes, the camera obscura, a sort of primitive motion picture, and— not least—a tapestry. We, meanwhile, are also finding art as we move through the story, for it has in it engravings by Tiepolo which seem to have been the inspiration for some of the scenes in which Perian becomes involved. (Aldiss's story is in part an extended set of variations on the pictures.)

The word *tapestry* in the title is indirectly explained. One of Perian's friends tells him about a story he heard.

> "Somebody told me that Satan has decided to close the world down, and the magicians have agreed. What would happen wouldn't be unpleasant at all, but just ordinary life going on more and more slowly until it stopped absolutely."
>
> "Like a clock stopping," Armida suggested.
>
> "More like a tapestry," Bedalar said. "I mean, one day like today, things might run down and never move again, so that we and every-thing would hang there like a tapestry in the air for ever more."
>
> (167)

Even a tired brain recognizes that Aldiss is having his characters describe the story he is writing: his story opens with Perian waking, and it closes with him falling asleep. *The Malacia Tapestry* is a tapestry hanging in the air for the gods—us, in this instance—to examine.

The closest Aldiss risks the novel to a theory appears in a discus-sion between Perian and the greatest artist in Malacia. Perian has been shattered by disasters and visions, and he is fumbling toward an under-standing. " 'Nicholas, this visitation I'm talking about persuaded me that we may never be able to understand reality, owing to perhaps merciful limitations in our perceptive powers.' " The artist pays little attention. He is trying to chase a bird out of his studio, but he does give the ancient reply of the working artist: " 'Never mind understand—*master.*' " Perian, who like his father is a natural philosopher, cannot be content with this; he blunders on: " 'You devote your life to transcribing what you believe to be real. I fear that what we regard as real is itself a transcription, something sketched by Powers as much beyond us as we are beyond that luckless bird. That there are pentimento moments, when one layer shows through another. That art and life, fact and fiction, are linked transcriptions of each other' " (356–57). But the artist is not interested in theory. Nor, while reading this story, are we: we are held by the wealth of arts on display before us and by the echoings of life in the arts, by the echoings of the arts in Perian's life, and by artifice mocking both. *The Malacia Tapestry* was not written to carry a discursive theory of art. If we want that, we must construct it for ourselves, and we might do that: all the materials we need are in the novel, waiting.

Red Harvest and stories like it seem to offer only reassurance, but they are disturbing in ways in which their readers choose to be intellectually disturbed. In some cases, we can tell ourselves that the writers have designed "unreliable narrators," people designed with incoherencies in them that interest us. Often—perhaps more often—we encounter stories like Hammett's that have come from "unreliable writers." We feel that the writers themselves did not understand—or at least had not yet worked through—certain intriguing difficulties that we readers see very clearly. If the problems the stories dramatize are intriguing enough, we do not care much whether they emerged in the story because of the writers or in spite of them. It is the problems that hold us and bring us back for more.

Slow minds read paperbacks, and juvenile minds read paperbacks, and sick minds read paperbacks. Some writers are sick or juvenile or slow and write for people like themselves; but paperbacks as a class are written for minds wearied—sick minds wearied, slow minds wearied, good minds wearied. All of our minds—even the sick, the slow, the immature—are human minds, and human minds require mental activity.

In this chapter we reviewed the most easily visible evidence of this: those nuggets of lore and advice that writers embed in their narratives; those caricatures they invent of our private notions of the good and the bad and the would-it-could-be; and—not least—their dramatizations of unresolved incoherency in such domains as the law and art and man-in-the-universe and man-in-society. The stories are incoherent not because their writers have failed but because they have triumphed over that human impulse to make things tidy by making them simple; few lessons are more valuable than the lesson that we are confused about an issue that counts and that we had better do some hard thinking of our own.

My friend Herbert Weil, a Shakespearean scholar, has defined a *problem play* as a play in which Shakespeare dramatized the problem more successfully than he did its solution. Most pulp fiction is problem fiction in this sense.

The paperback genres are a device the human race has invented to permit it to think even when it is tired, so tired it does not suppose that thinking is any longer possible. Looking through these story surfaces at what lies behind and beneath them—the traditions that generate them —we find the ultimate justification for the existence of the paperbacks, however, for it is not by means of the stories a genre writes but by means of the interplay of its stories that a genre wins its readers' respect for its intelligence. A genre's greatest value lies precisely where its critics find it weakest.

reading in
a system

. . . .

A paperback genre does not look the same to a doubtful new-comer as it does to one of its enthusiasts, of course. In *Two-Bit Culture*, Kenneth C. Davis quotes Walter Kendrick's angry rejection of the romance: "Escapist, masturbatory, exploitative—romance is all these things. It's a typical mass-produced American product, catering to a public so dull and timid that even when it dreams, it can only conceive what it's dreamt before. All the lines of thought romance seemed to initiate lead straight to the expected conclusion, without a twist or turn or spark of interest" (364–65). That is what a vernacular genre looks like from the outside. From the inside it looks entirely different. In an essay in the *New Yorker*, Gerald Jonas quotes Philip Klass on another vernacular genre, science fiction, which he wrote as "William Tenn": "We had the sense that we could go on endlessly, constantly topping each other's ideas, getting into whole new areas, creating things that didn't fit into any of the familiar literary categories" (69). What we see in a vernacular genre depends upon whether we are reading with a story focus or with a genre focus.

Every story in any genre—vernacular or literary—is the product of a system. It is one realization of that system's potentialities—as each English sentence is its own unique realization of that underlying system we call the English language. In reading any single story, then, we are reading the system that lies behind it, that realizes itself through the mind of that story's writer. And here lies the fundamental distinction between reading one book after another and reading in a genre, between reading with that story focus and reading with the genre focus. Genre reading is system reading. That is, as we are reading the stories, we are exploring the system that created them.

Further, the system is always changing, and in reading the new stories the system is writing we are following the changes in that system. Consider, for instance, a simple exchange between Nick and Nora Charles in Dashiell Hammett's *Thin Man*, published more than fifty years ago.

> "Tell me something, Nick. Tell me the truth: when you were wrestling with Mimi, didn't you have an erection?"
>
> "Oh, a little."
>
> She laughed and got up from the floor. "If you aren't a disgusting old lecher," she said. "Look, it's daylight." (691)

Reading *The Thin Man* in the 1980s, we hardly notice that exchange; it does little more than tell us that the relationship between husband and wife is easy and comfortable. Yet even into the 1940s, readers of *The Thin Man* were finding that reference to an erection remarkable, possibly unique for detective fiction. The words shouted from the page, not because readers were outraged (they had all heard the word *erection*, and most of them had experienced it in one way or another) but because the use of the word was an announcement that the tough-guy detective story would now speak frankly and easily about sexuality. The coyness, the suppression of sexual motive and act would now pass away. The next detective story they read would go through that newly opened door into new areas of human motivation and behavior.

I choose this brief example because I remember the disappointment some of us felt as we came to recognize that we had been given a false dawn. The next generation of stories did not go through that door Hammett had opened. To protect the excitable, unwashed masses, presumably, editors helpfully closed that door: in some later printings of *The Thin Man* that exchange was suppressed. Like our initial delight, our disappointment revealed that while reading the story we were also following the system behind the story; we sensed that possibilities the system might have explored were going to be ignored. It was not for some fifteen years that sexuality would be reintroduced into the paperback novel, with great

promise and great underlying timidity. Even then we were getting nothing more than, for example, this scene of sexual climax in Wade Miller's
1950 thriller, *Devil May Care:* "He discovered response and delirium and
explosion and then a placid infinity through which they drifted, hugged
close together" (141). Miller could have used the same sentence to describe two people sharing a religious vision, or an epileptic seizure. It
took ten more years for writers and their editors to go beyond the early
shock value of sexual references to get to the point Hammett had already
reached twenty-five years earlier. The inertia of the system in place in the
1930s had been too great for a single bold stroke to overcome. *The Thin
Man* remained, nevertheless, a character within the system rather like a
minor character in a story who makes a shrewd suggestion that everyone
ignores—a Lord Gro in *The Worm Ouroboros*, who correctly explains to
the other characters where true heroism lies but whose remarks have no
effect because no one is listening but the reader.

In this chapter, we examine features of a genre that experienced
readers notice because they are following a system but that inexperienced readers miss entirely. I gather my observations under the three
words that we all use when we reject an unfamiliar vernacular genre:
simplemindedness, *predictability*, and *absurdity*.

Simplemindedness

Not surprisingly, science fiction seems childishly simple to
outsiders. Science fiction seems simple because its stories are so simple.

This special kind of simplicity, story-simplicity, has made it possible
for every reader to find a different science fiction. The genre is notorious
for its interest in science and technology, for instance, but also (especially among scientists) for its ignorance. Do its critics want to show that
the genre's writers are ignorant? They say so with sufficient strength and
passion and then illustrate their claims with citations of scientific clownishness. Edgar Rice Burroughs, for instance, seems to have borrowed
from Rudyard Kipling's "With the Night Mail" the notion of flying ships
that run on that mysterious new scientific thing of the pre–World War I

era, *rays.* In "With the Night Mail," the rays made sense, but Burroughs apparently misread that story. It is hard to know what he thought rays were, but his travelers to the moon, to Venus, and to Mars keep their own power-giving rays in large tanks. *A Princess of Mars* first appeared in 1912, but it is still in print and is still being read: John Carter's fighting ships of Mars are still running on rays they carry in tanks.

It is just as easy to demonstrate that the science-fiction writer is uniquely sophisticated about science and technology. The apologist puts forward a selection of paragraphs such as the following, from Robert L. Forward's *Dragon's Egg.*

> Although many times hotter than the Sun, the neutron star was not a hot ball of gas. Instead, the 67-billion-gee gravity field of the star had compressed its blazing matter into a solid ball with a thick crust of close-packed, neutron-rich nuclei arranged in a crystalline lattice of a dense core of liquid neutrons. As time passed, the star cooled and shrank. The dense crust fractured and mountains and faults were pushed up. Most crustal features were only a few millimeters high, but the larger mountain ranges rose up almost ten centimeters, poking their tops above the iron-vapor atmosphere. The mountains were the highest at the east and west magnetic poles, for most of the meteoric material that fell on the star was directed there by the magnetic field lines. (4)

Robert L. Forward, like some other science-fiction writers, is a working scientist.

This characterization of a genre through vigorous assertion supported by selective quotation is a game anyone can play with the paperbacks. It is not a game we can play with serious fiction, whose stories are unsimple, ironic. Paperback stories are often sarcastic, but they are not structurally ironic. The works that do have interesting internal anomalies, works like Aldiss's *Malacia Tapestry* and Le Guin's *Dispossessed,* are very uncommon. Readers who cannot take pleasure—and profit, too—from simple stories cannot read in any of the paperback genres.

The simplicity of the stories is strategic. Every paperback genre works with complexities by means of simplicities. More than any other genre, science fiction used to be a byword for simplemindedness to the readers of serious fiction, and nothing seems to have angered its critics more than its writers' interest in technology.

We can claim anything we like about this genre's attitude toward technology and the machine. We can insist, as many of its critics have, that science fiction has fallen in love with the idea of the machine. Evidence of this development can be found in *The Science Fiction Hall of Fame*, the collection of short stories that Robert Silverberg edited for the Science Fiction Writers of America. Lester del Rey's "Helen O'Loy," for instance, tells of two men who fall in love with a female robot. One of them marries Helen, and the other remains sadly faithful to her all his life: there is machine worship for you. In another story, John Campbell's "Twilight," a man goes far into the future and discovers that humanity has lost its energy and curiosity and is dying out. We are not surprised at all at the solution Campbell provides; for by the time we have reached the last pages of the story, he has already told us that our time traveler's hair was "like fine copper wire," that his eyes were "like etched iron," and that his voice "sounded like an organ talking" (53). A writer who conceives of his human hero in those images will be satisfied with only one kind of solution:

> So I brought another machine to life, and set it to a task which, in time to come, it will perform.
> I ordered it to make a machine which would have what man had lost. A curious machine. (60)

That curious machine (which, we note bemusedly, will not even be made by a human) is obviously a descendant of Helen O'Loy and her human husband: in "Twilight," John Campbell makes the machine the successor and heir to humanity, the next step upward in human evolution. Plainly, science fiction does love the machine.

Perhaps, however, science fiction knows the machine so well that it can see its danger and in its heart of hearts detests technology. It would certainly be easy to show that, for the genre has always looked back with deep pride to Mary Shelley's *Frankenstein* and to Nathaniel Hawthorne's "Rappaccini's Daughter" and to all those other stories of the nineteenth century in which science was made to look ugly. Its mistrust of science and technology did not end in 1900. In 1968, science-fiction fans awarded a Hugo, the genre's most important prize, to Harlan Ellison for "I Have No Mouth and I Must Scream." Ellison's story may be characterized for those who know classic American literature as a technological sequel to Jonathan Edwards's "Sinners in the Hands of an Angry God," the sermon that terrified the men and women who first heard it and can still send a chill through the surprised reader. Ellison describes the fate of the last five human beings left on Earth, caught and tortured by the greatest of all man's machines, a computer that hates them with the ferocity of an Old Testament Jehovah. Ellison leaves the last person alive, now a featureless blob of jelly, facing an eternity of torment. To save them from their agony, he has killed his four friends; but he cannot kill himself, he cannot even cry out.

Science fiction sees the subtler dangers, too. In *The Divine Invasion*, Philip K. Dick gives a disturbing, technological answer to Christianity's rhetorical question, "Death, where is thy sting?"

> Although dead and in cryonic suspension, Herb Asher was having his own problems. Very close to the Cry-Labs, Incorporated, warehouse a fifty-thousand-watt FM transmitter had been located the year before. For reasons unknown to anyone the cryonic equipment had begun picking up the powerful nearby FM signal. Thus Herb Asher, as well as everyone else in suspension at Cry-Labs, had to listen to elevator music all day and all night, the station being what it liked to call a "pleasing sounds" outfit.
>
> Right now an all-string version of tunes from *Fiddler on the Roof* assailed the dead at Cry-Labs. This was especially distasteful to Herb Asher because he was in the part of his cycle where he was under the impression that he was still alive.   (3)

Offered a choice between eternal torture and eternal elevator music, some would hesitate.

What is it in a tradition that permits it to accommodate both the knowledge of *Dragon's Egg* and the ignorance of *A Princess of Mars*, both the machine love of "Helen O'Loy" and the machine hatred of "I Have No Mouth and I Must Scream"? Plainly, the writers and readers of science fiction share more than a deep interest in technology itself, in technology for its own sake. What they share is a probing, exploratory interest in human-machine relationships; for underlying these one-dimensional stories is a many-sided image of what Australians might call the "mateship" of man and technology. This genre shares many interests with other genres, but in its interest in man-machine mateship it is unique.

It is the only genre we think of when the matter of humanity and the machine comes up—when someone remarks, say, that the ratio of animals to machines on the surface of the Earth is changing in some curious and disturbing ways. On the one hand we recognize that, for all their ingenuity, theatricality, and wit, none of the hundreds of science-fiction stories about aliens invading Earth matches in queerness that other invasion of Earth which even people outside science fiction are watching with the corners of their eyes: the flooding of machines out onto the surface of our planet, machines coming not from Mars but from inside our own brains. Nothing in fiction matches this real-life invasion, we recognize, but only when we are inside science fiction do we see the invasion clearly. It is science fiction that shows us that there are more tractors in the world now than tigers, more Boeing 747s than whooping cranes, more microcomputers than rhinos.

Some of us—the more doctrinaire of the humanists—feel that we should express unswerving opposition to everything that "Helen O'Loy" represents and even that the very theatricality of machine hatred in "I Have No Mouth and I Must Scream" grants a dignity to technology it has not earned. This is a response that might have been predicted. There must have been sixteenth-century Aztecs who became angry when their neighbors took an interest in those odd-looking Spaniards who had begun to appear all around them. The reactionaries could see that the Spaniards were bringing with them some of the less-attractive features of European civilization, but the kinds of Aztec who found the hoe less rewarding than the book would not have felt the Spanish invasion was an unambivalent horror. They would have seen that the Spaniards were also bringing Homer and Virgil and Augustine and all the glorious art and music of the Renaissance church.

Some years ago, Robert O'Brien's *Machines* offered a few numbers he found in the report on the 1960 census.

. . . .

Machine technology has boomed so swiftly and all-encompassingly that the 10,967,285,000-horsepower which America produced to run its machines in 1960 alone represented roughly the work-equivalent of 1,200 slaves for every man, woman, and child in the nation. Machine population has long since outstripped human population. At our latest census in 1960, when there were 179,323,000 people in the United States, there were 73,769,000 motor vehicles, 74,057,000 telephones, 55,500,000 television sets, 154,600,000 radios, and 574,178,000 electric clocks, coffee makers, mixers, ranges, shavers, vacuum cleaners, washers and other home appurtenances—a stupefying total of 932,104,000 machines.   (14)

These figures can be reduced to the following schema:

Human beings	180 million
Machines	930 million
Humans to machines	1 to 5
Citizens to slaves	1 to 1,200

There is good reason to suppose that man is addicted to machines. (The workers in Kurt Vonnegut's *Player Piano* fix broken machines and invent new ones in their free time while they are on strike against the machines that cost them their jobs.) But let us suppose that we were to set out to rid the world of machines. We might be able to agree to melt down the aircraft carriers, machine guns, and bombs; but what shall we get rid of next? Shall we destroy the machines that print our copies of Shakespeare's plays and Blake's poems? The machines that make the pencils and pens and paper and typewriters that our poets use? Shall we destroy the music machines: the clarinets and organs that future Mozarts and Bachs will use? Shall we destroy the cameras that Henri Cartier-Bresson and Akira Kurosawa used?

For science fiction, the answer to the question, What shall we do about the machine? is not at all obvious. All of the alternatives any of us might suggest are already being weighed in its stories.

The Luddites among us advocate a return to the primitive, and science fiction is already exploring that possibility. The post–World War III stories once greatly in fashion—Walter Miller's *Canticle for Leibowitz* is generally agreed to be the best of them—give us humans in a world that had stripped itself of technology; and such ambiguously science-fiction/fantasy novels as Gordon R. Dickson's *Dragon and the George* shift people from the twentieth century into worlds of swords, dragons, and magic that they sometimes choose over ours.

Probably most of us feel we ought to recognize what the machines have given us, accept them, and improve them—even make it impossible for them to harm us. Science fiction is exploring that alternative, too. Isaac Asimov's *I, Robot* offers us humanoid robots so designed that they not only cannot harm us, they cannot let anything else harm us, either. This, surely, is a splendid idea—but in "With Folded Hands," Jack Williamson suggests that Asimov's solution is not without its dangers. Williamson offers us androids with Asimov's safeguards built into them. Williamson's robots will never try to conquer mankind, and they, too, are so made that they cannot let us harm ourselves—but, as every parent knows, any sport, indeed any activity at all can lead to an injury, and so Williamson's androids will let us do nothing. They love us. They want only to serve us. They cannot understand why we would want to do anything for ourselves. They cannot let us cook for ourselves because they cook better than we do and, anyway, we might accidentally cut or burn ourselves. They think it best that we sit quietly, with folded hands, and let them do everything. If this puts us into a state of depression, that too could lead to injury, and so they surgically alter our brains to guarantee that we will always be joyful. In Williamson's grim little fable, humanity loses itself through its own investment of good intentions in pedantic machines.

Perhaps we feel that the currently simple man-machine relationships are best, that we should leave things as they are. But science fiction is not sure those relationships are so simple as either the man-machine love of "Helen O'Loy" or the man-machine hatred of "I Have No Mouth and I Must Scream" suggest.

Alfred Bester's "Fondly Fahrenheit," also in *The Science Fiction Hall of Fame*, appeared in 1954, twenty years after John Campbell had his hero invent the machine with curiosity. Vandaleur, Bester's central character, has wasted his inheritance and now flees from one planet to the next with his last remaining possession: an android of advanced design that he rents out. He must keep moving, for the android is defective. When the temperature rises above 98 degrees it starts to kill people, and the android is leaving behind them a long trail of brutal murders. He and the android are having other difficulties: neither is quite sure which of them is man, which is android. When the android is destroyed, Vandaleur escapes; but he carries with him, as a psychosis, the temperature-dependent murderousness of that android, and he is now killing people. He buys another, simpler android, but somehow that machine picks up Vandaleur's psychosis. At story's end, Vandaleur is dead, but the murders continue. The new android thinks it is Vandaleur and kills whenever the temperature is above 10 degrees.

Bester's story is troubling—at least to any of us who have ever been amused to discover that we felt better about *ourselves* when driving a new car or when using a typewriter with luxury features, who notice—not without additional dismay—that we remember the first bicycle we ever owned more vividly and with greater affection than we do some of the human friends we had then. Plainly, some machines are not emotionally invisible: some of them are influencing us. Science fiction raises the possibility that inventors may transmit their own neuroses through their machines to those of us who use them and that we, in our turn, may pass them on to other machines and, through them, to other people.

People who read science fiction know every one of these stories, the stories as rigorously—and adventurously—scientific as *Dragon's Egg* and those Edgar Rice Burroughs stories about battles inside a hollow Earth and trips through space in machines that have fuel tanks with gallons of rays sloshing around in them. They know *I, Robot* and "With Folded Hands," "Helen O'Loy" and also "I Have No Mouth and I Must Scream" and "Fondly Fahrenheit." The stories are ideological enemies, and yet they appear together in anthologies and in those recurrent series of the best science fiction ever written. The stories may seem to hate one another, but their readers love them all.

When we look at the readers of the other genres, we find very much the same thing. The readers who like the Westerns that favor the Indian (Marie Sandoz's *Cheyenne Autumn*) also like the Westerns that favor the cavalry (Ernest Haycox's *Bugles in the Afternoon*). The readers of the gentle school of detective story (A. A. Milne's *Red House Mystery*) also admire the best of the tough-guy stories (Ted Lewis's *Get Carter*). Every few years a spy story like John Le Carré's *Spy Who Came in from the Cold*, a western like Walter Van Tilburg Clark's *Ox-Bow Incident*, or a science-fiction novel like John Brunner's *Stand on Zanzibar* succeeds in capturing a larger than usual part of one of the images implicit in its genre, and then nongenre readers hail it as a book that rises above its genre; but the writers of those books know—or should know—better. The experienced readers of the traditions the books emerge from recognize that the books are hasty harvests from the riches of their genres, that they merely make evident to an unknowing public a small part of the unending and ever-changing debates that are the true lives of those genres.

The strategy by which any genre—vernacular or literary—explores a volume of meaning can be outlined by analogy with another art: the art of the animated cartoon. As we all eventually discovered, those magically delightful animated cartoons we watched as children were drawn on transparent overlays. Part of every frame we saw in the theater was drawn on one overlay, and other parts were drawn on other overlays. If we had only one of those transparent overlays, or cells, from Walt Disney's *Pinocchio*, say, we would see only part of the image that moviegoers saw when the film was shown in theaters. That cell would seem very simple—no background and perhaps only part of the figure. Some of that overlay would be entirely blank. If we did not know how animation is done, we would not know that the rest of the picture was on other overlays, and that moviegoers saw the partial image superimposed on other partial images, the whole creating a single, complete picture. The part glaringly absent from the figure on our overlay would already exist, on another overlay.

The monumental work of fiction offers us richly explored images captured within its pages. This is the case with the canonical works of fiction (*Moby-Dick, Middlemarch*), and it is also the case with works from the vernacular traditions that nevertheless have monumental ambitions (*The Malacia Tapestry, The Dispossessed*). The paperback genres do not often aim for the monumental, however, and work with a different strategy. Each individual work is the equivalent of one of those transparent overlays. It is designed to be placed on top of earlier, related works so as to produce with them those rich images that are characteristic of its genre.

The individual stories create, over time, richer volumes of meaning

. . . .

than any one of them can carry—even richer than those captured by the more visible and more honored monumental works. In 1959 Robert Heinlein's *Starship Troopers* offered the professional soldier's heroic myth of himself as standing in harm's way between the enemy and the civilian —the myth of the soldier as seen by the soldier. In 1965 Harry Harrison responded with *Bill, the Galactic Hero,* a satiric novel that offered a comic parallel of Heinlein's plot line but presented the myth of the soldier as seen by the civilian, an image that has more in common with Bertolt Brecht's *Mother Courage* than with an Annapolis commencement address; Harrison gave us the story of an innocent man turned by the military into a brute. In 1975 Joe Haldeman answered both novels with *The Forever War,* a story that also paralleled Heinlein's plot line and gave us the myth of the soldier as seen by a Vietnam draftee, an image of intelligent men and women caught within a self-perpetuating military system crippled by its own rhetoric, a system which is neither heroic nor brutal but is irredeemably stupid. Each of the stories is simple enough. If we read only one of the stories, we think the genre is simple. Each story seems to be claiming that it is offering the definitive image of the professional fighting man, but *Bill, the Galactic Hero* and *The Forever War* were written explicitly for people who already knew *Starship Troopers.* The three stories do not offer images, they offer counterimages, correctives to simplicities. No matter which of the three notions of the soldier we begin with, the other stories make us uncertain, less hasty to judge, and certainly less persuaded that science fiction is simple. The genre is not simple; but, like all other paperback genres, it proceeds by means of simplicities.

The effect of these opposed story-simplicities is to create those meaning-volumes and also to create profound though unparaphrasable questions; for when several answers are proposed for any question and each shows every other to be inadequate the result is increasingly sophisticated redefinition of the question.

We may speak of the questions indigenous to each of the genres or, alternatively, of the "matters" of the various genres in the somewhat old-fashioned but still useful literary sense of *matter* as "the elements that constitute material for treatment in thought, discourse, or writing" (*Webster's Seventh*). When we turn to the detective story, we are turning to the matter of legality and morality, the matter of the civilian and the police, the matter of error-finding intelligence. When we turn to science fiction we are turning to the matter of humanity and technology, the matter (in some stories) of the civilian and the soldier. And when we turn to the romance, the western, the spy story, we are turning to other matters— that is, to other questions. In this more adequate view of the content of the paperback genres, each simplistic story is playing its role (albeit, unconsciously) in making its genre's matters, or questions, more sophisticated. It is because the paperback genres make us feel we understand the baffling questions that we feel we have profited. It is not the answers (the lore about silencers, etc.) that enrich us: it is understanding why it is difficult to find answers to any of the central human questions.

Predictability

Walter Kendrick's complaint about the romance—that the stories "lead straight to the expected conclusion, without a twist or turn or spark of interest"—has been brought against science fiction, the western, the detective story. Their critics say that all the stories in a genre are effectively the same.

This is not literary judgment, however. It is impatience. If the romance offered not a twist or spark of interest, why would its readers spend their money on new titles? If they were clever enough to learn how to read, they are clever enough to recognize that when every story is effectively the same they can save money and time by rereading the same book. (If they cared about this sort of complaint, they would point out that readers of canonical and serious fiction, who do reread the same books many times, elsewhere blame readers of paperbacks for always wanting something new.) If the romance is so simple, why do some writers fail to get their books published? Why do only a few writers sell hugely?

The experienced truth of the romance and of the western and of all the other vernacular genres is that the stories are *all* twists and sparks of interest. They are predictable in one sense, of course. We know what we are getting when we buy a paperback; we know what we are refusing when we pass the book over. If the titles and cover illustrations do not warn us, the publishers do. Here are four back-cover blurbs. Not one of us has the slightest uncertainty as to what we are being promised.

Sam Vetch didn't know that his wife had been the woman of Salvaje, The Ghost—that she had borne two sons by the Apache chieftain. When Salvaje came to claim his own, the duel began: a deadly contest between two men of strong will, courage, and different standards of honor—a duel that must end in tragedy.

(Blurb for Olsen, *The Stalking Moon*)

A tale of human emotion that lays bare the heights and depths of love, passion and desire in old and new worlds . . . as we follow Virginia Brandon, beautiful, impudent and innocent, from the glittering ballrooms of Paris to the sensuality of life in New Orleans to the splendor of intrigue-filled Mexico.

A tale of unending passion, never to be forgotten . . . the story of Virginia's love for Steven Morgan, a love so powerful that she will risk anything for him . . . even her life.

(Blurb for Rogers, *Sweet, Savage Love*)

Tree Frog is charged with menace and high adventure. It races from an intelligence briefing session in London—to a terrifying torture ordeal in the Austrian Alps—to a heart-thudding test flight above the Sahara.

Tree Frog has an unlikely heroine. Red-haired Binnie Abrams is not a beauty. She's just 140 lbs. of sure-fire sex appeal.

Tree Frog has an unconventional hero. Giles Yeoman is a scientist who *knows* he's passing wrong information to the other side —information about a spy plane that makes the U-2 look like a Piper Cub.

(Blurb for Woodhouse, *Tree Frog*)

Sir Eustace was surprised when the box of chocolates arrived at his club. It was an ideal gift for a man of taste, but he didn't have a sweet tooth. So he gave them to George Bendix, who gave them to his wife, who gobbled them down. They were perfectly fresh. Perfectly delicious. Perfectly poisonous.

Was this the fiendish work of a lunatic or an ingenious murder? And who was his intended victim? The famous Crimes Circle Club is determined to help Scotland Yard find out. Each member has a theory. One will be right. One will be "dead" wrong.

(Blurb for Berkeley, *The Poisoned Chocolates Case*)

That fourth blurb is as unmistakable as the three that preceded it. When people buy *The Poisoned Chocolates Case*, it is not because of their interest in chocolates or in the Crimes Circle Club, either. They are buying it because they have been assured that the novel comes from the genre of the tale of detection, and because they can predict that the writer used the classic pattern for that type. That pattern was established long ago and has been outlined many times. Here is John G. Cawelti's account from *Adventure, Mystery, and Romance:*

> As Poe defined it, the detective story formula centers upon the detective's investigation and solution of the crime. Both "Rue Morgue" and "The Purloined Letter" exemplify the six main phases of this pattern: (a) introduction of the detective, (b) crime and clues; (c) investigation; (d) announcement of the solution; (e) explanation of the solution; (f) denouement. These parts do not always appear in sequence and are sometimes collapsed into each other, but it is difficult to conceive of a classical story without them.   (81–82)

Anyone who reads at all has read a dozen stories that honor that pattern, and some report that they are reading a hundred novels like that every year. How do they manage to read so many stories with the same pattern?

This is not so strange as some would have us believe. The following is from Lewis Turco's excellent *Book of Forms: A Handbook of Poetics*. It is the pattern for a distinctive verse form, the Spenserian stanza, which has been used in some memorable poems, among them Spenser's *Faerie Queene*, Byron's *Childe Harold's Pilgrimage*, and Keats's *Eve of St. Agnes*.

lines	meters and rhymes
1.	xx́ xx́ xx́ xx́ xá
2.	xx́ xx́ xx́ xx́ xb́
3.	xx́ xx́ xx́ xx́ xá

4.   xх́ xх́ xх́ xх́ xb́

5.   xх́ xх́ xх́ xх́ xb́

6.   xх́ xх́ xх́ xх́ xá

7.   xх́ xх́ xх́ xх́ xá

8.   xх́ xх́ xх́ xх́ xb́

9.   xх́ xх́ xх́ xх́ xх́ xá

There are hundreds of these stanzas in Spenser's *Faerie Queene*. No one asks why lovers of Spenser, Byron, and Keats do not become bored with that underlying pattern repeated again and again. The patterns in vernacular fiction have the same character and purpose as those Spenserian rhythms—and other rhythms, too: the predictable alternations of *episode* and *stasimon* in the ancient Greek play; the certainties of the past in such historical novels as Walter Pater's *Marius the Epicurean* and William Makepeace Thackeray's *Henry Esmond;* and the hundreds of other patterns in canonical literature that make monumental texts predictable, too.

We do become bored when these patterns tyrannize the materials, as they do when invoked by uninventive writers. The poet who writes stanzas that duplicate the Spenserian pattern exactly—with every accentuated syllable in the right place and every rhyme exact—will have us nodding off within a few minutes. The mystery writer who scrupulously follows that sequence Cawelti describes is a writer whose books we do not return to and never recommend.

As we saw in our discussion of design, readers in a genre find claims of predictability puzzling. Most of the writers who interest them are not very predictable even in the skeletal patterns they use. Writers like Ursula Le Guin use entirely untraditional patterns; writers like John Le Carré cross-fertilize the genres by combining patterns; writers like Maj Sjöwall and Per Wahloo honor the familiar designs but create larger designs that embrace whole series of books; and, of course, there are so many designs traditional to any genre that it is often difficult for readers to determine, at first, which design is governing the story.

Even when readers recognize the pattern that is carrying the story— that classic pattern of the tale of detection, say—it is rarely the case that the pattern is pure. As suggested earlier, the pattern seems to play much the same role in vernacular fiction that the metrical scheme plays in a poem. In both cases, readers sense the formal scheme as the norm that permits them to appreciate the figural variations. The writers are like the jazz musicians who give us a familiar melody at the opening of the piece so that we can understand the variations that follow. We do not listen for that melody. We listen for the variations.

The analogy is especially apt for the classic detective story. Readers in this tradition are alert to the pattern, anticipate the sudden shifts, try to guess the solution that is getting closer as they turn the pages. They insist that the design be honored. In no other tradition would readers have become so upset as they were in 1926 by Agatha Christie's *Murder of Roger Ackroyd*. They said that the novel broke an implicit promise to its readers that certain characters—and especially the fictional detective's biographer—be trustworthy. (This protest had its own lovely ironies. Readers had blithely accepted the murder of thousands of men and women in the stories but were outraged when one of the stories wounded the genre's own conventions.) This trickiness has always been the appeal of the Agatha Christie novel, winning the reluctant loyalty even of readers who find her social vision innocently appalling. In *Mortal Consequences*, Julian Symons caught it precisely: "She shows us the ace of spades face up. Then she turns it over, but we still know where it is, so how has it been transformed into the five of diamonds?" (62).

Critics of detective stories emphasize their sameness, but it is unpredictability that their readers remember. The crime novelist whose readers guess the solution before they reach the author's explanation is dismissed immediately. And, as Cawelti remarks, the possible variations are unlimited, though this is hidden, somewhat, by publishers' efforts to make every new book look like a revision of some admired older book. Every one of the four blurbs quoted above is inaccurate in fact or in emphasis, for instance. *The Poisoned Chocolates Case* is everywhere recognized as one of the dozen or so classics in the tradition of the tale of detection, and yet it does not exemplify those six main phases of the detective-story formula that Cawelti and others have identified. The story knows that formula, of course. The writer demonstrates his mastery of that formula by ringing changes on it. Eight plausible solutions—each ingenious and witty—appear on stage in succession, each a definitive rejection of every earlier solution. The novel is like all the better novels in its genre—in being different from all other novels in its genre.

Predictability is an important part of that reading experience, of course. Readers think they know what is coming next, but they are always slightly wrong—which creates the disappointment, surprise, and delight that they associate with the stories.

In stories like Le Guin's *Dispossessed*, with its alternations between present and past, or Philip K. Dick's *Man in the High Castle*, which offers us four parallel and intersecting time streams, the patterns themselves are intriguing; but in most paperbacks the patterns are carriers of materials rather than forms experienced for themselves. The patterns bring to readers certain kinds of characters and events. This is true of the tale of detection, but it is also true of every other paperback genre. There is no event in a vernacular story that is not a variation on what has come before, an invitation to further variation in the books that will follow. We see this when we turn to the western, for instance. If ever there was a convention-governed fictional event, it is the gunfight between two men of the West. One would think that the possibilities for variations on that confrontation were exhausted long ago; but writers are still designing new insides for that theatrical moment.

Jeni Calder's delightful study of the western, *There MUST Be a Lone Ranger*, gives us two versions that suggest what writers have done. The first, from J. T. Edson's *Ysabel Kid*, is the gunfight as seen through the eyes of the loser.

> Flame tore from the barrel of the Ysabel Kid's rifle. Giss felt the sudden shocking impact as lead struck him. He reared up and through the whirling pain haze saw the Kid get up, take out a bullet and push it towards the breechplate of his rifle. Then the Kid lifted his weapon again, his right eye sighted along the smooth blue barrel, and his finger squeezed the trigger lovingly. Even though Giss was staggering, the Ysabel Kid shot and hit. Giss rocked back on his heels, threw his rifle to one side and crumpled forward. He lay there on top of the Lookout Rock dead without ever finding out how he came to make the mistake which cost him his life. (118)

The second, from Ernest Haycox's *Free Grass*, gives us muted violence and a view through the eyes of the winner.

Nothing was said between them; that time had come when there were no words to carry any meaning either would understand. They were, the both of them, thrown back on instinct, back to the stark and ancient promptings. So they closed the interval, and for all the emotion they displayed they were as men coming up to shake hands. San Saba's body swayed forward on his feet, and his little nut round head nodded. Gillette advanced erect, watching how the ex-foreman's eyes grew narrower at each pace. Time dissolved into space and, save for the sound of his own boots striking, he would never have known himself to be moving. Somewhere a spectator coughed, the sunlight drew dim, the spotted dog ran between them. And then all his range of vision was cut off and he saw only San Saba. San Saba had stopped. His arm rose slowly away from his belt; a bull whip snapped twice, sounding to Gillette strangely like guns exploding. The spotted dog raced back, barking, and men ran out into the street and made a circle round a San Saba who had disappeared. Gillette stood alone, wondering. His arm felt unusually heavy, and he looked down to find a gun swinging from his fist; the taste of powder smoke was in his throat.   (118)

And here, from Jake Logan's *Slocum's Debt*, is the sort of gunfight we have been getting lately in the Western. It makes no concession to readers who find violence distasteful.

The first gunny was still upright. He had taken a solid hit in the chest and although he must have known he was already a dead man he still struggled to bring his Colt level so he could get off a dying shot into the man who had killed him.

Slocum took the time for careful aim and peered down the sightless barrel of his reworked Colt, to look the gunman square in the eyes before he squeezed the trigger and sent his third bullet into the bridge of the man's nose, squarely between his eyes.

The gunman's head snapped back with a suddenness that broke

bone and tore tendons, and Slocum could hear the loud crack of splintering vertebrae before he heard the solid thud of the body fall.

(189)

If readers unfamiliar with the western think that account unpleasant, they might remind themselves that stories that look at violence do actually look at it sometimes. Here is Richmond Lattimore's version of one of Homer's more physical moments in *The Iliad*, a work famous for its glory and for its grimness:

He hit him at the joining place of head and neck, at the last
vertebra, and cut through both of the tendons, so that
the man's head and mouth and nose hit the ground far sooner
than did the front of his legs and knees as he fell.

(14.465–68)

(The violence in some of the vernacular genres is much misunderstood by people who, as Conrad remarked in *Heart of Darkness*, have their own violences done for them by the butcher who lives at one end of their street and the policeman who lives at the other. The most searching study of the problematic relations between art and violence is John Fraser's *Violence in the Arts*, which looks thoughtfully at both monumental and vernacular art.)

We have already seen something of the range of possibilities that the crime novel, in its largest sense, admits. Its patterns bring us odd bits of lore, for instance. In John D. MacDonald's *Cinnamon Skin* we looked bemusedly at a collage house trailer; from Hammett's "Big Knockover" we learned about the names that thieves gave one another when Hammett was still a private investigator; from Gash's *Grail Tree*, how to look at suspect watercolors; from Hare's *When the Wind Blows*, about the laws governing the marrying of sisters-in-law; from Forsyth's "No Comebacks," about silencers for handguns.

There was more: Georges Simenon's oeuvre gives us "the panorama of France"; Hammett's *Red Harvest* dramatizes a conflict between legality and morality; Ross Macdonald's *Chill* gives us urban antipoetry; William Marshall's *Hatchet Man* gives us the good-humored O'Yee family in Hong

Kong; Sjöwall and Wahloo's novels detail the spread of bureaucratic duncedom.

In spite of the publishers, even the blurbs cannot make them look all the same. Here are two from the shelves on which science fiction is kept —one of them a novel we have already met.

> Dick Seaton and Marc DuQuesne are the deadliest enemies in the Universe—their feud has blazed among the stars and changed the history of a thousand planets. But now a threat from outside the Galaxy drives them into a dangerous alliance as hordes of strange races drive to a collision with mankind!
>
> Seaton and DuQuesne fight and slave side by side to fend off the invasion—as Seaton keeps constant, perilous watch for DuQuesne's inevitable double-cross!
>
> (Blurb for E. E. Smith, *Skylark DuQuesne*)

> Philip K. Dick's latest novel starts out on a lonely planet in the star system CY30-CY30B and ends up in Hollywood on a future Earth which is not quite ours. Along the way we encounter God, His Son, Elijah the Prophet, and the demon Belial, who controls Earth. Through the course of the book we have an opportunity to deal with the problems of Good versus Evil, reality and illusion, and how it feels to listen to canned music for ten years without being able to turn it off.
>
> (Blurb for Dick, *The Divine Invasion*).

The following blurb for one of Chester Himes's Harlem novels will take the taste of chocolates from us and eliminate any notion that the world of the crime novel is populated only with Sir Eustaces.

> Somebody was giving a bloody new twist to the old-time religion. The case started in a gigantic Harlem revival meeting where the as- sembled sinners suddenly discovered that one of them was a corpse. It led to a hellish fight in a pitch-black building where no one was sure who was killing whom. It took a wild detour in a swank apart- ment house where an old man was seduced by a teen-aged hooker, his young wife was led astray by a handsome stranger, and a killer made hay while the others made love.

And following every step of the way through sin city were Coffin Ed
Johnson and Grave Digger Jones, two black supercops who preached
their sermons with long-barreled pistols and big, hard fists.

(Blurb for Himes, *The Big Gold Dream*)

Plainly, *Skylark DuQuesne* is not the same as *The Divine Invasion*, and
The Poisoned Chocolates Case is not the same as *The Big Gold Dream*.
Probably what its critics mean when they say that all the stories in a
particular genre are the same is that none of the stories piques their
interest. That is true of a genre's stories when we do not know how to read
them, when we are unconsciously looking for the wrong things.

Some readers spend most of their reading lives in the bookscape of the
serious novel and make only brief, occasional visits to the bookscape of
the paperback. What they seem to find disturbing is an intrusiveness of
rhythm, which they identify as predictability. Paperback fiction is form-
intensive; the serious novel is not, and so experience with the serious
novel does not prepare one for the paperback novel.

One useful definition of the serious novel is that it is fiction written
outside any genre. Serious novels are the consequence of writers' attempts
to produce something unique, and so the underlying patterns are less
visible than in the paperbacks. Serious writers find encouragement in the
study of such mountainous works as *Moby-Dick, Don Quixote, Nostromo*,
and *Ulysses*. These and books like them seem genre-independent today to
all except scholars. Only the literary historians remember now that there
was a popular genre, the High Society story (in England, the Silver Fork
school), when Henry James wrote *The American* and *The Ambassadors* and
that his works did not seem nearly so original when they first appeared.
The masterworks of the past were anomalies within their genres when they
first appeared, and the genres that did inspire them have now vanished.
Their indebtedness to those genres is no longer visible. Such works can
hardly be said to have form in anything like the sense that the sonnet
and *rime royale* and the epic—and paperback stories—have form. John
Dryden spoke of the delightful surprise we get when a writer gives us an
appropriate but quite unexpected ending; but in fact the surprises come
all along the way. Paperback fiction is fiction that invites readers to predict
what they will get but then surprises them. If they are not surprised, they
are disappointed; but of course they cannot be surprised if they have not

unconsciously been predicting as they read. This is not a fiction that lacks any twist or turn or spark of interest. This is a fiction that is read for its twists and turns and sparks of interest.

Absurdities

What we think of as absurdities when we first visit an unfamiliar genre are only its conventions, and their apparent silliness disappears when we continue to read. Until that silliness does disappear, however, those conventions, hardly noticed by the regular reader, stand out like so many assurances of clownishness—a formidable barrier between new readers and the pleasures the genre offers.

In an earlier chapter, we examined an inventory of science-fiction clichés, but any of us can write a list of paperback absurdities. There are, for instance, those insistently happy endings of certain kinds of romance; that implausibly quick recovery time for any detective who receives a beating in one of the hard-boiled stories; the newly discovered planets in an older style of science fiction, planets so implausibly well fitted to Earthmen that they can go out the air lock in their shirt sleeves; in tales of detection, those professional policemen so awed by their social superiors that they humbly ask their help in solving crimes; and many, many others.

A genre convention is most usefully thought of as an enablement—a device that makes it possible for writers within a genre to do things that they otherwise could not do. All conventions appear first within a particular genre, and so all conventions are genre-specific and must inevitably appear absurd—be it delightfully absurd or embarrassingly absurd—when we first encounter them.

Although all conventions are genre-specific, they do not all remain tied to the traditions that invented them. Some are needed so badly, apparently, that they are borrowed by other genres. Some become free-floating figures with lives of their own. These last are of special interest here because we do not have to know their genres to see the kinds of enablement that all such conventions provide.

Two immensely successful absurdities are Sherlock Holmes and Tarzan of the Apes. They are not the first figures to become widely known in modern times even to nonreaders: Robinson Crusoe preceded them, for instance. Yet for every one person who has met them in print, ten thousand people who have never read a story by Conan Doyle or Edgar Rice Burroughs can recognize even distant allusions to Holmes and Tarzan. However absurd we may think them, we are interested enough to watch them in films and on television, and no doubt our descendants will someday be watching them in music videos on laservision. Sherlock Holmes is from a genre—*the tale of detection*—that seems to be fading in popularity after an incredibly long run. Tarzan comes from another genre—the *scientific romance*—that was replaced by the tradition we now call *science fiction*; but though the genre that invented him is dead, Tarzan lives on. What have these two absurdities enabled for both the people who do and the people who do not read in those traditions?

Conan Doyle's Sherlock Holmes did, of course, have ancestors and a fertile cultural ground in which to grow. First, Holmes enabled the trail-following and sign-reading fun of James Fenimore Cooper's Deerslayer to take place in urban European settings. Second, Holmes fit in well with the increasingly glamorous notion of rational intelligence as manifested in science; he did not think in metaphors and images but worked with itemizing, analytical intelligence. Third, he was a genius who failed to terrify because he was comically or embarrassingly eccentric; Holmes's strange combination of genius and oddities is a distant echo of that earlier odd genius, Samuel Johnson. Fourth, Holmes appeared in the 1890s, in the midst of what puzzlers today call—after its most eminent writer —the Sam Lloyd Era, a great period for amateur puzzling, when most of the puzzles we encounter today (though not the crossword) first took shape (Martin Gardner 78–84). Holmes dramatized inside fiction the kind of problem solving that contemporary readers were doing for recreation outside fiction.

These and a dozen other threads came together in Sherlock Holmes, but he did something else for the reading class that very badly needed doing —and still does, apparently. By means of Sherlock Holmes, Conan Doyle domesticated the police force. It is quite plain from the immense, immediate popularity of all those stories about gentlemen detectives humbly deferred to by the working-class police just how frightening and confusing the newly invented police force was to the middle and upper classes—to the people who had enough money to buy books.

The police were a group of men newly brought together—men from the laboring class—who were uniquely licensed for domestic violence (they could use fists and clubs in England, guns in the United States) but who had no natural loyalties to the reading class. It must have been plain to all that a good police force was disinterested and that while it was the protector of every man, woman, and child, rich or poor, it was also potentially the enemy of every man, woman, and child, rich or poor, for any persons who harmed or endangered or even threatened anyone else would find the face of the police turned against them. And when questions of right and wrong were difficult to decide, the middle class would find that it was the police, a group with laboring-class origins, who were making the decisions. To turn loose in the imaginations of the reading class those armed men who were not from the reading class was to create a threat that had to be tamed. Conan Doyle tamed that police force with his Sherlock Holmes stories. The crimes were too clever (in his stories) for the police (in his stories) to imagine, and they had to turn to Holmes and publicly acknowledge their inferiority to a person from the readers' reference group. Every new story with a gentleman or lady detective was a reassurance to the reading class that they were safe from the police. Sherlock Holmes himself, with his eccentricities and his specialized intelligence, is a continuing reminder even to nonreaders that the police can be outwitted—a somewhat dubious proposition, admittedly, but a solace nevertheless.

What did Tarzan enable? Why was Tarzan so quickly popular, and why did translations of the Tarzan image into the comics and the films and television prove so popular? Perhaps the first thing that should be said is that, like Sherlock Holmes, Tarzan is not for the reader the simple creature he seems. He does have predecessors in all the isolated and feral children who have fascinated us: Kaspar Hauser, for instance, and Kipling's Mowgli. He is also a reinvention of the Robinson Crusoe myth and, indeed, goes Robinson Crusoe one better. Crusoe was mature and highly skilled when he was shipwrecked on his island, but Tarzan was an infant who had to teach himself everything, who even had to teach himself how to read. Still, these parallels and provenances do not sufficiently explain the continuing popularity of the figure of Tarzan of the Apes.

. . . .

The most likely stimulus for the invention of Tarzan was the investigations in nineteenth-century geology and biology that culminated in the work of Charles Darwin, whose theories of the evolution of species offered a direct, apparently unanswerable challenge both to religious cosmology and to the quiet smugness of homo sapiens in a proud age of invention. The mere notion of a Tarzan of the Apes allowed the popular imagination to live with the Darwinian hypothesis even in its most easily remembered (because most frightening) vulgarization: that man was descended from apes. It may seem odd that an uneducated writer should casually have succeeded where the more thoughtful laboriously failed, but no other writer managed to create an image of man in a Darwinian universe that matches the naive response of Edgar Rice Burroughs. Tarzan, absurd or not, is still our most successful dramatization of the quintessential human being. Raised by apes, he rose to his full human potential.

There is more to the appeal of the image of Tarzan than that, of course. With that first of the Tarzan books, Burroughs created the paradigmatic Freudian *family romance*—that dream familiar to all our childhoods that the people who tell us they are our parents are not our real parents, and that we shall eventually discover that we are descended from the noble, or the supremely wise, or at least The Rich. And Tarzan has proved highly elastic. When he was played in the films by the tongue-tied Johnny Weissmuller, Tarzan became the nonreader's Billy Budd—an inarticulate man who could not speak out against injustice but who could strike out against it, and with all the forces of outraged nature behind him.

Tarzan is no less absurd than the singing shepherd of the pastoral tradition, the knight errant of the chivalric romance, the revenger of Shakespeare's era, but he is no more absurd than they. Each figure was a nexus within a network of recognized and unrecognized concerns—a solution to several problems. Tarzan and Sherlock Holmes and the clones of the Ysabel Kid and Mike Hammer are no less interesting as indicators of social and psychological and emotional pressures than all of the conventions that preceded them. The images from vernacular fiction that we borrow out of the genres that invent them—the Robinson Crusoes, the Deerslayers, the Sherlock Holmeses, the Zorros, the western marshals—are always resolutions in a network of darker concerns that transcend genre boundaries.

Sometimes, however, the resolutions occur inside a genre, and then they do seem absurd to occasional readers. A convenient example of this is the *body shield* of science fiction, which may have *only* intrageneric value. It is not difficult to guess what some scientists think of people who can read stories about faster-than-light spaceships and the body shield and shirt-sleeve planets. In each of these instances, however, it can be shown that science fiction needed the convention.

To understand why science fiction needed the body shield, it is necessary to return to Edgar Rice Burroughs. In his *Princess of Mars* of 1912, John Carter is transported to Mars "by means science has yet to explain" (by pure will power, apparently) and finds himself in a desert menaced by green-skinned hominoids who are twelve feet tall, have six limbs, and are riding dinosaurlike thoats. They carry spears, and they carry radium guns; those radium guns are accurate at two hundred miles. John Carter is a fighting man already, and his Earth muscles in this lighter gravitational field make him the most athletic fighter on this violent planet; he quickly becomes the greatest swordsman Barsoom (Mars, of course) has ever known.

Fair enough: as the reviewers say, if this is the sort of thing you like, you will like this sort of thing. Ingenious, even: though it was apparently not original with Burroughs, the simple elegance of the Earth-muscles solution to the problem of making readers feel they have something in common with an athletic hero is worth separate recognition (Pierce 57). Of interest at this point in our inquiry, however, is that curious juxtaposition of spears and radium rifles.

We may first have come across this story when we were eight years old. (Burroughs did not write the story for eight-year-olds, but eight-year-olds read it, too.) Even if we did read this novel when we were very young, a certain incredulity insinuated itself into many of our minds. Why, we inevitably asked ourselves, would warriors carry heavy spears if they already had rifles accurate at two hundred miles? True, we had been assured that Burroughs's Barsoom is caught in a culture of heroism and that its warriors actually preferred to fight with primitive weapons at close range. Still, many bookish girls and boys must have asked themselves whether they would lug that spear around when they had one of those marvelous rifles and must have confessed, with some secret embarrassment, that they would not: they would be too lazy. Further, they would have been certain that there would be Barsoomian warriors like themselves— warriors who would pick up the rifle and conveniently forget to bring the spear along. (Even at eight, one learns about oneself. Apparently, some of us can suspend our disbelief in radium rifles, in gorgeous red-skinned princesses, and in six-limbed warriors, but we cannot conceive of a planet on which no one is lazy.)

And would all Barsoomians patiently wait until John Carter, the Greatest Swordsman Barsoom Has Ever Known, came close enough to kill them, dying for the greater glory of the culture of heroism? Again, some of those eight-year-old readers would have had the sad conviction that they, at least, would not. The moment John Carter lifted his handsome white head above the distant horizon, those eight-year-old warriors would have lifted their radium rifles and taken out the man's left eyeball. As Huck Finn might have said, they didn't mind dying but there was no point in *wasting* their lives.

Spears and radium rifles: Burroughovian silliness, of course. All readers saw that it was silly, and yet they continued to turn the pages. They wanted what the novel was giving them. It was giving them magical technology (that radium rifle: *Gosh!*) and it was giving them hand-to-hand resolution of moral issues (*Wow!*). And if the two are not consonant inside the universe of the story, the bits and pieces of the universe outside the story in our own universe do not always fit snugly together either.

Burroughs never did find a way to permit man-to-man combat inside high technology; and his successors spent thirty years in the search for a solution. Meanwhile, their readers simply swallowed the anomalies, mocking them later in their parodies of space adventure.

Some science-fiction writers played interesting games with the juxtaposition of old-fashioned physical *virtú* and futuristic weaponry. Brian Aldiss refers in *Galactic Empires* to the love for both ray guns and sword play. He gives us Alfred Coppel's picturesque marriage of cavalry and faster-than-light spaceships in "The Rebel of Valkyr." The paragraphs can be relished: the image of horse manure on the decks of an FTL ship is probably unique.

The spaceship was ancient, yet the mysterious force of the Great Destroyer chained within the sealed coils between the hulls drove it with unthinkable speed across the star-shot darkness. The interior was close and smoky, for the only light came from oil lamps turned low to slow the fouling of the air. Once, there had been light without fire in the thousand-foot hulls, but the tiny orbs set into the ceilings had failed for they were not of a kind with the force in the sealed, eternal coils.

On the lower decks, the horses of the small party of Valkyr warriors aboard stomped the steel deck-plates, impatient in their close confinement; while in the tiny bubble of glass at the very prow of the ancient vessel, two shamen of the hereditary caste of Navigators drove the pulsing starship toward the spot beyond the veil of the Coalsack where their astrolabes and armillary spheres told them that the misty globe of Kalgan lay.

Many men—risking indictment as warlocks or sorcerers—had tried to probe the secrets of the Great Destroyer and compute the speed of these mighty spacecraft of antiquity. Some had even claimed a speed of 100,000 miles per hour for them. But since the starships made the voyage from Earth to the agricultural worlds of Proxima Centauri in slightly less than twenty-eight hours, such calculations would place the nearest star-system an astounding *two million eight hundred thousand* miles from Earth—a figure that was as absurd to all Navigators as it was inconceivable to laymen. (162)

We helplessly salute that lovely, wry solution to the problem of having ray guns, and all they stand for, and sword play, and all it stands for, in the same story.

The commonest early solution was to have the ray guns jam up or run out of atomic power at the climactic moment (Paul A. Carter 19). Writers did experiment with other evasions, but only one is worth special mention: the writer turns the ray gun into a sword, as in *Star Wars*, where the light sword is a high technology marvel that permits personal duels. (Presumably, a code of chivalry is again invoked to put the true ray guns away. Or it may be that those guns are too inaccurate; no one in the film seems to be able to hit anything other than a doorjamb anyway.)

The most ingenious solution was the body shield. This device had appeared as early as 1940, in A. E. van Vogt's "Weapon Shop," though I think it was not immediately recognized as the solution it was. The body shield requires a bit of explanation.

In its classic form it was a device that surrounded those who wore it with a field of energy, a sort of invisible body halo. This field had two properties. First, it repelled any high-energy attack (bullets, laser beams, and the like). Second, it was transparent to low-energy attacks. Here, from Keith Laumer's *Galactic Odyssey* of 1967, is a standard account of a body shield in action: "I saw a lightning-wink and heard the soft *whap!* of a filament pistol. Fsha-fsha *oof!*ed as he took the bolt square in the chest; a corona outlined his figure in vivid blue as the harness bled the energy off to the ground. Then he was on the assassin; his arm rose and fell with the sound of a hammer hitting a grapefruit, and the would-be killer tumbled backward and slid down the wall to sprawl on the pavement" (224). As always, the fight ends with a manly punch—well, in this case, a manly alienly punch: Fsha-fsha is not human.

My own first acquaintance with the body shield came in the 1940s in a short story whose title and author I do not remember. In that story, the viewpoint character is a licensed assassin whose specialty is the throwing knife. This weapon is a popular one because assassins' targets wear body shields. Pistols are useless; the body shields simply bounce the bullets back. A thrown knife, however, approaches that shield at a low enough energy level so that it can go through.

The body shield is absurd, of course, but not because it is scientifically impossible. It is scientifically impossible for Glendower to call spirits from the vasty deep in *Henry IV, Part One*, but he does and we do not object. The body shield may even be possible scientifically. We live in a universe that permitted the invention of Silly Putty, which one of its admirers describes as "a piece of pink goo that stretches like taffy, shatters when struck sharply with a hammer, picks up newsprint and photos in color, molds like clay, flows like molasses, and—when rolled into a ball— bounces like mad" (Kaye 112). If our universe allows for the invention of Silly Putty, it may allow for the invention of the body shield. No. The body shield is absurd because it is absurd. Readers are asked to accept the postulate that some humans will invent and the rest of us will buy body shields. Aristotle's observation is as true now as it was in ancient Athens: "Probable impossibilities are to be preferred to unconvincing possibilities" (54). Glendower's powers are impossibilities, but they are probable impossibilities. The body shield is the unconvincing possibility.

Our objection is very simple. The device is worthless. Consider the battle of Agincourt. Henry V would have thrown his high-tech body shield away. The arrows and swords and spears would not even have known the body shield was there; a garbage-can cover would have given him better protection. We try to imagine ourselves wearing body shields in New York City or London. We would be safe from nuclear attacks (a plus), but not from muggers. Even if someone does invent a body shield, we are not going to wear it.

The body shield was not absurd in science fiction, however. Science fiction was working under the governance of the necessity of including both ray guns and sword play, and the body shield was a solution that validated their juxtaposition. The body shield *was* superscience that cleverly invalidated superscience and forced humans into personal resolutions of their differences.

Let us return to that forgotten short story. If it was intended to be a masterpiece, the story failed. It was an unexceptional adventure—no better, if no worse, than several hundred other stories. This is the test: it would look out of place in any collection of the thousand best short stories ever written. As a contribution to its genre, however, it was immensely important. It contributed to the genre the resolution of an internal anomaly that had defeated the best efforts of writers for at least thirty years.

Readers new to science fiction would not have noticed the body shield's significance. Its absurdity as a real-life device would have been all too obvious, and they would already know fictional adventures that were more exciting. The story would have seemed stale and uninventive, and those who read stories like it would have seemed far too easy to please. Those who did know science fiction, however, read the story and had the *Aha!* experience: at last someone had found a way to combine ray guns and sword play without embarrassing all the rest of us. As a paracharacter inside the oeuvre of that genre, this story was a major figure.

Literary conventions are solutions and enablements. That body shield saved for technological adventure the image of the purposeful individual.

Those FTL ships that ignored everything Einstein had taught us about the impossibility of exceeding the speed of light made it possible for writers to invent an unlimited number of strange worlds and cultures and to send people to them without our cringing at the thought of the time it really would take to get there at sub-light speeds. (To travel the 3.3 light years to Alpha Centauri at that unimaginable 100,000 miles an hour, it would have taken Alfred Coppel's Valkyrs and their horses not 28 hours but 22,000 years.)

There is a special pleasure that we take in watching a genre's stock of conventions change over time, a pleasure denied people who do not read with a genre focus. A genre's enthusiasts watch it devise new character types, new settings, new techniques, new problems. Watching this happen, we are watching the genre invent itself. We discover the new, watch it become standard, watch it become a cliché, and then one day notice that it has disappeared. Viewed as a system, a genre is like a ship always heading into strange waters. To the occasional visitor, the genre looks always the same, but for regular readers everything is changing: the crew, the conditions, the ship. Especially the ship. The crew is always throwing out older parts of the ship—once brave new additions—and always building new parts, parts that will enable it to enter new conditions, do new things. That is a rich part of the excitement: watching the genre invent itself.

It seems best to stop with that reminder of what it is like to watch a changing genre adapting itself to changing conditions. We have already examined the genres' strategy of developing intriguing questions by means of the opposition of story simplicities and their use of clearly established norms for the creation of delicate variations on those norms.

There are other features of genre reading that we might have examined, for enthusiasts can watch their genres change themselves in other ways, too. Writers are always importing into their genres information from the outside. In Robert L. Forward's description of the neutron star in *Dragon's Egg* we see a genre teaching itself through the agency of one of its writers. As readers were learning all that odd lore we looked at in the previous chapter (about silencers, driving on a superhighway, etc.), the other writers were learning it, too. The importance of the fingerprint for identification must first have appeared in one detective story before any other, for instance, and from there spread to other stories, and the latest information about the Apaches must first have appeared in some western and so become common property.

Enthusiasts also watch their genres change themselves through self-criticism. The criticism most easily recognized for what it is is the parody (as in the parody of the space adventure of E. E. Smith in Fredric Brown's *What Mad Universe*), but there are other kinds of criticism. Harlan Ellison's anthology of short science fiction, *Dangerous Visions*, explicitly set out to change the character of the genre by giving models of stories that successfully flouted all the unadmitted editorial taboos on style, tone, and content. Readers and writers recognized what Ellison's writers were trying to do, and argued fiercely—not about the stories themselves but about the genre consequences of those stories' having been written.

William Tenn said that science-fiction writers felt that they "could go on endlessly, constantly topping each other's ideas, getting into whole new areas, creating things that didn't fit into any of the familiar literary categories," and that is what he had in mind: the sense of a system firm enough to permit interesting rhythmic inventions and yet elastic enough to permit its writers to adapt it to any purpose, even to invent entirely new purposes for it.

There are other pleasures unique to reading with a genre focus. The exchange from *The Thin Man* quoted earlier gratified the story's readers not for itself but for what it promised, for instance. We cannot have that experience when reading with a story focus. Another kind of pleasure that is possible only to those who are reading inside a tradition can be seen in a short story by Philip José Farmer, "Sail On! Sail On!" This is a story that occasional readers—even readers new to science fiction—can enjoy, but Farmer wrote the story especially for people who know the genre very well.

"Sail On! Sail On!" is a curious story. (It is welcome in two different bookscapes, for instance. It is reprinted in anthologies of the best fantasy and also in anthologies of the best science fiction.) As the story opens, readers find that they are on the *Santa María* and are sailing across the Atlantic with the *Niña* and *Pinta* in Columbus's first brave attempt to reach the Orient. Readers quickly discover that this *Santa María* has screwdrivers, a slide rule, light bulbs, and even a radiotelegraph, however, and they learn that the church has not only encouraged Roger Bacon's scientific interests but devoted time and resources to furthering his work.

Plainly, this story is set in another time stream. We have already met a story about another time stream: Brian Aldiss's *Malacia Tapestry*. Aldiss's novel is about a parallel reality. Its universe was created by Satan, for instance, and its creatures are fashioned in his image: the humans are descended from reptiles. Magic works, people have true visions, some people have wings and can fly, and so on.

"Sail On! Sail On!" seems to come from a different subgenre, the tradition of the what-if story. Ward Moore's *Bring the Jubilee* and Philip K. Dick's *Man in the High Castle* are justly admired achievements in the what-if tradition. (The what-if story is also called the "branching time-stream" story, which presupposes that from every moment in history there branch off many time streams—that is, historical sequences—one for each occurrence possible at that moment.) *Bring the Jubilee*, for instance, tells about adventures in a twentieth-century America that resulted when the South won the Civil War. *The Man in the High Castle* tells us about an America that followed the assassination of Franklin Roosevelt: the Japanese now occupy the West Coast, the Germans and Italians occupy the East Coast, all blacks in the South have been killed, and only a weakened Rocky Mountain States remains of what once had been the United States.

The what-if story intrigues writers and readers because it permits an interesting kind of invention—a sort of contrapuntal history writing. Farmer's "Sail On! Sail On!" is typical in offering amusing variations on the familiar. Father Sparks, the monk in charge of the radiotelegraph, offers an elaborate theological explanation of radiotelegraphy. One of the crew asks him what "k.c." means:

> "*K* stands for the French *kilo*, from a Greek word meaning thousand. And *c* stands for the Hebrew *cherubim*, the 'little angels.' It is our concept that the ether is crammed with these cherubim, these little messengers. Thus, when we Friar Sparkses depress the key of our machine, we are able to realize some of the infinity of 'messengers' waiting for just such a demand for service.

"So, eighteen hundred k.c. means that in a given unit of time one million, eight hundred thousand cherubim line up and hurl themselves across the ether, the nose of one being brushed by the feathertips of the cherub's wings ahead. The height of the wing crests of each little creature is even, so that if you were to draw an outline of the whole train, there would be nothing to distinguish one cherub from the next, the whole column forming that grade of little angels known as C.W."

"C.W.?"

"Continuous wingheight. My machine is a C.W. realizer."

(199–200)

Readers are prepared to suppose that monks who had stumbled onto radio might explain things in just that way until theory had caught up with practice.

Readers are *not* prepared for the ending of the story, however. Columbus's crew see strange birds—birds with enormous wings but no legs. The crew hear a noise "like a finger plucking a wire" and then guess the truth, but too late to save themselves. In their reality, Columbus was wrong. In their reality the Earth is flat, and the three ships are carried by the ocean out into space, forever lost over the edge of that flat Earth.

It is only at this moment that readers discover that they have not been reading a what-if story at all, that they have been reading a parallel-universe story like *The Malacia Tapestry*. They discover that from the opening paragraph they have been misreading and misunderstanding the story. Farmer has tricked his readers into a subgenre misidentification: that is his entire purpose in "Sail On! Sail On!"—to share a joke with his readers.

Rereading the story, we discover that Farmer had warned us—by reporting on an experiment in that reality in which objects of different weights had fallen at different speeds. If we noticed this, we perhaps thought that scientific experiment was still crude in the times of this Columbus. Now we see that the physical laws in this reality really are different. We also find ourselves looking more charitably at that explanation of radiotelegraphy. Perhaps it is the case that in this reality angels do fly from one machine to another.

"Sail On! Sail On!" delights experienced readers of science fiction because the story recognizes their sophistication. It knows that they know the what-if story and can savor amusing variations on it. It knows how to trigger an identification of itself as a what-if story. It also knows that they know the parallel-universe story and can recognize the differences between the two. Lastly, it knows that they can take pleasure in having been misled into thinking the one was the other. The less experienced readers of science fiction like the story well enough; but they do not experience the comedy of the ending, for they do not know the system from which it comes. "Sail On! Sail On!" is not a joke that Farmer is playing on those occasional readers. That is, it is not an in-joke that makes some readers feel pleased because they think other readers have missed the point. It is a story that permits us to see how reading in a genre is different from reading story by story. Those who read in this genre only occasionally are reading the story, but they are not reading the genre.

literary bookscape and
paperback bookscape

· · · · · · · · · · · · · · · · · ·

Every bookscape grows its own distinctions. In Chapter 3, we examined some of the confusion we fall into when we bring to the unlearned bookscapes the distinctions and hierarchies native to learned bookscapes. Here we directly compare a learned and an unlearned bookscape: the literary and paperback bookscapes. They are not at all alike.

Three points of difference stand out. First, the two bookscapes recognize formally different texts; second, they have unlike notions of the people who write the texts; and, third, they differ in the visibility of their genres. We sum these differences up when we say that—to newcomers, at least—the paperback bookscape is a literature without texts and the literary bookscape a literature without genres.

These differences are conveniently approached through what is the simplest of all paradigms of the writing and reading transaction. When we are reading, we sense that certain *sources* produced a *text* that manifested itself in various *copies*, and that one of those copies has fallen into our hands. Adam Hall, a source, wrote *The Quiller Memorandum*, a text, which exists in thousands of hardbound and paperback copies. By means of one of these copies, we make contact with the text, and by means of the text, we infer the character of its sources.

For the reader, there is no part of this chain that does not have its significance. The copies are merely the carriers of the text; but they provide their own information. The cover illustrations of the paperbacks tell readers where to find the westerns, the fantasies, the romances—and trigger the dispositional sets appropriate to those genres. (The copies are the primary focus for the book collector, of course, who to the dismay of the reader may bring together a large library of copies, each of which offers that reader the same text as every other copy.)

As we have seen in the earlier chapters, readers sometimes value a text as an object and sometimes as a function. We say that the paperback bookscape offers readers a literature without texts, but there are times, even in the paperback bookscape, when they give their attention wholly to the text, to its characters and action and embedded lore or to its textural or design intricacies. They are then aware of that story as an object distinct from all other objects its writer and its genre have produced. At other times, they are reading the text as a function of the sources that produced it. Readers at home in several bookscapes have a wide repertoire of reading strategies available; for, as we shall see in the next chapter, a literature without texts does not encourage the same range of reading strategies as does a literature without genres.

Both bookscapes do have texts, of course, and the texts in both bookscapes did come from genres; but we can speak of each bookscape as limited in its own way because, as we saw in the last chapter, the enduring fascination of the paperbacks arises especially from the systems that are creating the texts, while the fascination of literature arises especially from those monumental texts readers meet in the schools and continue to explore in all their later years. To see this more clearly, we return to that simple paradigm of the source-text-copy-reader transaction and examine some of its components.

A text can have different shapes. It can be the work itself. Frederick Forsyth's *Day of the Jackal* appeared as a self-sufficient story and has had no sequels. In the paperback bookscape, however, many separately published works are parts of larger texts. John D. MacDonald's *Free Fall in Crimson*, a Travis McGee story, can be read all by itself, but it is part of an accretive text, a series that came to more than twenty volumes before MacDonald's death. (Students of popular fiction distinguish between *sequels* and *sequence novels* and embrace the form so enthusiastically that they publish bibliographies for other readers who want more. See the lists compiled by Elizabeth Margaret Kerr and by Janet Husband, for instance.)

The sources of texts are of two broad types, *human* and *superorganic*.

The human sources are the writers, of course: John D. MacDonald, Adam Hall, Jake Logan. But behind the writers lie other sources. These are dynamic systems—genres, for instance—that are used by more than one writer. When we take a meticulous theoretical interest in these traditions as systems of behavior-governing rules it is helpful to refer to them as *grames*—that is, as entities that belong to the general class in which we also find grammars and games (Roberts, "Critics' Conceptions" 4). Here, in the interests of term symmetry we shall follow the lead of cultural anthropology, however, and use *superorganic*, Alfred Kroeber's term, and point out that a genre is one form of superorganic source. As we saw in the last chapter, readers of paperbacks (many of whom have never heard the word *genre*) are tacitly recognizing the nature of a genre by the character of their reading.

The differences between human and superorganic sources are sometimes difficult to define, but it is trivially obvious that the two are different. Hal Clement and Roger Zelazny are different people, but they both write within the genre of science fiction: two human sources exploiting a single superorganic source. John D. MacDonald, one individual, could write a story within the genre of science fiction ("Escape to Chaos"), a second story in the genre of the crime thriller (*On the Run*), and a third story in the genre of the western ("The Corpse Rides at Dawn"): one human source, three superorganic sources.

Readers, viewers, and listeners in the other arts recognize this distinction between human and superorganic sources, but they do not everywhere give them the same quality of attention. In some arts, it is the superorganic source that is the more visible; the viewer sees the human artist as the agent—that is, as the voice—of that tradition. In others, they perceive artists as people who mine a tradition, with the best of them finding the richer veins of ore that the rest of us would miss entirely; in these arts, it is the artists, not the traditions, who win all credit. It is in just this way that the paperback and the literary bookscapes differ.

The Literary Bookscape: The Variorum Text

Distinctions among source and text and copy are sufficient for the discussion of paperback fiction, an unlearned bookscape, but a learned bookscape is radically different. In the literary bookscape we find attached to primary texts and sources secondary materials—*commentary*, texts that challenge, supplement, complement, or explain another source or text. A commentary may be as short as a one-word explanation of an archaic phrase in a Shakespeare play or as elaborate as John Livingston Lowes's delightful *Road to Xanadu*, which, in 1927, offered a study of two Coleridge poems, the 625-line *Rime of the Ancient Mariner* and the 54-line "Kubla Khan." To these 679 lines of poetry, Lowes devotes 434 pages of text, 16 illustrations, and 43 pages of notes—the whole requiring a 33-page index and no fewer than 12 pages just to explain Lowes's abbreviations. This is literary commentary in the magisterial mode, but it is by no means unique.

Learned readers respect (even if they do not always like) other learned readers and want to know what they see in each text and author and genre, and so readers' commentaries are collected, preserved, and transmitted along with the texts that inspired them. When we add to any text the commentary it has received we have what is known in literary studies as the "text *cum notis variorum*": the text with critical and scholarly commentary.

The literary bookscape is immensely difficult to map. It recognizes not only *literature* itself but also an *antiliterature* and a *literature by association* (Roberts, "Critics' Conceptions" 20–24). It gives effective recognition to works but also to *microworks, macroworks, megatexts*. Different parts of this bookscape are governed by radically different notions of literature, and each part disagrees with every other in its specification of literature. Still, all versions of the literary bookscape have certain features in common, and one of these is a general acceptance that *literature* is a collective term for individual works. Monroe C. Beardsley has been unusual among aestheticians in that he has taken as keen an interest in literature as in music and the visual arts. He has correctly recognized that, whatever literary theorists have said, the teaching, reading, and criticism of literature is predicated on a sense that it is a collection of independently valuable works.

> One of the less problematic remarks that can be made about the term "literature" is that it is a collective name for literary *works*. True, critics sometimes speak of a "literary quality," and even of degrees of such a quality, and this usage deserves study. But more usually, and intelligibly, "literature" marks off a species of the genus of discourses—i.e., written or spoken pieces of natural language. A discourse is either a literary work or it is not a literary work—or it is a borderline case that balks at classification (which is why we may be tempted to say that it has "literary quality," perhaps meaning that it has some claim, though not a decisive claim, to be called a literary work). (23–24)

The second feature shared by all versions of the literary bookscape is the tacit agreement that those individual works, or texts, are variorum objects: texts plus commentary. Not only is each poem, novel, and play given its own companion commentary; but each author comes to be perceived in terms of a primary set of texts (letters, memoirs, lectures, observations of contemporaries), a set eventually enriched with its own scholarly and critical commentary. Further, each genre comes to be perceived as the set of the texts it generated plus their commentary. In the universities, the *eighteenth-century novel* is not the system that generated the novels written between, roughly, 1700 and 1800 but something different: it is a text, a variorum object that comprises the novels written in that period and the commentary written about them since then.

There is nothing to compare with the variorum object in an unlearned bookscape, which shows no interest whatsoever in any commentary more sophisticated than reviewers' brief recommendations and warnings. Even in the literary bookscape there is little evidence of conscious recognition and no explicit description of the variorum object, but variorum objects are everywhere visible, and implicit in scholarly and critical commentary is the recognition of their importance.

In an excellent review of John Bayley's *Shakespeare and Tragedy* in *The Times Literary Supplement*, J. M. Cameron talks about one variorum object. He begins with this innocent sentence: "One is tempted to plunge into Shakespeare as into an inviting ocean."

Cameron seems to be preparing his readers for a remark on the mystery of Shakespeare's life, identity, and personality or for a quick reminder of *Twelfth Night, The Phoenix and the Turtle,* and the rest of the Shakespearean oeuvre. That is the sort of thing that readers of the detective story would get if a review spoke of plunging into Conan Doyle as into an inviting ocean.

Cameron does give a catalog, a list of the things that the word *Shakespeare* brings to mind in the literary bookscape, but it is not the list that outsiders had expected.

One is tempted to plunge into Shakespeare as into an inviting ocean. There is so much stimulation about. There are the classic commentators: Johnson, Coleridge, Bradley, Wilson Knight, Middleton Murry (this was perhaps his best critical work). Then there are all those who in the past fifty years have moved us to think more deeply about the plays and poems: Eliot, Empson, Clifford Leech, Danby, Kenneth Muir, G. B. Harrison, Dover Wilson, Derek Traversi, Tillyard, Maynard Mack, R. A. Foakes . . . to make an arbitrary selection. Then there are the fascinating single works: Anne Righter's *Shakespeare and the Idea of the Play,* Wyndham Lewis's *The Lion and the Fox,* Muir and O'Loughlin's *The Voyage to Illyria* (what a brilliant debut, in 1937, this was for the two young men), Michael Platt's *Rome and Romans according to Shakespeare,* M. D. H. Parker's *The Slave of Life,* M. M. Mahood's *Shakespeare's Word Play,* S. L. Bethell's *Shakespeare and the Popular Dramatic Tradition*—again, to make a quite arbitrary selection, for one could draw up long lists of works all valuable in their various ways.

Then there are the instruments of study, handbooks, monographs on law and medicine and botany, historical works, books on Shakespeare's predecessors and contemporaries, treatises on the structure of the theatre, and all the work on the life of the poet, genially presided over, one might say, by Samuel Schoenbaum. Finally, there are the works themselves, in many sizes, shapes, combinations, with many kinds and degrees of scholarly attachments: one might pick out the New Variorum editions of Furness, reprinted by Dover Books, the indispensable Arden Shakespeare, the one-volume editions—the Riverside Shakespeare lies before me as I write—and there is Professor Alexander's reliable text; and the humble nieces and nephews of the more elaborate editions, notably *two* Penguin Shakespeares, one for Britain, one for the United States.

Here is enough material to satisfy the gluttony of a lifetime and to excite ambition. Those who have gained a critical reputation in other fields are likely to conceive a yearning, to feel the temptation, to try a fall with Shakespeare.

Cameron began by speaking of all this Shakespearean commentary as "stimulation," but he ends quite differently: "Here is enough material to satisfy the gluttony of a lifetime and to excite ambition." What he has listed is only commentary—the best of everything ever said about Shakespeare and his works. *Shakespeare* is for Cameron and his readers a megatext that has the oeuvre of Shakespeare at its heart but also includes all that commentary. The reader new to literature who begins to talk about *King Lear* with a Shakespearean expert will be talking about one text, which is one of the versions of *King Lear* that Shakespeare left us, while the specialist will be talking about quite another text: a text-palimpsest which is a blurring together of all the variants of the play's text and all the commentary on it by Johnson, Bradley, Eliot, Empson, and others.

There is a polite convention by which scholars speak as though the commentary that gathers around primary texts and authors were all explanatory, all helpful: the sort of information that tactfully explains classical and biblical allusions, identifies topical references, outlines the conditions under which a play was produced or a poem was written. There is more (and less) to literary commentary than that, however, as is made quite plain in Andrew Wright's review of N. John Hall's *Trollope Critics*. Wright imagines someone in the year 2082 looking into the literary criticism of our own day to determine what Trollope was to us.

> Is Trollope a master of his craft? Yes (Gordon Ray, C. P. Snow); no (Bradford A. Booth, Lord David Cecil, Michael Sadleir). Is his focus on society or the individual? Society (J. Hillis Miller, Chauncey Brewster Tinker); the individual (A. O. J. Cockshut, David Skilton).

Is he a realist? Yes (Snow); no (Frank O'Connor). Is he a religious writer? Yes (Hillis Miller, Paul Elmer More); no (Ruth apRoberts, James Gindin). Is he a stylist? Yes (Gerald Warner Brace, Frederick Harrison); no (James Kincaid, O'Connor). Is he a political novelist? Yes (John Halperin); no (Booth). Does he accept the mid-Victorian world view? Yes (Brace, Cecil, Ker, Sadleir); no (apRoberts, O'Connor).

Literary commentary, in its largest sense, is anything that learned readers find interesting: useful information, of course, but also any observation outrageous enough so that other readers can use it as an excuse for offering their own observations.

If the gateway to the paperback bookscape is, say, a magazine stand or a paperback exchange, the gateway to the literary bookscape is the classroom; people do enter this bookscape after they have left school, but it is uncommon. The stages in which students in those classrooms are introduced to canonical literature are now well established. First, precollege students study those monumental texts that are designated "masterpieces," or classics. In college, they move on to the authorial oeuvre—the works of a Chaucer or a Cervantes or a Goethe. Or, third, they may find themselves studying a period oeuvre—the writings of the romantics or of the modernists. They do not come to the fourth type of text, the major critical statement—Aristotle's *Poetics*, Plato's *Republic* and "Ion," Samuel Johnson's *Lives of the Poets*—until late in their studies. Each of these last—the period oeuvre, the major critical statement, the authorial oeuvre—is a variorum object. The critical manifesto, the formal theory of literature, and all other literary commentary are "literature about literature." There is no "literature about paperbacks"; when a body of commentary begins to accrue around a text or an oeuvre, readers know that it is now being accepted as a part of canonical literature. While none of the other three types of text has a precise parallel in a paperback bookscape either, the fourth type—the major critical statement—is strangest of all to readers visiting from that bookscape. The evidence that there are readers who pause in their reading of great books to turn to the reading of books about books is, they feel, an unmistakable symptom of reading decadence.

The critical declarations of the past are honored in this bookscape because of the insights they provide into the traditions that generated an author's or a period's books, but it is also the case that Aristotle, Plato, Longinus, Samuel Johnson, and some fifty other men and women like them are the special heroes of the learned reader. In honoring those critics, the learned are indirectly honoring themselves. All these major critical texts together would occupy no more space on a shelf than two or three nineteenth-century novels. They do not bulk large, but their presence in this bookscape is significant—if only as confirmation of the importance of commentary and of the variorum text in this bookscape.

The paperback bookscape has nothing to rival either these works of theory or any of these other hugely intricate verbal objects—works monumental in themselves but now further enriched with at least half a century, and in the case of the Greek classics as much as two millennia, of explanation, analysis, controversy. It is not surprising that when readers who formed their expectations inside the literary bookscape visit a paperback bookscape they find the texts "thin."

The Paperback Bookscape: Writers versus Authors

Readers of literature leave the word *author* behind when they enter the paperback bookscape because that word is always silently urging readers to judge the writers of paperbacks by standards those writers do not recognize. *Author*, from the Latin *auctor*, "creator," connotes something much grander than *writer*. A true author, twentieth-century readers have come to feel, is not just creative but uniquely creative; the works of any true author can immediately be recognized as that author's and that author's alone. But a writer does not have that distinctively authorial ambition of being uniquely and eternally identifiable. The people who do have these ambitions today are comfortable only inside the bookscape of serious fiction, where they find readers who share their vision of the sacredness of fiction and of the dignity of the author. (One can be a true author without being aware of that ambition, of course. Readers today identify Chaucer and Shakespeare, Cervantes and Dickens, as true

authors, whether those writers were conscious of having that ambition
or not.) Zane Grey and Agatha Christie and Robert Heinlein and Rosemary Rogers and Eric Ambler have been something else: they have been
writers, which is to say that they have thought of themselves as making
stories for people—good stories, of course, even excellent stories, stories
with truth in them sometimes, and beauty, but not the kinds of texts being
made by those who would be authors.

The absence of professional solemnity guarantees that the paperback
bookscape will lack the atmosphere of reverential awe that is characteristic of all the high-art environments, including the literary bookscape.
(It is this awe that lies behind the acceptance of certain texts as sacred—
that is, as secular sacred—objects, a status we considered in Chapter 3.
Nothing is sacred in a paperback bookscape.) When people in that secondary readership are reading in the literary bookscape and find a classic
text unintelligible or boring, they assume that the fault lies in themselves.
When this happens in the paperback bookscape, they assume that the
fault lies in the writer.

The writers of paperbacks are not in awe of their readers nor are their
readers in awe of them. While the successful writer of serious fiction can
have a huge income and achieve the status and solemnity of the bard,
most writers in one of the paperback genres receive nothing much grander
than a comfortable living and the pleasure of having the deep affection
of a loyal band of readers. From these differences in the notions of the
writer and of fiction, two other differences follow. First, readers' interest
in writers is weaker in the paperback bookscape than it is in the literary
bookscape, a matter to which we shall be returning. Second, the readers
of the paperbacks are unperturbed when they learn that some of their
writers are playing tricks on them, tricks that would upset the exclusivist
readers of serious fiction and of literature. Inside a learned bookscape,
these tricks would indicate that the writers lack high seriousness and so
are without professional honor. Four of these games the paperback writers
play are worth examining.

1. The disguised writer. Writers have always used pen names: Vol-
taire, George Eliot, George Sand, Mark Twain. Where the writers of
paperbacks are different is in their use of several—sometimes a great
many—pen names. Barzun and Taylor tell us that John Creasey, who by

1968 had published no fewer than 521 books, most of them detective stories, had used two dozen names: John Creasey, Gordon Ashe, M. E. Cooke, Henry St. John Cooper, Norman Deane, Elise Fecamps, Robert Caine Fraser, Patrick Gill, Michael Halliday, Charles Hogarth, Brian Hope, Colin Hughes, Kyle Hunt, Abel Mann, Peter Manton, J. J. Marric, James Marsden, Richard Martin, Rodney Mattheson, Anthony Morton, Ken Ranger, William K. Reilly, Tex Riley, and Jeremy York (*Catalogue* 589–90). Frederick Faust was also famous for writing in different genres under different pseudonyms. The index to Robert Easton's *Max Brand: The Big "Westerner"* lists the most famous of them—Max Brand, of course —and seventeen others. Some writers are so prolific that their pseudonymously written books compete with one another in the marketplace: Elleston Trevor has been writing stories under his own name but also has been writing the Quiller stories as Adam Hall.

2. The writing team. In the bookscapes of literature and of serious writing, the art of fiction is practiced exclusively by individuals. This is not so in the paperback bookscape. Many readers of mysteries would not recognize the names of Frederic Dannay and Manfred B. Lee but would recognize Ellery Queen, the pseudonym that Dannay and Lee used for the books they wrote together. Henry Kuttner and C. L. Moore, a husband-and-wife team, had been writers before they met; after they met, according to James Gunn in *From Heinlein to Here*, "almost everything they wrote was a collaboration in some degree under seventeen different pseudonyms" (71). Frederik Pohl and Cyril Kornbluth (*The Space Merchants, Gladiator-at-Law*) wrote good science fiction stories together. Dorothy Sayers and Robert Eustace wrote a successful detective story, *The Documents in the Case*. Team writing seems dishonest to exclusivist readers in some other bookscapes, but people who think of themselves as writers only, and the people who read them, find nothing odd in it.

3. The ghostwriter. Betty Rosenberg lists as house-name writers of westerns Tabor Evans of the Longarm series, Jack Slade of the Lassiter series, and Jake Logan of the John Slocum series (64). To people who never leave certain other bookscapes, the existence of oeuvres produced under the rule of an editor supervising an ill-paid assortment of ghostwriters suggests galley slaves, the lash, and an insistent drum. Neither

the primary nor the secondary readership is greatly concerned when they discover that the names Jack Slade and Jake Logan stand in for editors rather than individual writers, and there is no compelling cause for them to be. It is very much like their knowing about a film (*King Kong*, say, or *Le Regle du jeu*) that one person produced it, another person scripted it, a third directed it, a fourth starred in it, a fifth photographed it, and a sixth edited it—to know all this and to love the film and to give all credit for it to its director, whom they declare its *auteur*. Nor is even this acceptance of artworks made by teams but identified with one person entirely an invention of these degenerate times. The museums honor works of art even when the historians can say only that they are "from the school of Rubens" or "from the studio of Cellini." It is neither new nor intrinsically absurd to enjoy stories as "from the school of Jake Logan" and as "from the school of J. D. Hardin," and apologists could translate into recognition of the creative role of the paperback editor anything that cineasts have ever said about the role of the *auteur*.

4. The jam session. In traditional American jazz, a jam session is a gathering of musicians who play both for and against one another, testing their skills in an unregulated competition in which they are both performers and judges of their performance. They compete with one another, but they compete for their mutual admiration.

Its verbal parallel, the writers' jam session, does not take place in the bookscape of serious fiction; and while it has happened in other eras (John Donne's circle wrote poems in amateur competition with one another) the literary bookscape does not single out those competitions for appreciation in their own right. The paperback bookscape does. Robert Asprin's science fantasy *Thieves' World*, a collection of short stories written by eight different authors about a common city, Sanctuary, give the secondary readership a special kind of delight. They can measure the writers' abilities as craftsmen against one another and savor the differences in the qualities of their imaginations. The writers' jam session can be highly sophisticated. Barzun and Taylor tell us that, for his *Ask a Policeman*, John Rhode brought in five other writers to compete in the solution of a murder: Helen Simpson, Gladys Mitchell, Dorothy Sayers, Anthony Berkeley, and Milward Kennedy. Each writer agreed to help in the solution of the mystery and to set his or her own detective aside and use another writer's detective instead (*Catalogue* 415–16). The result is a fiction concentrate: it is simultaneously mystery, parody, and criticism.

As I indicated in the last chapter, there are excellent reasons why the possibility of a jam session would attract the interest of the writers and the readers of paperbacks. A paperback genre could be defined simply and usefully as a writers' jam session with broad extensions in space and time. The writers know this: it was this image that William Tenn was offering when he spoke of the pleasure that writers of science fiction took in their writing—"constantly topping each other's ideas, getting into whole new areas, creating things that didn't fit into any of the familiar literary categories." Since scholars have searched out the true identities of the men and women who used pen names in the past, that sort of puzzle of authorial identity has been cleared up in the literary bookscape; and it is difficult for people who learned to read in that bookscape to see that other readers of literature who also read paperbacks may have good reason for not being greatly concerned about pen names, house names, and writing teams.

For casual but longtime readers of the paperbacks, Susannah Bates's book, *The PENDEX*, with its lists of real names, pen names, collaborative pen names, and house names associated with paperback fiction, solves mysteries of accreditation that never worried them much anyway. In the paperback bookscape, a writer's name is a label that the reader uses in the continuing search for the good read. It is quite possible to like the stories writers produce under one name and dislike the stories they write under another: to enjoy the Quiller stories Elleston Trevor writes as Adam Hall but not to enjoy the stories Trevor writes under his own name, to enjoy Erle Stanley Gardner's A. A. Fair stories about Donald Lam and Bertha Cool but not his Erle Stanley Gardner stories about Perry Mason. The knowing reader uses the names Adam Hall and Elleston Trevor as though they were brand labels on so many cans in a supermarket. The reader who likes the one kind of Elleston Trevor product will buy the Adam Hall soups and the reader who likes the other kind will buy the Elleston Trevor soups. If the stories that come from the Jake Logan factory offer more satisfaction today than the stories that were handmade for an earlier generation by Zane Grey, shall we expect readers to feel so loyal to writing as the art of individuals that they will choose to read books that give them less pleasure? The most successful writers of paperback fiction are well known and are followed as closely as are the best-known serious writers—though without that special devotion which is the author's reward. Readers do speak of "early Robert Heinlein" and "late Agatha Christie" and of this third writer's persistent inability to create interesting women and of that other writer's gift for the phrase. Readers do savor the work of individual writers, as their interest in those jam sessions indicates, but none would mistake the critical discourse of the paperback bookscape with that of any of the learned bookscapes. Since the readers of the paperbacks are not in awe of paperback writers, they are not greatly disappointed when they learn about these disguises, joint ventures, and fiction factories.

The Genres in the Two Bookscapes

As I remarked earlier, those readers who have been taught to measure all texts against the variorum text and all writers against the higher dignity of the author are not satisfied with the bare texts of the paperback bookscape and with writers who have no sense of the ancient honor of their profession—and they are puzzled when they learn that some others who read literature very well do find satisfaction in the paperback bookscape. We should not be surprised when we discover that the other kind of reader—the primary readership of the paperback bookscape—experiences a matching dissatisfaction when he or she visits the literary bookscape. Literary exclusivists suppose that literature need only be encountered for a conversion in taste to occur, but readers from the paperback bookscape have difficulty distinguishing between seriousness and pomposity in the talk about literature, and they certainly do not understand people who are sometimes more interested in talking about books than they are in reading them. Others, traveling back and forth between the two bookscapes, will sometimes feel they are shuttling between Kansas and the Land of Oz—and be unclear occasionally as to which is Oz, which Kansas.

Genres are plainly visible in the paperback bookscape. Are genres visible in the literary bookscape? The secondary genres—the genres of literary commentary—are visible; and, as we shall see in the concluding chapter, it is these genres that advanced students of literature have in view when they read by genre in this bookscape. The primary genres— the genres of literature—seem to be on view to specialists, but as we shall also see, that is a somewhat different matter. Students of literature use the word *genre* frequently, and they write books on the nature of genres (Dubrow's *Genre*), and readers enroll in university courses that have the names of genres (The Epic, The Eighteenth-Century Novel); but when we look more closely we discover that students of literature are using that word *genre* carelessly. The plainest definition I have seen appears in Heda Jason's *Ethnopoetics: A Multilingual Terminology*, which explains that in ethnopoetry a genre is "A group of ethnopoetic texts which share syntactic and semantic narrative patterns" (36). Holman and Harmon's *Handbook to Literature* tells students of English and American literature that *genres* are "the distinct types or categories into which literary works are grouped according to form or technique" and gives such instances of genre names as "novel," "short story," "essay," "television play." Cesare Segre's *Introduction to the Analysis of the Literary Text* provides a thoughtful history and survey of the uses of the word *genre*, and it, too, makes it plain that the word is used as a synonym for *type* (199–222). This is disturbing. Students of literature already have the words *class* and *set* and *category* and *form* and do not need another synonym, and none of those words suggests a system of changing rules, which is the criterial characteristic of a genre and which, when people set out to explain it, has them turning not to set theory but to language theory.

The word *genre* is not a synonym for words like *class* and *set* and *category*. A genre is a tradition; a category is something else again. All texts that have a prime number of *e*'s in them (if there are any) do belong to the same category, or class, but we would not say that they were products of the same genre unless there has been a text-writing tradition that recognized that feature. That *Handbook to Literature* is providing an unuseful definition, but it is not the fault of the editors: they are reporting accurately on the verbal definitions given this word throughout the literary bookscape, where many are confused about the differences between a class and a genre.

When we examine course descriptions and class reading lists, we discover that phrases that name genres, phrases like "The Victorian Novel" and "The Topographic Poem," do in fact refer to classes, or categories, rather than to traditions: they refer to sets of texts, sets that include not the texts with highest significance in terms of the evolutions and mutations of their genres but (inevitably) those texts that still have the power to hold readers' attention: Fielding's *Tom Jones,* Sterne's *Tristram Shandy,* Pope's *Windsor Forest.* And when we look into the learned journals we find that an essay on the "epic" is only rarely about the system that generated epics in Europe for twenty centuries; it is about those epics themselves— that is, Virgil's *Aeneid,* Milton's *Paradise Lost,* perhaps even Joel Barlow's *Columbiad.* The people who wrote those poems and the people who first read them were reading the "epic" in the same sense in which people earlier in this century were reading a tradition they spoke of as "experimental fiction," in the same sense in which people today are reading the "crime novel." The twentieth century does not read the "epic," however; it reads the texts that the tradition of the epic left behind when it disappeared.

When Ezra Pound characterized literature as "news that stays news" (29), he, like Monroe Beardsley, was reflecting the widely accepted image of literature not as a system or even as a set of systems but as a set of texts. Readers do not speak of literature in the way Pound did unless they have a text-by-text conception of the literary bookscape.

This "enumerative" conception of literature is inevitable. Nothing is canonical literature until it is half a century old and more, which guarantees that readers of literature cannot experience a literary genre in the same dynamic sense in which readers of serious contemporary fiction and readers of paperbacks do. Robert Escarpit plausibly claims that

> the "life" of a literary genre—Elizabethan tragedy, classical tragedy, the realistic English novel of the eighteenth century, romantic forms —is generally from thirty to thirty-five years, or half a lifetime. An experiment . . . appears to corroborate this observation. We superimposed curves, each representing in our sampling the respective number of novelists, poets, playwrights and other writers, composing the whole literary population (the polygraphs each counting several times). It is clear that the chart changes radically every 70 years

and partially every 35 years, as one genre dominates the others or
diminishes.   (26)

If genres do mutate ("change partially") into something else every thirty-
five years and die after their allotted three-score years and ten, none of
the genres that did generate the primary texts in the literary bookscape
will survive with those texts into any period that accepts them as parts of
literature.

In any event, the books that do survive were either monumental to
begin with (*The Iliad*, Goethe's *Faust*, George Eliot's *Middlemarch*) or they
became monumental as commentary was attached to them and they were
transmuted into variorum texts. The sheer size and complexity of these
variorum texts distract the reader from any interest in the superorganic
sources that produced them.

Further, authorship—in the special sense of the glorification of individual creativity—is so honored and the roles of impersonal, superorganic
sources so suspect that readers while in the literary bookscape always
bestow their attention and their admiration on authors—that is, on people
—rather than on anything so nonpersonal as genres.

In the paperback bookscape, however, readers find the genres easy
to see. First, the stories are rarely monumental and the riches of the
variorum text are unknown; the stories speak in the idioms of the readers'
times and so the reading is effortless. The result is that there is less in
the stories to distract readers from taking an interest in the writers and
genres that made them. Second, because the stories are easier to read and
usually short, readers see more of them. They are always being confronted
with similarities and differences among those stories, and that sends their
minds out into the story sources and permits them to follow a drama that
readers in the literary bookscape rarely see clearly: the interplay between
human sources and the superorganic sources they have inherited and are
now reinventing.

Third and last, the significance of the human sources of those stories
—their writers—is much weaker. This is in part the consequence of the
writers' images of themselves. The writers think of themselves as artist-
craftsmen rather than as artist-prophets. In other times people thought of
prophets as god-visited; in our own time, prophets still retain some sense

of having a sacred task and status. It is therefore a part of their responsibility as prophets that others be made to know their true identity and character—and names. The writer-craftsmen invoke other metaphors. They want readers to use that modern honorific: *professional.* That is, they would like their readers to think of them as having rare natural gifts; as having developed those gifts through discipline; as having a clear-eyed recognition of the differences between the glamour and the realities of writing; and, especially, as having the capacity for writing, for rent money or by invitation, the kinds of stories that will make the very editors who commissioned them and established the parameters sit up in surprise at the depth and power of their storytelling. There is nothing in the conception of the writer-as-a-professional that speaks against using pseudonyms or writing with others or joining a jam session or even doing ghostwriting with others under house names.

Most of the secondary readership of the paperbacks come from other learned bookscapes, but even when it is the law that they come from or sports or business or medicine it is the bookscape of literature against which they are measuring paperback fiction. Sometimes they think of it as failed literature, but paperback fiction is no more an unsuccessful imitation of literary fiction than is Dublin English an unsuccessful imitation of Oxford English. If the paperback bookscape really were the realm of Caliban, those Prosperos who are finding pleasure in Melville and in Austen and in Dostoevsky would not also be finding pleasure in the westerns of Elmer Kelton or the Regency romances of Georgette Heyer.

The literary bookscape offers readers discernible magnificences: monumental texts, magisterial authors. It does not offer to the amateur the opportunity to read by genre, for the genres that once lay behind those authors and texts have evaporated. Unlike the paperback bookscape, the literary bookscape does offer readers the opportunity to share their reading, not only with their contemporaries but even with readers of the past. (That the paperback bookscape misses this sociability in reading is evident in the spontaneous generation of the hundreds of fanzines that spring up around the vernacular genres.)

The paperback bookscape rarely offers its readers the monumental text, and when it does they may be annoyed that the text is asking them to give it careful attention. The writers often have quirkily interesting minds, but they do not *loom* with an authority that makes experienced readers humble. It is the systems, the traditions, the genres, that keep people reading through the work they themselves think mediocre. The literature it offers is that literature without texts that we spoke of before. It is a literature that would not hold thoughtful and experienced readers if the objects it offers were not also functions of something larger than themselves.

Each bookscape grows its own distinctions. Each educates readers in its own way. The literary bookscape teaches readers a specialized style of reading that students of literature name *studying*. The study mode maximizes the pleasure and the rewards of literature. The paperback bookscape teaches quite another, equally specialized style of reading—I shall be calling it *thick reading*. It maximizes the rewards of vernacular fiction. The two styles of reading are bookscape-specific.

We considered earlier what it is like for people who learned to read literature before anything else to come upon the paperbacks. They are looking for books and authors to study, and they are deeply disappointed, for the texts they find are thin, obvious, repetitive. They say that the texts are not worth rereading, but they mean, rather, that they are not worth studying. The people who learned to read vernacular fiction before any other kind of book are equally disappointed in the literary bookscape at first. They do not have the study mode in their repertoire, and so the literary texts seem heavy, lumpish, and needlessly difficult, and readers' interest in literary commentary seems decadent. For the nonspecialist reader, the mode of thick reading is no more successful in the literary bookscape than the mode of study reading is in the paperback bookscape. It is to the differences between these two reading modes that we now turn.

reading

thickly

· · · · · · · · · ·

Janice Radway noticed that when her informant on the romance said a book was "well written" she meant only that the writer had invented a good story. Her informant "made it clear," Radway reports, "that she believes that success in writing has nothing to do with elegant phrasing or the quality of perception but is a function of the uniqueness of the characters and events intended by the most familiar of linguistic signs." Radway adds that readers of romance speak as though the page were "a transparent window opening out onto an already existent world" (189). We all invoke this windowpane image when we talk about certain types of books (cookbooks, for instance, and dictionaries and Radway's own study of the romance), but when people talk about novels as though they were only windowpanes through which the reader sees what is important, we become doubtful of their judgment and sophistication. The image that Radway found in discussions of the romance dominates the discussion of science fiction, the western, and other paperback stories, too.

Even the people who come to the paperbacks from a learned bookscape talk as though they read thinly, as though they were only dimly aware of the words themselves, as though they were affected only by the stories they saw through those words. They do not read that simply, though. If they did, they would not be admiring the books and writers they do admire.

Even the primary readership, the people who never read outside a paperback bookscape, read more sensitively than their styles of speech suggest. It does not require literary or legal or medical training to learn how to read a text with full consciousness of the writer and of the shape and texture of that writer's sentences, after all. However unsophisticated these primary readers may be, they all read job announcements with excited concern not only about the job itself but about the phrasing and the meaning of the lists of qualifications and duties. Later, when they do get the job, they certainly read the annual appraisals of their work with keen interest in the people who wrote those reports. They read those personal advertisements in which lonely men and women describe themselves and the people they are trying to find, and they wonder aloud what kind of woman would characterize herself as quiet and what kind of man would announce to the world that he thinks of himself as witty. And it hardly needs saying that they give this kind of attention to letters from the people about whom they care deeply. They are not satisfied with asking, "What does the letter say?" They ask, "Why did she put it that way?" "What does *that* mean?" "Is she just being polite?" or, alternatively, "How does he feel about the women in the city in which he is working? Why does he mention (or never mention) them?" Whatever our education, we are all capable of reading with a wide-ranging alertness to the writer of a document, the words that writer uses, and the denotative and connotative implications of those words. University training helps some become aware of what they have been doing as readers, but it could not instill this capacity for many-faceted reading alertness if it were not already in them.

Although they have an expanded awareness of story, writer, text, and more, paperback readers are so private in their reading that they do not develop styles of commentary that are adequate to their experiences. They do read with heightened awareness, but they talk as though they did not. Some will even deny the richness of their responses. Thus, Radway's romance readers assured her that they read purely for escape—but then also insisted that one of the chief appeals of romances is that readers learn so much from them and insisted, too, that their reading of these romances had profoundly changed them, making them stronger, more self-reliant, and more competent (101, 107). They saw no inconsistencies in these claims. Whatever allergics may feel about the romance or the thriller, reading is not simpler in the paperback bookscape than it is elsewhere.

It is different, however, and only those who develop the necessary skill can remain in that bookscape.

The literary bookscape teaches one rich form of response to books that I shall be calling *study reading* here or, when the word is unambiguous, *studying*. The paperback bookscape teaches a different style of reading, also many-minded. I shall be calling this *thick reading* when confusion might otherwise result and, less solemnly, *reading* whenever it is plain that it is study reading and thick reading that I am comparing and contrasting.

In these chapters, we have been asking ourselves what this secondary readership has been finding in books we associate primarily with what we think of as a far simpler readership. We shall review here some of what we have discovered and add certain critical distinctions that prove useful when we set out to make ourselves aware of what it is like to read inside a system, to read by genre. We shall be looking quickly once again at the paperbacks as stories, as information carriers, as patterns, and as revelations of their writers' minds. We shall also look at some other matters, however: the experience of mapping a new genre while reading its stories, the reader's awareness of the "canon jostling" that is a queer by-product of following any genre, and the excitements provided by the quirky mutating and evolving and regressing that a genre manifests over time. Finally, we shall look once again at the matter of reading sociability. The reading of paperbacks is not so thin an experience for this secondary readership as they allow themselves to suppose.

Stories

Of course, the paperback novel tells a story that includes characters, settings, events, and everything else that stories involve. It is the story that readers feel they are witnessing through word transparencies that look out on invented versions of the real world. The novel recognized as canonical literature also tells a story, of course, and almost always the story it offers is superior. Some apologists for the paperbacks become angry when critics say this, but it is true. One unpretentious but useful definition of canonical fiction is that it is "the best stories written before we were born." It is when readers compare the typical story of their own time with the atypically superior stories of the past that they come to feel that the paperback bookscape is offering a literature without texts—that is, that the paperback bookscape cannot compete on a text-for-text basis with the literary bookscape.

Even though the quality of the story lines is higher, on average, in other bookscapes, we owe it to the paperbacks to recognize that some valuable story forms do not exist in other bookscapes or, at least, are difficult to find. We do not find elsewhere those writer jam sessions; or those sequence stories in which a sharply defined personality-construct (Adam Hall's Quiller, Ed McBain's 87th Precinct) is moved into different settings and problems; or the common-background stories of writers like Cordwainer Smith (*Norstrilia, Space Lords*) and Maj Sjöwall and Per Wahloo (*The Terrorists, The Laughing Policeman*), who hold our attention with fairly simple stories in the foreground while their writers are outlining more elaborate histories in their backgrounds. Some of these forms were invented in other bookscapes and then abandoned but still offer writers uniquely powerful opportunities for the construction of stories.

Information

As we saw in Chapter 1, the images of outer reality that the paperbacks reflect include at least the following: the kinds of images the newspapers provide of the daily flow of events in this piece of space and time; the kinds of images contemporary readers have of the past (including images of the works of art they have inherited from the past); the kinds of images that their own eyes and ears and noses and fingers provide; and, finally, those images they have of the unique shapes that human personalities take in this time. While readers are not normally aware that they are mirror peering, they can afterward see that this was what was happening, for the passing of the years turns a novel into a sort of two-way mirror. Reading that novel a century after it was written, readers become time-spanning voyeurs, curiously watching its original readers as they study anxiously the book's selective mirrorings of the reality that they sense around them. (It is an odd, licensed form of the invasion of the privacy of their ancestors' minds. Sometimes—as in the nineteenth-century use of racial stereotypes—later readers are embarrassed by what they see.)

Canonical works of fiction offer their mirrorings of other people's pieces of the space-time continuum and thus provide the reassurance that our times are not unique; but only the contemporaries of a generation of readers recognize the world that generation has inherited and made, and readers need that, too. Beyond the fact that some of the information may be useful—the explanation of a confidence trick to which someone might otherwise fall prey, for instance—there is the matter of being recognized.

The writer's recognition of the reader is rarely given the attention it deserves. Few readers live in the popular settings for fictional action—the New York or London or Paris of the spy stories, or the Los Angeles, Detroit, or Boston of the private-investigator stories. Sometimes they do come across a story set in the very towns in which they live: Minneapolis, Cleveland, Birmingham, Halifax. If I can judge by my own experiences, readers find it oddly pleasing to read stories in which familiar buildings, streets, and parks appear by name, stories in which all the action takes place inside the maps they already have in their minds. It is a curious experience: strangers are showing a deep and respectful interest in what their provincial readers have been doing. It is much this experience that readers have when they turn from literature to contemporary fiction. To shift from immersion in Homer and Chaucer and Shakespeare and Dickens to stories—even when they are weaker stories—that at least know superhighways and Boeing 707s and Mahler and adrenalin by name does for readers in time what home-town fiction does for them in space: it helps them remember who they are.

There is more to this matter of the stories as information carriers than the recognition of their readers' existence. In Chapter 7 we read the claim that Georges Simenon gives his readers the vast panorama of France, and we read paragraphs in which John D. MacDonald told readers how to drive and Cyril Hare told them why the English do not marry the siblings of their living spouses and Frederick Forsyth explained why silencers are not effective with automatic pistols; we even learned how to blow our brains out.

This pleasure in learning odd bits of lore—"pure" knowledge in the sense that people take pleasure in having it even though their lives do not require it—is less prominent in the literary bookscape. Coming out of that literary bookscape to the paperbacks with the hierarchy of expectations their own bookscape put into them, students of literature deprecate those who read fiction for instruction; but, as I remarked in that earlier chapter, people do not read paperbacks for the instruction—not, at least, in the sense that they read a textbook or a cookbook for instruction: they read paperback fiction because it also provides odd blocks of quaint and curious lore and because the acquisition of information is in itself a pleasurable experience. This informational part of stories is less evident in the books read in literature classes, but those books were written for people who died long ago. The information they brought their original readers is visible when modern readers begin to look for it. Those unintelligible catalogs of weaponry and men in *The Iliad* and those tiresome genealogies in works like the Icelandic *Njal's Saga* were, for our ancestors, intriguing blocks of information.

There does not seem to have been much interest recently—at least, not in humanistic studies—in what we might call *everyday curiosity*, but our ancestors recognized and honored it. When Chaucer's Host, in *The Canterbury Tales*, invites the Pardoner to tell a funny story, the other travelers protest. They do not want to hear ribaldry. They want to listen to something that will give them moral guidance, something that will make them more intelligent. They do not ask for specific instruction—how to ride a horse, or how to tithe, say, or how to control their own lust. They ask only that they be given the chance to learn *something*.

> "Nay, let him telle us of no ribaudye;
> Tel us som moral thing, that we may lere
> Some wit, and thann wol we gladly here."

In *The Poetics*, Aristotle observed that philosophers take higher satisfaction from learning than others do but that they are not unique: "Learning is a great pleasure, not only to philosophers but likewise to every one else" (20). We need only look around us to see that humankind is as curious today as it was in ancient Athens. (It finds its apotheosis, perhaps, in "the eternal student," the person whose curiosity is politely insatiable and who would be perfectly content to take one college course after another throughout the long stretch of eternity.) The improbably immense popularity of *The Guinness Book of World Records* and of yearly almanacs and encyclopedias and dictionaries (and, recently, of the game Trivial Pursuit) are unavoidable indications of the huge hunger people have for raw, pure information. Radway's readers of the romance are not unique in expressing the satisfaction they take in what they learn from the stories. Some crime novels, science fiction, westerns, and spy stories are from 10 to 20 percent description and explanation. Many short stories in these traditions are 50 percent explanation.

· · · · **Forms**

Genre allergics are most confident when they declare that paperback stories are not interesting on the level of pure form, and surely they find verification of their judgment in the failure of even the admirers of the stories ever to comment on what art historians used to call "the life of forms." But readers do participate in the life of forms while reading vernacular fiction, for when they are savoring genre variations (the many varieties of the amateur detective) and genre closures (the body shield), they are having formal experiences that are less purely formal but not finally different in character from the experiences they have with the fugue and the villanelle.

The individual text, too, provides formal experiences; for, as we saw in Chapter 6, the individual texts manifest the same interest in verbal texture and narrative design that are wrongly thought to be the exclusive province of literature and of serious fiction. George V. Higgins, Dashiell Hammett, and Damon Runyon played delightfully on variations in verbal texture; and, though one would never guess this from the science-fiction films, those who read science fiction love design intricacies. Even in the books that tell their stories in a straightforward manner (as popular fantasy usually does and also the tale of detection), their readers find formal variations in the designs of those stories themselves. The stories vary in the selection and size of sets of characters: in matters so fundamental as the narrative time spans (the story of a western may cover months, even years; the story in a tale of detection rarely more than a few weeks); in the number and variety of settings and incidents; and so on. Students of the paperbacks have rarely given any attention to these matters, but the paperback genres look as though each had been designed to appeal to its own group of readers, differing from all other groups in the precise character of its tastes in texture and in design.

Even if the minds of readers did not lift themselves beyond the individual text, their experiences with story shapes, with odd blocks of information, and with variations in texture and design on both the narrative and the rhetorical level would be rich; but as they are reading, this secondary readership is looking through those stories at their sources—especially at the superorganic sources but also at the human sources.

Writers

The literary bookscape offers better opportunities to look into the minds of the people who create texts than does the paperback bookscape, for variorum texts supplement primary texts with biographical data and with the commentary of scholars that helps them see the mind behind the text. By contrast, the reader of a paperback cannot always be confident that the name of the writer given on the cover is not a pseudonym —or is even spelled correctly; readers are often looking, unknowingly, through two different names at the same person.

Still, some paperback writers have such distinctive styles and personalities that their presence is keenly felt. Robert Heinlein lectured the readers of his science fiction with huge delight in defense of positions they wholly rejected; but he did this so shrewdly, so wittily, and gave and took such pleasure in the argument that even his ideological opponents would support him in the annual awards competitions. The subgenres themselves have distinctive voices: no one would mistake a story from the hard-boiled tradition of the crime novel—by Jim Thompson, say, or Chester Himes—for a tale of detection by Agatha Christie or Dorothy Sayers. Even within a single subgenre, however, the styles of many writers are distinctive: experienced readers do not mistake Chester Himes for Jim Thompson or Agatha Christie for Dorothy Sayers.

Their readers do not reverence paperback writers, but they do care about them. Even in those brief notices that pass for book reviews, the reviewers always manage to find room for writer scorekeeping, telling readers whether the writer's book this year is as good as last year's, whether this writer is improving, whether that writer is beginning to repeat. In any case, publishers believe that the name of the writer heavily influences the buyer's decisions—which, presumably, is why they develop such house names as Jake Logan and Tabor Evans.

Still, it is the superorganic source, the genre, that commands readers' attention in this bookscape; for stories from an unfamiliar genre have that same object-function appeal that the first Indians to arrive in Europe had for the natural philosophers. The Europeans wanted to know what those Indians were as individuals and what they represented. It is at this point that the models for reading that are encouraged by the literary bookscape begin to fail, for the reading-by-text learned in that bookscape does not prepare people for the reading-by-genre that best rewards people in the paperback bookscape.

We examined certain features of the experience of reading inside a system in an earlier chapter. Here we can add to them three other features. Readers who come to the paperback bookscape from one of the learned bookscapes seem to engage in at least three different types of mental activity. They are mapping the genres they enter; they are identifying their canonical sets and watching them change; and they are watching the genres themselves change. When people speak of *following* a genre, it is these activities that they have in mind. The people who read a genre exclusively follow that genre, and the users of that genre follow it, too. It is the people who read in a genre only occasionally who can see the stories as objects but cannot see the genre itself.

Genre Mapping

When James Gunn suggested that a teacher could get a sound background in science fiction by reading about a hundred books, he meant, presumably, that it took that much experience for readers to acquire the internal map of the genre that they need if they are to get full pleasure from the books of that genre (see Gunn, *From Gilgamesh to Wells* 396). That number, one hundred, both is and is not absurd. It is absurd if it is taken to mean that we cannot understand one science-fiction story until we have read ninety-nine others. Plainly, readers do understand the stories as objects from their moment of first encounter. When they do not enjoy the first story in a new genre, they do not read the second.

Gunn is speaking of being able to understand stories as functions, however, of being able to read pleasurably inside the system. The ability to read competently in a genre is the ability to recognize in a story what is new and what is not. People who are just coming into a genre are always getting excited about the wrong features of a good story. Inevitably, they see the features that distinguish the stories in this genre from the stories in other genres; experienced readers are focusing on what distinguishes this story from other stories in the same genre.

The claim is absurd, too, if it is taken to suggest that there is some precise moment of critical mass when an ignorant reader turns abruptly into a skilled reader. It is a matter of a reader's gaining familiarity with a genre's potentialities and achievements with experience. Each new western, each new spy thriller, each new romance, gives its readers additional insight into the larger system that is its superorganic source. After readers come to know twenty or fifty of the stories in a genre, they begin to feel at home; but they do not fully understand the genre's directives (its rules and its dynamics) and its achievements (the texts the genre most admires) until they have reached that one-hundred-book level in their reading experience— for, as an order of magnitude, the number is not absurd.

When its learned readers turn to recommending titles to people new to a vernacular genre, they soon find themselves passing the number fifty with the sense that they are just getting started. In their publisher's brochure for *Fifty Classics of Crime Fiction: 1900–1950*, Jacques Barzun and Wendell Hertig Taylor apologize:

> Obviously, the choice of 50 titles does not exhaust the riches of the period 1900–1950; it *does* attempt to represent the varieties that flourished within the genre during that span—short and long, straight and inverted, pure crime and pure detection, "tough" and civilized, humorous and sober-sided, psychological and scientific

inference, male and female (author as well as protagonist), English and American. It gives, moreover, a fair idea of the formal and stylistic differences characterizing the successive decades, through the contributions of no fewer than sixty-four authors.   (4–5)

This reprint series, *Fifty Classics of Crime Fiction: 1900–1950*, contains only one novel each by Agatha Christie, Dorothy Sayers, and Raymond Chandler and no stories at all by Dashiell Hammett or James Cain—and does not pretend to offer a sampling of the stories and story traditions that flooded out after the end of World War II in 1945. Experienced readers would declare that the selection of stories that Barzun and Taylor made to represent this genre was outrageously inadequate—unless, that is, those readers tried to represent the genre with only fifty titles themselves. Outsiders do not guess how diverse such traditions as the crime novel and the romance really are.

In the literary bookscape, the reading of primary texts by genre is denied to any but the most specialized readers. The segmentation of that bookscape into major texts surrounded by commentary together with the disappearance of the genres that produced those texts ensure that the perception of a primary text as the function of a genre is available only to readers of the minor writers and the forgotten works of the periods from which the masterpieces have come.

Canon Disturbances

As readers move through the stories and learn a genre's dynamics—its rules and potentialities—they are encountering the texts accepted in that bookscape as genre classics. Once they have gained a certain amount of knowledge of that genre, they are prepared for certain tremors in its canon of classics. This is a familiar experience in the literary bookscape and, in fact, the best description of it was provided by that revolutionary traditionalist, T. S. Eliot. He was not thinking of paperback fiction when he wrote the following sentences, often reprinted, but they are as true of vernacular fiction as they are of art.

What happens when a new work of art is created is something that happens simultaneously to all the works of art which preceded it. The existing monuments form an ideal order among themselves, which is modified by the introduction of the new (the really new) work of art among them. The existing order is complete before the new work arrives; for order to persist after the supervention of novelty, the whole existing order must be, if ever so slightly, altered; and so the relations, proportions, values of each work of art towards the whole are readjusted; and this is conformity between the old and the new. (5)

Part of the pleasure readers take in paperback fiction lies in feeling those perturbations in a genre's canonical set that follow the appearance of a remarkable story. Once readers have come to know the best stories the genre has written, that set of the best comes to have a character of its own, always, however, subject to revision. Outsiders can watch the pushing and shoving that goes on inside a genre's canon of classics by means of revisions of those lists-of-the-best that fans and writers and editors make up—of, for instance, "The Greatest Science Fiction Ever Written." In *The SF Book of Lists*, by Maxim Jakubowski and Malcolm Edwards, we find the results of such ballotings in science fiction for 1952, 1956, 1966, and 1975 (174–77). We can watch individual titles changing places within the hierarchy of preferences. In 1952 A. E. van Vogt's *Slan* (1946), a story of the difficulties a superspecies has with humanity, was voted the second-best science-fiction book ever written; it lost first place to Raymond J. Healy and J. Francis McComas's anthology *Adventures in Time and Space*, but it had managed to edge out an anthology of no fewer than seven of H. G. Wells's best novels. In 1955, *Slan* came in fifth; in 1966—twenty-six years after its first appearance in a magazine—it had recovered and was now third; but by 1975 it had disappeared: it was no longer included even among the top twenty-six. *A Canticle for Leibowitz* (1960), Walter Miller's tale of the aftermath of World War III, was in tenth place in 1966 but had risen to fifth place by 1975. George Orwell's *Nineteen Eighty-Four* (1949) was appearing on these lists in the 1950s but by 1966 had dropped from sight. In August 1987, the science-fiction fanzine *Locus* published the results of its first balloting for "Best All-Time

Novels" since 1975 ("Best All-Time Novels," 32). Van Vogt's *Slan* is not among the top forty-five vote-getters; Orwell's *Nineteen Eighty-Four* is barely visible, in thirty-fourth place; but Miller's *Canticle for Leibowitz* is holding its position among the top ten: it is seventh. In the paperback bookscape, books come and go, but some do not go as quickly as the others. The drama of their comings and their goings and the drama of their rankings and changes in rankings have their own narrative values for experienced readers. In this there is nothing unusual. In unbuttoned moments, intellectuals have been known to get excited with one another also when they found they did not agree on "The Ten Greatest Film Musicals" or "The Ten Greatest Film Westerns."

Genre Mutations

As new readers' maps of a genre become more detailed, they find it easier to place each text against the system of rules which is the genre itself. They begin to sense how it is that this one text came into being and can even guess at the effect that its appearance will have on the rules that govern that environment. Every text changes its genre.

Even if it has nothing more to recommend it, each new text is a declaration that what might have been done has now been done and cannot be done again. An old set of possibilities is being exhausted. A new set of possibilities is being created. A new tone has been found, new textures, new possibilities in design. Perhaps a cliché has been definitively identified for what it is; perhaps another cliché has been invested with vigorous new life. To its readers, the spy thriller was never quite the same as the decades passed. From the days of Kipling's *Kim* (1901), where a child is taught to play the Great Game, and Erskine Childers's *Riddle of the Sands* (1903), where two amateurs wander around in the North German mud flats (surely the least romantic scenery ever chosen for a thriller), through the decades when the genre was dominated by John Buchan (*The Thirty-Nine Steps*, 1915), E. Phillips Oppenheim (*The Great Impersonation*, 1920), and Sapper (*The Return of Bulldog Drummond*, 1932), changes took place with a glacial slowness. Then the appearance of Eric Ambler's *Coffin for Dimitrios* in 1939 modified the genre utterly and irreversibly. It changed again when Ian Fleming's James Bond stories (*Casino Royale*, 1953) brought back some of the silly, charming glamour of the pre-Ambler days, and it abruptly changed once more, in 1963, with the success of John Le Carré's *Spy Who Came in from the Cold*. In Chapter 8 we saw that Hammett's *Thin Man* (1934) seemed to its first readers to be opening a new system of possibilities for its genre; its accomplishment lay not in its presentation of sane images of sexuality but in offering itself as a precedent that would make it possible for other stories to do that. We saw that in 1965 Harry Harrison's science-fiction novel *Bill, the Galactic Hero* began talking back to Robert Heinlein's *Starship Troopers* of 1959, and that ten years later, in 1975, Haldeman's *Forever War* began to talk back to both of them. And we saw that a narrative oxymoron (the appearance in the same stories of both the disintegrator ray and the punch in the jaw) that had embarrassed writers and readers of science fiction for decades was finally resolved in those works that presented the genre with that absurdly ingenious body shield.

As these books appeared, readers were discovering further possibilities that had been hidden from them inside the genre's dynamics; they were watching older classics making room (in some cases, giving place) to new works; and they were sensing opportunities opening up as someone successfully breached the limitations of the genre. These dramas are invisible to those reading the stories only as objects.

Sociability

Of all facets of all the many types of reading experiences, sociability, surely, is least well understood. Nonreaders think that when people turn to books they are withdrawing into themselves. (When readers are young, the adult nonreader assures them solemnly that they read because they cannot face Life.) The readers themselves think of books as offering not solitude but a private sociability. They are joining a *virtual fellowship* of characters, readers, and writers.

As with all other kinds of reading, there are two kinds of fellowship available in the paperback bookscape. Fandom offers one kind. Inside

. . . .

fandom, with its letter columns in the professional magazines, its fan-zines, and its conventions, people know one another by name and address and interact as more than readers, as individuals who like and dislike and interest one another as individuals. These fandoms are not without their importance. They indicate, for instance, that people can care enough about fiction to take the trouble to find others who share their enthusiasms. In this respect, the fandoms are indirect validations of institutionalized literary study, for they show us that the study of literature is not just a function of the existence of schools, as some cynics have claimed (Spar-shott 14). They make it evident that even if the schools were to disappear or to change radically, there would be people who care enough about the books of the past to form their own associations—fandoms, then—for the reading and discussion of literature.

It is the other kind of fellowship that interests us, though—the virtual fellowships of readers who sense one another's existence but do not know one another individually. Most readers of pulp fiction do not know anyone who reads in the same genres they read; and, everything considered, they would prefer not to know or be known. More likely than not, they become conscious of other readers only when they are embarrassed. Every now and then, they are forced to admit that they would prefer not to be part of a company of readers whose taste is so undiscriminating that they are pleased by writers with nasty minds and by other writers who are disappointing even in their choice of clichés.

What is especially to be remarked about the people who are doing this reading and who do form these virtual fellowships is that they are not ruled from above. That is, the primary readers of pulp fiction are usually characterized as the victims of the manipulative editors and writers who pretend to be their servants, and those editors and writers do give them-selves the credit when a genre, a writer, or a book is successful. They are wrong, however. It is the readers who should be taking both the credit and the blame for pulp fiction. It is the readers, after all, who invent genres—by becoming so enthusiastic about an odd new book that publishers and writers make other books resembling it; it is the readers who change the genres—by passing over stories that are too much like those that have already appeared; and it is the readers who kill genres—by leaving the genres' stories unbought on the bookstore shelves.

That notion that publishers, editors, and writers are manipulating the tastes of a vast, unthinking mob is one more echo from the literary bookscape, in this case an echo of the notion of arbiters of taste. In the literary bookscape, men and women of specially developed sensitivities—from Petronius in the time of Nero through Samuel Johnson in eighteenth-century England to Edmund Wilson in mid-twentieth-century America—have been studied carefully by people who were learning their way around inside a bookscape that is ancient, large, confusing, and awesome. We find this pervasive concern about correctness of taste—an international literary concern—neatly evident in Matthew Arnold's approving quotation of Sainte-Beuve's characterization of the French. " 'In France,' says M. Sainte-Beuve, 'the first consideration for us is not whether we are amused and pleased by a work of art or mind, nor is it whether we are touched by it. What we seek above all to learn is, whether *we were right* in being amused with it, and in applauding it, and in being moved by it' " ("Literary Influence" 236). Learned readers may sometimes wonder whether they should be spending their time reading paperbacks, but the notion that in preferring one paperback over another they might be manifesting anything more than personal preference is utterly foreign even to them.

In the literary bookscape, there are arbiters; in the paperback bookscape, there are only guides. The distinction between arbiter and guide is implicit in the everyday uses of the more familiar terms *critic* and *reviewer*. Critics tell writers whether their new books are well written, where they have gone wrong, why their books are not as good as their earlier books; and they tell readers which books they should be reading and how to read those books. Reviewers, on the other hand, are content to look for books their readers will enjoy and to share with them the excitement of reading. (They do not bother to tell their readers about the books they read but did not enjoy.) Simply put, critics try to make the world better; reviewers try to make the world happier. There are no critics in the paperback bookscape, there are only reviewers—and not very many of them. (Anyone who would like to read typical reviews of pulp fiction can find them in two magazines that understand the reading fellowships of the paperbacks perfectly. *Romantic Times* reviews romance novels; *Rave Reviews*, just about everything else in paperback. Their pages persuade us that the writers thoroughly enjoyed the books they are praising and hope that we will enjoy them, too.) Without criticism and the commentary that accrues from it, there can be no instruction in taste. The readers of pulp fiction do not want it anyway.

These virtual fellowships embrace the writers, too—virtual companions, as it were. In this respect, readers in the paperback bookscape are indistinguishable from readers in the learned bookscape. Wayne C. Booth talks about the pleasure of sensing the companionship of both the author and that author's readers while reading Jane Austen's novels.

> The dramatic illusion of her presence is thus fully as important as any other element in the story. When she intrudes the illusion is not shattered. The only illusion we care about, the illusion of traveling intimately with a hardy little band of readers whose heads are screwed on tight and whose hearts are in the right place, is actually strengthened when we are refused the romantic love scene. Like the author herself, we don't care about the love scene. We can find love scenes in almost any novelist's works, but only here can we find a mind and heart that can give us clarity without oversimplification, sympathy and romance without sentimentality, and biting irony without cynicism. (276)

Change a dozen words in that paragraph and we have a reader of paperbacks explaining how he feels about his favorite writer. Change those words again, and we have another reader of paperbacks explaining how she feels about still another writer. The relationship the reader has to the writer of paperbacks is not always so devotional as Booth's own sentences, of course. More often, there is a measurable gap between the reader's mind and the writer's, as when a conservative reads a radical or a radical reads a conservative, say, with a surprised mixture of pleasure, dismay, admiration, and baffled satisfaction.

That sense of the presence of another mind is only part of the pleasure, though, for readers of pulp fiction also have an interest in the writers as performing artists. When they have been reading in one of these genres for a little while, they come to feel that each new paperback—a Ruth Rendell mystery, a Louis L'Amour western—is one more episode in the career in art of its writer; and as they are reading their books they are following the writers' struggles, triumphs, failures. After a few years, some of that genre's writers are more securely established in their readers' imaginations than any of their characters. It should be emphasized that readers' interest has very little to do with their favorite writers' commercial success. Looking through the books, they are watching fierce struggles between writers and their always refractory materials. They do not care much whether anyone is making money; their interest is in whether the writer is writing well or badly, whether the writer *qua* writer is getting better or getting worse. It is rather like watching the animal trainers and trapeze artists in a circus. Will the trainers get their animals to do their tricks, or will the animals eat their trainers? Will the aerialists fall? Often the animals win, and all of the aerialists fall now and then.

This shadow drama, a drama whose character readers infer as they read, can be quite as fascinating in its own way as the stories they are reading. James Gunn provides a reflective headnote in *From Here to Forever*. Trying to explain the impact that John Varley, a new writer, had on the science-fiction readership, Gunn begins with a distinction between "innovators" and "realizers," a distinction that we also encounter when reading histories of scientific invention, reviews of popular music, studies of war strategy—and, of course, histories of literature. Then Gunn slips away into reflections on some of the writers' careers, as though the writers themselves were fictional characters.

Edgar Rice Burroughs was both an innovator and realizer, but E. E. "Doc" Smith was an innovator. Robert A. Heinlein was an innovator; A. E. van Vogt was a realizer. Both were recognized as superstars from the moment of their first publication.

Not so many have blazed so unequivocally: Ray Bradbury brightened slowly; Alfred Bester exploded; Frederik Pohl, after a long pseudonymous apprenticeship, formed a spectacular double star with Cyril Kornbluth and then had a new burst of creative fire in the middle and late 1970s. Ursula K. Le Guin certainly belongs among the novas, and probably Larry Niven. Others, such as Jack Williamson, Clifford Simak, Fritz Leiber, L. Sprague de Camp, Frank Herbert, Brian Aldiss, Philip K. Dick, Robert Silverberg, and Harlan Ellison, have burned more evenly.   (375–76)

None of this writer following (even more noticeable among the readers of serious fiction) receives much explicit attention, but a reader's discovery of an unread novel by a favorite writer or a reader's learning that the writer has published a new novel can bring cheer to the day. The books sometimes look from the outside as though they were coming off an assembly line; but there are people behind those books, and the people in front of those books look through those books at the people behind them, and they care about them. If that is only a virtual fellowship or companionship, it can be more rewarding than some of the other fellowships life throws us into.

Everything we have considered, and more, is involved in this many-minded reading of the paperbacks, but moments of single-minded reading frequently occur. Some stories are intended to make their readers excited, and readers are altered physically by the words. Their breathing becomes shorter, their heart begins to beat more quickly, extra adrenalin enters their bloodstream—or, at least, they feel that this is happening (and they do seem to have more trouble falling asleep afterward). The most obvious occasion for this glandular experience is the moment when younger readers first encounter well-written erotica. Sexually aroused, they are hardly aware of the writer's skill in character development or in the variations that writer has introduced into the book's tradition. They are doing windowpane reading at this moment. This sort of single-mindedness in reading is common enough, though. Any well-written page of life-and-death tension, any page of stirring denunciation or of rousing affirmation reaches down through and below readers' minds to trigger glandular response to terror, exuberance, despair.

Similarly, the characters or the setting or the events may be so intriguing in one book that readers have no interest in anything else. More often, they are more interested in one of these story elements than the others on one page and less interested on the next. As they move through the book their attention shifts from plot to subplot and back again. If there is any puzzle at all in the story, readers are framing, discarding, and reframing their expectations as they turn the pages. This happens to readers of the tale of detection, of course, when the writer challenges readers to guess the identity of the murderer before the fictional detective announces it. As readers' suspicions shift from one character to another, the earlier suspect dims a bit in the story for them and the new suspect becomes a bit more vivid. Meanwhile, their minds are scribbling and revising scenarios of the murder. We know that they do this because they complain of some writers that the solutions to their mysteries are too obvious or too farfetched; the murder scenarios the writers are providing are no better than the ones the readers' own minds are inventing.

But if their minds shift their focus within the realm of the story, they also shift out of the story temporarily to the odd bit of useful or merely intriguing information that the story has yielded, or to a strange bit of verbal texture or a challenging design, or to some revelation of the moral posture of the writer, or to a new bit of insight into the genre, or to a recognition that one of the genre classics is being seriously challenged for preeminence, or to the revelation that the genre is taking a new direction, or to the sense that this is an experience that only the readers' own sort —whoever they may be—could possibly enjoy sharing. As I noted in an earlier chapter, popular fiction is a device that permits secondary readers to engage in serious thought even when they are tired—but the stories enable other forms of pleasurably intense mental activity, too.

It is a matter of knowing how to read. The bookscapes we have been looking at do teach those two different styles of reading: *studying* (study reading) and *reading* (thick reading). These are the lessons to be emphasized: that there are two such styles, that they are natives of different bookscapes, that neither is an imitation of the other, and that the differences between them are valid. Studying gives the readers of fiction valuable experiences they do not get from reading; reading gives them valuable experiences they do not get from studying.

As we have seen, the differences between studying and reading are not absolute; it is the students of literature, such as T. S. Eliot and Wayne Booth, who have written the most useful descriptions of reading.

Both styles of reading require an expanded alertness within which readers' narrower reading focus can range, looking now at one matter and now at another. There are other points of similarity. In both we find not only awareness of story but also awareness of texture and design; in both we find awareness of the human source of the story and of other readers of the story; in both, the awareness of a personal canon of valued texts whose claims to readers' affections and loyalties are put at risk whenever they read another book.

Study reading does offer uniquely valuable experiences: the individual texts yield more to study reading, the minds of the writers come more plainly into view. Thick reading and study reading have similarities, but study reading and genre following are utterly and forever different. If either activity were ever pursued in isolation, then study reading would see the thing created but never see the creating of that thing, and genre following would see the creating but never see the thing that is being created. Which reading strategy came first? Is it the focus on the object itself that is the more ancient, or did focus on the object as a function of an activity precede it? Which of the two strategies yields the greater rewards? Perhaps these questions are unanswerable.

Readers map a genre by examining its products—the stories—and by extrapolating from those stories the systems that produced them. When the system is simple, they do not find this difficult. Some paperback stories are produced to what are indeed properly called *formulas*. Sword-and-sorcery fiction (Robert E. Howard's crude and splendid *Conan the Warrior* and Michael Shea's *Nifft the Lean*) and the locked-room mystery (especially the novels of John Dickson Carr) honor patterns only slightly more complex than the Petrarchan sonnet. The people who read these stories know about formulas, for they want their writers to accept the challenge to their powers as inventors and as craftsmen that is a consequence of their choosing to write within the limitations of those formulas. If the reading of paperbacks were only a matter of coming upon works written to formula, as some suppose, there would of course be nothing more (or less) challenging to the mind than there is in the formal appreciation of the Renaissance sonnet. Formula following is not especially difficult.

A genre, however, is not a formula; it is not even a set of formulas. Genres contain formulas—for example, the genre of the crime novel includes the formula of the locked-room mystery—but genres themselves are (or, rather, include) traditions of formulas that are mutating, formulas that are evolving. And, of course, some genre stories do not honor any formula at all, though they may be so admired that they are used as the basis for a new writing formula by emulators and imitators. (The tale of detection grew out of the success of Conan Doyle's Sherlock Holmes stories in this way, and the sword-and-sorcery formula grew out of writers' and readers' ambivalent fascination with the Conan stories of Robert E. Howard.)

For readers to grasp the character of internally inconsistent genres—traditions as complex as the crime novel, say, and the romance—requires that they recognize by inference that a single system does lie far behind the many different stories by the many different writers working within the many different subsystems of that system. Readers learn this without outside instruction, unselfconsciously, almost inadvertently. They make themselves competent in the genre by the simple and time-consuming (but satisfying) expedient of exploring and mapping for themselves the genres that interest them, by developing their private canons of their genres' highest achievements, and by allowing the stories to teach them how to savor both the changes in their personal canonical sets and the changes in their genres' rules, lexicon, and themes.

Linguists have sometimes spoken of our learning of our native languages while we are still very young as the single greatest intellectual feat we ever perform; but this is a feat this secondary readership performs whenever it learns a new genre. From a small number of that genre's products they develop a familiarity with a subcultural code so complex that even when they are expert in it they cannot explain it. As the grammarians would put it, they can tell when an utterance—a romance or a mystery or a science-fiction story—is well-formed and when it is not; but they cannot explain how it is that they know that.

Readers who are following a genre are creating maps of that genre which they are continually redrawing as that genre changes. The capacity to do this must always have been in the human nervous system, of course; developments in mathematics in the school of Pythagoras must have had that kind of appeal to those who took an interest in them, for instance, and changes in fashion in armament and in decoration have always been rapid enough to be visible to observers. Genre following by readers, though, may never have been pursued so intensively as it has been in the past couple of hundred years. When we look back at earlier eras, we are struck by the close parallels between the reading of such scriptures as the Bible and the Koran in earlier times and the study reading of literature today. We find in that earlier reading of scriptures a depth of reverence that is uncommon in the literary bookscape but is certainly not unknown. The differences between scripture reading and study reading are not differences in strategy; they are differences in the scale of emotional response. Our ancestors seem to have felt that object focus in reading was superior to genre focus and, therefore, that the monumental objects that elicit study reading were unique in having value.

Our ancestors did not have as many opportunities as we have to follow changes within the kinds of cultural systems that are carried in language. Living in an age of print, we are swept each day by tidal waves of information interchange. In the oral cultures of the past, information exchanges on this order were possible only in cities, where diverse populations interacted. Until fairly recently, the rate of cultural change in rural areas was too slow to be visible as more than a sequence of mysterious disasters and salvations. It was the development of ever-cheaper forms of print that made possible an appreciation of cultural changes as valuable in their own right. Certainly, the kind of genre following we have been studying, though familiar to those inside literary circles in the past, must have been uncommon for the average reader. Today, it is hard to avoid becoming genre followers in one way or another.

For all the claims made recently that humanity has left the culture of the letter and entered a culture of the image, humans are living now in an environment saturated with visible language as it never has been before. Even the people who never open a book may be reading more words each year than did the scribes of ancient Egypt, the librarians of Alexandria, or the monks of the Middle Ages: they see those words on billboards, on cans of corn, on television screens, in store windows. Today, people who do read books do not find it difficult to obtain and read one hundred books a year in the hours after they have completed the day's work and fulfilled their obligations to their families. That is fewer than two books a week.

Some of the reasons for this are material. People with poor eyesight do not read as much as people with good eyesight. People who must read by the light from a wood fire do not read as much as people who have electric light. People living in an area that has few books do not read as much as people who live where books are plentiful. The shorter workdays that readers now have, the adequate lighting in the evenings, the reading glasses, the public libraries, the inexpensive books, and the saturation of the culture with books began to appear only within the last two hundred years. It was not until then that cheap fiction in the form of the dime novel and the penny dreadful, the ancestors of contemporary pulp fiction and nonfiction, began pouring off the presses and into the lives of our ancestors. It was not until then that people had the time, the conditions, the equipment, and the skills that make reading in bulk possible.

Some impatient readers of these last few paragraphs will have been finding this claim for a previously unrecognized sophistication in the reading of paperbacks absurd. There is dining, they will be thinking, and there is gobbling. When we are dining, we savor each meal and each part of each dish of each meal, and we are keenly aware of the gifted person who cooked that meal. Gobbling is something else. When we are gobbling, we are eating snack foods (potato chips, popcorn, crackers) and fast foods (hot dogs, hamburgers, fish and chips). When we are gobbling, we are hardly aware of what we are doing; and, anyway, the stuff was not cooked by a human being, it was cooked by a stopwatch. Are we expected to agree that in the moments of our gobbling there is a sophistication in our taste we do not know as diners?

It is a false analogy, this contrast between dining and gobbling—though we find such an analogy thinly hidden by much that is written about these materials. A western by Elmore Leonard is not a bag of potato chips, and a romance by Kathleen Woodiwiss is not a hamburger. If we want to find a parallel in the reading of these secondary readers to the gobbling of snack foods, we shall find it in that message scanning we have just looked at—in their half-unaware reading of political slogans, one-line jokes, advertising tags, greeting-card sentiments, bumper stickers, and all those other messages that make up so large a part of a landscape supersaturated with visual language. The gulf between the reading of a memorable slogan and the reading of even the simplest novel is immense. (This is not to say that all can see the differences: some of the Puritan contemporaries of Shakespeare were opposed to all plays, poems, and novels because they could not distinguish between the open let's-pretend of fiction and the sly falsehood of the lie.)

When readers are in the literary bookscape they are gourmets of reading, but they do not turn into mindless gobblers when they move into the paperback bookscape. Their thick reading, so confusingly like and so confusingly unlike study, is a qualitatively different mode of text response. If it has come to seem odd and wrong even to the people who are skilled in it, that is because the most searching accounts of the experiences that readers have with fiction have been coming from specialists in study reading who—from deep inside the literary bookscape—have been emphasizing monumental texts and magisterial authors at the expense of larger systems. Even specialists in study reading read thickly, however, and they read thickly in the literary bookscape.

reading
learned essays
and watching
television

• • • • • • • • • • • • • • •

In the plainest—and, ultimately, the only *reliable*—sense of the terms, the primary readers of paperbacks are the people who read only paperbacks and the secondary readers are the people who read learned materials as well.

We have been assuming that people who can read comfortably in a learned bookscape are good readers and that their minds do not become less effective when they turn to the paperbacks, and we have found that when we look at the ways in which those readers read vernacular fiction we get an entirely different image from what we have been led to expect. Still, there are those other readers of the paperbacks who do not read comfortably in any of the learned bookscapes. Do they read paperbacks differently?

When we speak about these primary readers, we seem to have two groups in mind. We think of some of them as inexperienced, as readers who admire some paperback stories more than they would if they had read more widely and knew how much more they have a right to expect from books. We recognize, from our own reading histories, that readers who are only inexperienced will outread that limitation in time. We think of others as less resonant readers, as people who have one limitation or another in their capacity to respond to prose. These verbal limitations, we say, will prevent their ever taking pleasure in materials that less limited readers enjoy easily. We feel that these other readers will not outread their limitations and are forever barred from entry into a learned bookscape.

Readers do differ individually in these two ways; but I am not at all sure how important these differences are, and I am not sure that we can generalize from individual differences to groups. I am not persuaded, that is, that either the primary readers or the secondary readers of pulp fiction can usefully be said—as a group—to be less experienced or less resonant than the other. We shall look first at the individual differences and then return to the question of group differences.

Since all experienced readers were once inexperienced readers and remember the reading they did in those years with affection, they know very well that inexperience is neither shameful nor a bar to pleasure and growth. They also know, however, that inexperienced readers are marked by their inappropriate enthusiasm for paperbacks as objects in their own right. Readers new to the novel are much more likely to be awed by, say, Frank Herbert's *Dune* than are the readers who know the classic English, French, and Russian novels of the nineteenth century. As it happens, I feel that the admirers of that science-fiction novel *Dune* need not be ashamed to compare it with those earlier novels, but it is certainly the case that readers' sense of what a novel can be is different when they have *Emma* and *Dombey and Son* and *Anna Karenina* also in mind as they read *Dune*.

No one feels uncomfortable when people speak of some readers' being limited by inexperience, but the claim that some readers are limited in their capacity to respond does make many of us uneasy. Still, I would remind other readers that one of the more painful lessons that we all do learn as we become more experienced is that we are indeed forever different from one another as readers and that some of the differences we do discover in ourselves are limitations. We discover that we do not have so subtle an ear as one of our friends or that our visual imaginations are not so responsive or that when we encounter compound-complex sentences (what someone once called semicolon-intensive prose) we find the book more tiring than others do. We have probably already learned by that time, however, that some people are more gifted with numbers than we are and that others have better musical imaginations, and it is no longer quite so painful as it might once have been to admit that while some of our friends read some verbal materials less richly than we they also read other materials more successfully. In short, we learn that we readers differ from one another at least as widely in our strengths and limitations as the athletes on football and basketball and baseball teams do. (I am not persuaded that this has much to do with social origins, and I am quite confident that it has nothing whatsoever to do with intelligence in any more general sense. All readers know some men and women who find reading boring but are brilliant nevertheless.)

Once we have admitted that some readers are less experienced than others and that some readers are less resonant, we find it easy to suppose we now understand why some people are content with reading only paperbacks while others need materials in the more learned bookscapes as well. We assume that primary readers (the paperbacks only) are less experienced and less resonant and that secondary readers (the paperbacks also) are more experienced and more resonant. We might then conclude that those primary and secondary groups read the paperbacks differently: the primary readers are enjoying them as objects in themselves; the secondary readers are enjoying them as functions of underlying systems.

This elegant division does not bear up under scrutiny. The two readerships are not so different as most of us have too hastily assumed. Two types of difficulty face us when we try to claim that the readerships are fundamentally different.

A difficulty that the people who read only paperbacks will not see but that the people who know the learned bookscapes cannot avoid seeing is that these same distinctions—these distinctions between experienced and inexperienced and between more and less resonant readers—are evident inside every learned readership as well, including the people learned in literature. There is a vast plenty of materials inside the literary bookscape, for instance, which will please inexperienced readers and a vast plenty which will reward less resonant readers. If all those people we think of as being part of a primary readership of the paperbacks were abruptly pushed into the literary bookscape, they would soon find themselves just as comfortable as the readers who already are roaming freely inside that bookscape. They would not read everything in literature equally well, but no other readers of literature read everything equally well, either. That is one reason why we find it difficult to accept the distinction between primary and secondary readerships as a distinction in styles of reading.

Another difficulty, evident to primary and secondary reader alike, is that the paperback bookscape itself changes every reader who comes into it. Just as every learned bookscape teaches study reading, so the paperback bookscape teaches every person thick reading. People who cannot learn to read thickly do not continue to read paperbacks.

When we examine popular culture, it is useful to keep always in mind its secondary readerships—those readers who have earned our respect as readers elsewhere—for that makes it more difficult for us to please ourselves too quickly with the easy answer. Finally, though, the other people, the people who use only the vernacular traditions, are not different in their strategies of reception from the people beside them who are visiting from the worlds of science and high art. Neither group is so simple —not in this century, at least—as to make the task of understanding its behavior simple.

In these last pages, we shall be examining two activities that are usually felt to be at the opposite ends of the intellectual spectrum: the reading of learned essays and the viewing of television. Neither is quite what we think it to be, and while they are plainly different they are much more alike than we have supposed them to be.

Reading Learned Essays

I noted earlier that the literary bookscape offers a literature without genres and that it teaches people how to study rather than how to read. This is not quite true. It does teach some people to read thickly, and they are reading genres.

The literary bookscape is a learned bookscape that is prepared by experts for the profit and pleasure of amateurs. It is the experts, for instance, who search out the texts that amateurs will enjoy, and it is the experts who transform them into variorum texts. Elsewhere, the distinction between expert and amateur is felt to be a distinction in competence ("expertise" vs. "amateurism"), but in the literary bookscape an expert is anyone who has command of a special kind of knowledge, while an amateur is anyone who is driven by a special kind of love. The expert loves, too; the expert loves learning, but the amateur loves literature.

No one will suppose that the work of the experts is selfless in its preparation of this bookscape for amateurs, for it is plain that almost all literary experts are amateurs of literature as well. As the workday ends, the expert Chaucerean becomes a passionate, nonexpert reader of the Latin American novel, and the expert in the literary modernism of the 1920s turns eagerly to the major works of Alexander Pope. Six months later, they will be reading, as amateurs, in other parts of this bookscape.

The pure amateur is different from the pure expert, of course; but even the same person is different when he is reading as an expert from when he is reading as an amateur, as we can see when people finish one text and turn to another. When the amateurs close Austen's *Pride and Prejudice* they turn next to George Eliot's *Middlemarch*, perhaps, or to Richardson's *Pamela*. When the experts close Austen's novel, however, they turn to something quite different. Either they turn to the popular novels that Austen and her readers had read, or they turn to the essays that other Austen experts have written about her and about her novel. They are not turning to another masterpiece but to parallels, in the literary bookscape, of vernacular writing. Why do they do this? They are doing the work of the expert. They are professionally curious as to how much in *Pride and Prejudice* comes from Jane Austen herself and how much from the traditions within which she was writing, perhaps; or they want to compare their own mappings of the novel with others. For the one, they turn to the books that were written by Austen's predecessors and rivals; for the other, they turn to the essays that were written by other experts.

The amateur (nonexpert, lover) studies for the pleasure of those monumental variorum texts, but the expert (specialist, professional) reads for the pleasure provided by the primary genres of times now gone and by the secondary genres of our own times. No amateur who is not also an expert can guess how different the literary bookscape is to those experts.

The MLA is the best-known of the organizations that literary experts have formed. It has some twenty-five thousand members; but this is only a fraction of the total corpus of all experts in literature. Many professional teachers, scholars, and critics do not join any organization, and some join organizations that focus more tightly on their areas of interest. The MLA is the largest of all the professional organizations, however, and its character and its annual reports on the activities of literary experts provide a convenient insight into the topology of the literary bookscape as experts know it. The MLA itself has regional subdivisions, each active in its own way, and it has intricately subdivided itself into some one hundred officially recognized virtual communities it names Divisions and Discussion Groups and it recognizes scores of other groups—societies, associations—that its members have formed outside the MLA's embracing arms. These virtual communities differ in size, but all are actively—and independently—teaching, discovering, disputing, writing, editing, and meeting. Most have their own newsletters, and many have their own journals.

One of the services the MLA provides is its annual bibliography of literary commentary. So much is written about literature (and about the enterprise of writing about literature) that the list of studies done on literature in modern languages now fills five volumes each year. The pure amateur would find any one of those volumes bewildering. The volume devoted to publications in 1986 of General Literature listed 2,716 separate items: notes, editions, essays, collections, monographs, books. That volume recognized Genres, Literary Forms, and Criticism, among others, as categories into which publications fall. The amateur might have expected that. The volume also recognized nineteen different types of literary theory: Feminist, Hermeneutic, Linguistic, Marxist, Narrative, New Historical, Philosophical, Postmodernist, Poststructuralist, Pragmatist, Psychoanalytic, Psychological, Reader-Response, Reception, Rhetorical, Semiotic, Sociological, and Structuralist. Two in this list were being newly recognized: New Historical and Pragmatist. Two others had just been dropped: Formalist and Phenomenological. Many of these labels—Feminist, Hermeneutic, Linguistic, Marxist, Psychoanalytic, for instance—refer to virtual communities with their own identities, shifting interests, conventions of discourse, honored writers, special outlets, and classics of achievement (MLA, *General Literature*).

The pure amateurs of literature would also find that those formally named divisions—there are seventy-six of them—are looking at literature through different lenses. They will not be surprised to learn that some divisions focus on the major literary forms:

    8. Drama
10. Nonfictional Prose
11. Poetry
12. Prose Fiction
14. Literary Criticism

They will learn that Division 23 is devoted to Chaucer and 25 to Shakespeare and that there are calendrical divisions. British literature has ten, and American literature has four:

17. American Literature to 1800
18. 19th-Century American Literature
19. Late 19th- and Early 20th-Century American Literature
20. 20th-Century American Literature

Some divisions address themselves to different reading-writing communities, such as

    6. Women's Studies in Language and Literature
    7. Ethnic Studies in Literature
16. Asian Literature
75. Gay Studies in Language and Literature
76. Black American Literature and Culture

Some of the divisions are less interested in which parts of literature are worth studying than in how one goes about studying any of it, and they use the all-purpose word *approach:*

35. Anthropological Approaches to Literature
36. Linguistic Approaches to Literature
37. Philosophical Approaches to Literature
38. Psychological Approaches to Literature
39. Religious Approaches to Literature
40. Sociological Approaches to Literature

The discussion groups are other virtual communities, ones that found the divisions either too broad or too confining. Their names recognize additional distinctions:

American Indian
Anglo-Irish
Asian American
Arthurian
Folklore
Computer Studies in Language and Literature
Interdisciplinary Approaches to Culture and Society

These lists hardly suggest the intricacies of the Modern Language Association's overlapping interests; see MLA, "Divisions and Discussion Groups" for a fuller picture.

The program for the 1987 meeting of the MLA listed associated meetings for the convenience of its members. In the list we find that each of the following authors has a "Society" devoted to it: Samuel Beckett, Byron, Cervantes, Paul Claudel, Joseph Conrad, Dante, Dickens, George Sand, Robert Frost, Ellen Glasgow, Goethe, Nathaniel Hawthorne, Hemingway, Langston Hughes, Brecht, Henry James, Kafka, D. H. Lawrence, Doris Lessing, G. E. Lessing, Malraux, Marlowe, Melville, Milton, Vladimir Nabokov, Eugene O'Neill, Pirandello, Poe, Spenser, Wallace Stevens, Thoreau, William Carlos Williams, and Virginia Woolf (MLA, "Allied Organization Meetings").

This is the topography of the world of the expert in literature. The literary bookscape comprises several hundred of these virtual communities, or intellectual neighborhoods, in which the experts have their being (Roberts, "Network"). It can differ markedly from one intellectual neighborhood to another. In Chapter 9 I discussed the arguments swirling around the novels of Trollope. Do those novels focus on society or on the individual? Was Trollope a realist? Was he a stylist? Was he a political novelist? Compare that debate with what R. Howard Bloch tells us about debates in Old French literature:

No issue in the study of Old French literature has invited greater interpretative license than the question of the sources of Chrétien

de Troyes's *Conte du Graal.* Some explanations are indeed difficult
to believe. Take the following for example: that the episode in which
Perceval visits a mysterious castle, meets an invalid king, sees a
graillike dish and bleeding lance, forgets to ask what they mean, and
awakens to find that both castle and king have vanished—that this
aventure is: part of early Aryan literature, derived from an ancient
Babylonian cult, the survival of an archaic Indian vegetation ritual
or of an esoteric Islamic initiation ceremony; or, that the mysterious
meal is, in reality, a Sephardic Jewish Passover seder, that the old
king is a secret emissary of the Cathar faith, a medieval version of
the Egyptian god Thoth, or a historical image of Baldwin IV afflicted
with elephantiasis; or, finally, that the graillike dish represents a
"sex symbol of immemorial antiquity," the pearl of Zoroastrian tradition, a talisman of heretical Albigensians worshiped in caves in
the Pyrenees, a secret religious relic originating in Hellenic Greece
(and preserved in the medieval *corpus hermeticum*), or a genuine
"Great Sapphire" kept in the sacristy of Glastonbury Abbey. And,
further, we are asked by the scholarly workers at this building site
of Babel to believe that all of the above sources of Chrétien's tale
reached the medieval poet without leaving any visible trace.   (255)

The amateurs see the literary bookscape differently, of course. For
them, it is not so much a linkage and overlapping of intellectual neighborhoods as it is a heroic landscape of mountains and monuments, of
rich valleys and awesome waterfalls, of terrifying chasms, of flowering
meadows, of live volcanos. The amateurs wander here and there within
this bookscape as whim directs, moving from one of these heroic objects
to another, from a monumental text to a magisterial author to a brief but
brilliantly lighted decade of literary production, and then on to another
monumental text.

The literary expert (even when it is the nighttime amateur in a daytime
persona) has one or two or three local residences; for to be an expert is
to have local residence in the literary bookscape. The amateurs travel
around in the literary bookscape, but the experts live there. If a learned
bookscape is a clustering of virtual communities, or neighborhoods, it is
like a continent, too, though the pure amateur cannot see that. Experts

. . . .

are not experts in some hypothetical "literature-at-large," just as people are not citizens in some "Europe-at-large." People live in Europe by virtue of their living in Paris or in Munich or in Milan. It may be that they maintain residences in Paris and in Munich and in Milan and divide their year among them; but then they are not living in Oslo or in London or in Amsterdam or in Rome. So, literary experts live in Shakespearean studies and perhaps in studies of Asian-American literature as well; but if they do, they do not have the interest, the capacity, or at least the time to live also in Old English studies and in Sociological Approaches to Literature and in Edgar Allan Poe studies. To live in one virtual community in the literary bookscape, which is to know and to share in the minutiae of the intellectual life of that community, is to use the time that would be needed to know and share in the minutiae of the intellectual lives lived in other virtual communities in this bookscape.

Inside many of these virtual communities of criticism there are people reading in the oeuvres left by ancient genres: the epic, the topographical poem, the epistolary novel, the beast fable. Some of the traditions that shaped the works that remain were the high genres of the past and some were the analogues of the modern paperback genres. The books the experts read are not works they can recommend to the amateurs of literature; for the amateurs want to remain in that bookscape of the monumental and the magisterial.

It is not while reading these oeuvres that the literary experts are reading by genre; for the genres themselves—which is to say the patterns and rules and tendencies that governed their writers—disappeared when the minds in which they resided disappeared. Today, the experts are reading oeuvres, not genres; and the experiences they are having are far different from those that the writers' contemporaries had. The modern readers read these minor works of the past like the gods. They are reading from outside the thin slices of space and time, from outside the cultural moments, within which those texts took their shapes. When they lift Edward S. Ellis's dime novel *Seth Jones; or, The Captives of the Frontier* off the library shelf, or the first American comedy, Royall Tyler's play *The Contrast*, they are unlike the works' original consumers. They read a text as a historian reads one of Napoleon's letters. For the Napoleon who wrote that letter, the future had not yet been fixed, but for his twentieth-century biographers that letter is one discrete point inside a defined and immutable sequence of points in a when and a where whose every part those biographers already know. Unlike Napoleon, those biographers have free access to every one of those points, can visit any of them at any moment and can move between them in any sequence. Napoleon, and the writers of those books the amateurs never see, had the sense that they were shaping a future that was still undetermined. Modern readers cannot recover that sense of contingency, for they know what that future was.

Whatever the potentialities of those genres, whatever the dime novel or the epic or the revenge tragedy might have produced, what those genres left is all that they did produce and they will never write anything more. The stories are unremarkable as objects, and the death of their genres left them devoid of value as functions. The total genre oeuvres are not without their own exotic beauty, however. Northrop Frye has spoken somewhere of the contrast between the insignificance of the individual coral coelenterate and the magnificence of the coral reefs that those individual insignificances unknowingly conspired to leave behind. When exploring a genre oeuvre of the past, experts sometimes feel like divers swimming through a dead but vividly colored and oddly shaped underwater reef, a structure whose wholeness no writer or reader or publisher in those times could ever have imagined from their knowledge of the individual stories without which, nevertheless, that reef would never have existed. These are experiences the paperback bookscape does not offer, but our own paperback genres will be leaving behind just such structures for our distant descendents to explore with widened eyes.

The experts are most like the readers of the paperbacks not when they are reading the popular fiction of the past, then, but when they are following contemporary literary commentary. It is then that they are reading by genre. Indeed, every feature of the reading of paperbacks listed in the last chapter has its parallel in the expert's reading of that "literature about literature" we are calling commentary. Many of the terms we looked at earlier can be used in the study of the expert's reading, too.

When studying those virtual communities, for instance, and the genres of commentary that flourish within them, we might usefully speak of *exclusivists* (people who have no interest in criticism other than in the work that scholars do on, say, Samuel Johnson), of *users* (who follow several genres of commentary), of *occasional readers* (who dip appreciatively but intermittently into many different genres), and of *allergics* (who avoid studies of William Blake, say, or the scholarship devoted to Old English poetry). If it were not felt to be a diminishment of some valid activities, we might speak also of *fans:* the people who publish their own small-circulation newsletters devoted to a cherished writer.

Almost everything we found in the paperback bookscape has its queer parallel in the literary bookscape. Each of these genres of commentary has its own slowly changing canon of classics. (We can see which they are because of the citation patterns inside the genres. Some studies are never mentioned after their appearance, but some are cited repeatedly for a decade or more—only to be replaced eventually by later works as new discoveries make old studies obsolescent or as the research preferences change.) Like the paperback genres, each critical genre has its private library of those earnest efforts that managed to produce nothing better than the *clownish*, and each has the inevitable human response to clownishness: a library of *clownings*, or parodies.

It would be tedious to trace out all the parallels, but it is worth mentioning the formal experiences literary commentary offers and the ways in which they differ from one of these virtual communities to another. The graceful essay of appreciation has its own syntax and shape, as does the carefully argued interpretation that knows it is going to be challenged by other readers. The tone of the essay in Marxian analysis is unlike the tone of the study of Christian elements in a canonical work. Some forms seem clownish to unlearned readers but have their own odd pleasures: the learned essay with elaborate footnoting can be curiously satisfying in its own right. (The experts themselves are always condemning the footnoted essay, but if they did not enjoy writing and reading them, the editors of the professional journals would not always be pleading with them to reduce their footnoting.) The bibliographer's edition of an ancient work that includes many variant readings is another form not found outside the learned bookscapes, and it, too, offers its somewhat exotic formal gratifications.

Most notable, however, are those features that parallel the practice known as *following* a paperback genre. Young scholars go through the three phases we looked at in the last chapter as they learn to be at home in the genres they follow. As they read more and more of the materials recognized by the virtual communities they have entered, they are mapping the tradition's directives, its past, its proclivities, and its potentialities. Meanwhile, through personal experience and through the respectful references of others they identify the traditions' classics: the works everyone in a community is expected to know and to emulate. Finally, they reach a level of sophistication at which they can recognize what in a new essay is criterially different from what has come before.

In the paperback bookscapes, people educate themselves as readers privately, but this other style of reading is so much a part of literary commentary that it is explicitly recognized in the essays and books that experts in different critical genres write to help newcomers and to help experts in other areas understand them. They write essays that introduce newcomers to that "world" of Shakespeare studies, to psychological studies of literature, and so on. There are glossaries to explain the technical vocabularies these traditions develop to cope with the distinctions they discover. There are bibliographies of essential commentary at the ends of essays and books; and each learned essay opens by sending readers to a bibliographical footnote that cites the works that are currently recognized in the genre as classic. There are discursive annual reviews of new work in the area in which what is significant is identified.

If the experts in literature would understand the people who read paperbacks, they need look only into their own reading of literary scholarship and criticism. If the readers of the paperbacks would understand the fascination of professional literary criticism they need look only into their own reading of paperbacks.

How similar are the other learned communities and their bookscapes (in some cases, artscapes)? History and philosophy and art have both masterpieces and commentary and seem to have that same division of amateurs and experts. Only the experts in the other learned communities can report confidently on intellectual life in those communities, but those communities do seem to be somewhat different. In music's many worlds, for instance, the term *interpretation* seems centrally to refer to a contemporary musician's way of playing an older work; but there is a savoring of these interpretations by the experts, and that parallels some of the reading behavior found in the literary and the paperback bookscapes. Mathematics and the experimental sciences may be wholly governed by genres (under other names: *traditions, disciplines, areas*), for it is apparently only the historians in mathematics and in the sciences who take an interest in the texts of the distant past.

. . . . Viewing Television

We think of television as simple, and the stories usually are simple, but the experiences we have watching them are not simple. When the first episode of the comedy-adventure series *I Spy* appeared in September 1965, viewers were aware of that episode in at least three different ways.

That first episode—"So Long, Patrick Henry"—told a story about a black athlete who had defected to Communist China earlier but now wanted to return to the United States. It was dramatizing the dilemma of black Americans who had earned success through their talent and their long hours of hard work but had been denied the rewards white men and women could expect for the same achievements. This story was drawing upon the newspaper reality of the moment, for the black civil rights movement was then highly visible. This, the episode's story, had then and still has its own interest.

That first episode of *I Spy* was also presenting a new actor, Bill Cosby, who had established his reputation outside of television and as a comedian, not as an actor. His story, a part of history rather than fiction, was also present in viewers' minds as they watched that episode. Bill Cosby was the first black actor to win a leading role in a television series other than as a clown, and he was playing a noncomic part. Though it all seems absurd now, much depended on how well he filled that role—for his own career and for the careers of other black actors. If Cosby did a poor job, it would damage his career, and producers might use his failure as an excuse to deny other black actors opportunities. Would Cosby be deferential when the counterspy he was playing was decidedly not a deferential black? Could Cosby be funny in the style the show required—

intelligently, lightheartedly—without invoking images of the subservient clowning that earlier black actors had perfected to please their white audiences? In fact, his performance was a splendid success, and he went on in later years to triumph after triumph on television. The original viewers of that first episode of *I Spy* could not know that then, of course.

The show had its own story, too. As the first show to feature a black actor in a leading role, *I Spy* was a risk for all who had invested their money and their time and—most valuable and most rare—their career opportunities. Newspapers reported that some local television stations were refusing to broadcast *I Spy*, confident that their viewers would not accept this mixing of blacks and whites on an equal basis. The show itself faced difficulties no other show had had to face. Its viewers included angry blacks as well as angry whites, both of whom would be watching closely for missteps, and another and larger audience that had little interest in the black-white questions but did insist upon an entertaining show. Would all three groups accept a black actor in a show that mixed adventure and good humor in the style that the recent James Bond movies had managed so successfully? The show featured two bachelors and had to show them interacting with women, for instance; how would it introduce love stories when one of the two spies was white and one was black? Could the writers and directors produce a comedy that mixed blacks and whites without the show's degenerating into a farce or into angry, message-preaching satire? That is, could that production team prove that black actors could be introduced into a show that was unlike other comedy adventures only in its combining of black actors and whites? In fact, that production team and especially Robert Culp, the featured white actor, did brilliantly successful work. The show's own story was a happy one: it was triumphantly successful by every measurement. It delighted its reviewers; it won awards from the television industry; it won over even the suspicious viewers; it lasted for three years; it went into syndication; and it is still being rerun in all the odd corners of the world. The original viewers of that first episode of *I Spy* could not have known all that, either.

The viewers of that first episode were aware of more than the story the episode itself was presenting, more than their grandchildren will be able to infer from study of that episode alone. Those viewers were aware of several stories simultaneously. I do not know of any term for this conjunction of stories; I shall refer to it as a *story space* and to the three kinds of stories as *the episode's story, the actors' stories,* and *the show's story.* Though it is uncommon for a story space to be as charged with drama as was the story space of that first episode of *I Spy,* every episode in every television show creates a story space when the stories it presents and the stories it activates in viewers' minds intersect.

The viewers of that episode could see that the episode story about the black American counterspy talking to a black American defector about making an adjustment to an unjust America was a visual icon for the other stories in that space—"a sign," to cite Wimsatt again, "which somehow shares the properties of, or resembles, the objects which it denotes" (x). Partly by design, partly because the episode story appeared within the same space as the other stories, that story seemed to be about that talented black actor and about that show. It may not be visible today, twenty-five years after *I Spy* came on the air, but the original viewers knew that the actors and the show itself were taking as many risks as those fictional counterspies the episode was about. Those viewers were less confident of the endings of those nonfictional stories than they were of the ending of that episode story.

We might have spoken of such story spaces in connection with the paperbacks, too, for—as we saw—the writers' careers in art have their own story values, and a series like Donald Hamilton's stories about Matt Helm—one of many answers in prose to the James Bond series—can have an interesting history in its own right. Neither of these is so unavoidably present to the reader of paperbacks as those actors' and shows' stories are to the viewer of television, however. Viewers today cannot watch a rerun of a show in which Ronald Reagan played a part without being aware that they are watching someone who was later to become president of the United States. Further, though we think of the shows themselves as forgettable, some are not forgotten. Their names evoke for viewers histories and qualities and fond memories: *The Howdy Doody Show; Omnibus; Sesame Street; Star Trek; Mission Impossible; M.A.S.H.; Gilligan's Island; Columbo; Upstairs, Downstairs.* Television programming encourages unique strategies of analysis. The paperbacks do not offer anything quite like that. Still, everything we noticed in our examination of the readers' lives inside the paperback bookscape is evident in the viewing of television programming, too.

The shows in which the episodes are parts are also written under the governance of one genre or another, of course. They are in the tradition of the tale of detection (*Columbo*), in the tradition of the police procedural (*Hill Street Blues*), in the tradition of the western (*Gunsmoke*), in the tradition of the hospital story (*Marcus Welby, St. Elsewhere*), in the tradition of the situation comedy (*Three's Company, All in the Family*), and in many other genres and mixtures of genres. As do the readers of paperbacks, television viewers look through the episodes' stories to follow the genres those shows are honoring. The earlier shows about doctors in which deeply caring physicians gave viewers medical information (*Dr. Gillespie*) are replaced by a show in which a deeply caring forensic pathologist gives viewers medical information (*Quincy*) and then by a show in which doctors and nurses are egregiously nonangelic (*St. Elsewhere*).

Students of television could speak here, too, of variations in aversion levels among us viewers and of those inversion levels that separate the shows we find we cannot watch from those other shows, even worse, that are so badly done that they have their own horrid fascination for us. Scholars could label us addicts, users, occasional viewers, fans, allergics —to this or that type of show, to this actor, to television generally. They could speak, also, of the sense of immediacy that the programs give through their invocations of those four images of reality we examined in the opening chapter: viewers' newspaper reality, their current sense of the past, the reality their own eyes and ears touch (especially when the cameras go on location), and their current sense of the shapes that human personalities are taking. Students could also speak of television's searching out of complexities by means of simplicities, of its variations on familiar formats, of the competitions of the programs with one another and with the programs of the past. All of this does influence viewing preferences and viewing loyalties. And, of course, there are also those familiar explanations: about escape, about fun, and about the daydream factories the Walter Mittys are supporting. Those explanations, which promise so much, collapse here, too, under even sympathetic scrutiny.

The rewards that television programming offers to thoughtful people, including people who also read, go far beyond what we can identify through traditional analysis of those episodes' stories, with their wit and violence and exemplary character types and fantasy and gritty realism and obviousness and surprising sensitivities and conscious absurdity and warmth. Viewers have an interest in the actors' life stories (their loves, their marriages, their divorces) and in their performance stories (their creation of an intriguing character, their winning of awards, their stealing of shows from one another). The shows' publicists, knowing this very well, create vivid—but of course wholly unreliable—images of those actors for the newspapers. Sometimes, viewers find an actor or a new show so intriguing that the episode stories themselves have little bearing on the interest viewers are taking in them. The show itself or its principal actors are then deemed "stars."

In Chapter 9, I spoke of a superorganic source (a genre) being invoked by a human source (a writer) to produce a text (the individual story), which appeared in the form of copies (the physical carriers of that genre's writer's text). Those copies deserve more attention. Their covers trigger in readers the responses appropriate to paperbacks, and they are not without their own pleasure. Kathe Robin has written about romance readers' complaints about the covers of the books they have been buying:

Cover Controversies

We all know how important a beautiful cover is to a book's appeal. There's also the necessity of cover art denoting specific genres.

A couple in a clinch says ROMANCE. A portrait of a woman usually hints that the story is a SAGA. An anxious looking heroine fleeing from a brooding mansion indicates a slightly scary GOTHIC.

But what happens when the cover illustration says something else? Readers have written in with three major complaints:

1. The covers for several recent gothic/suspense novels, including Lee Karr's for Leisure, look decidedly like straight historical romances. Where's the light in the window not the low cut bodice!

2. Why was Rebecca Brandewyne's fantasy *Passion Moon Rising*, from Pocket not presented as such?

3. Lots of mail came in about the latest Sandra Brown novel, *Slow Heat in Heaven*, because of the "sizzling romance" quote printed

on promotions. It's a raw contemporary novel (a modern Plantation
novel, to be exact), not a romance. Readers say they wish they were
warned! (73)

A book is an object with physical properties that tell us what it is, cue
our reading, and—sometimes—please and amuse us in their own right.

The TV episode also comes as an object with physical properties,
and these physical properties, too, help select the show's audience and
shape the viewers' experiences. An episode may be in color, or it may
be in black and white; the black and white is a stylish suggestion of an
old movie or of a newsreel. This episode was filmed in front of a live
audience. The background music for one episode seeks only to influence
its viewers' emotions; the background music for the episodes in another
show is among its most prized features. The lighting is clean, even, and
clear; the lighting for a competing show's episodes is dramatic in its con-
trasts. The vocal sound track of this episode is simple; each speaker
waits to talk until everyone else has finished. The vocal sound track of
the show that follows it is many-layered; people talk over one another,
and half-intelligible background speech replaces another show's musical
accompaniment. Some of the features of this other show's slackly produced episodes annoy attentive viewers: the sound track is slightly out
of synchronization with the pictures; a microphone boom is visible; the
show has a laugh track.

Physicality plays a more decisive role in the television viewers' experiences than in the readers' experiences. It is the episode stories that yield
most quickly to our analyses, our comparisons, and our generalizations;
and so—however reluctantly—many of the most thoughtful students of
television have focused on only that one part of the story space. For many,
however, a show's physicality may be as important as its potential for
creating interesting story spaces. The physical properties of some shows
make their episodes confusing to some viewers, who experience the dis-
comfort of information overload; other viewers find that it is only when
shows provide visual and aural information at that level of density that the
shows have enough physical texture to hold their attention.

We need not turn to the visualized poems of William Blake or the
concrete poetry of our own era to discover how important the physical

properties of texts can be, for there is ample evidence within vernacular culture itself. We have all heard "The Star-Spangled Banner" played by marching bands, by organists, by symphony orchestras, and by pianists; and we all know that it is a different piece of music each time. Radio's dramas in sound could not compete with television's dramas in sound and picture. The silent films were replaced by the talkies; the black-and-white talkies, by color talkies. There is currently great interest in the practice of adding color to old black-and-white films. The fiercer admirers of *The Maltese Falcon* and *It's a Wonderful Life* feel that the color damages the films, but most television viewers, who will not watch those films in black and white, will watch them if they have had color added to them. Plainly, that gross matter of the physicality of the presentation does count.

No one has yet devised a language of critical analysis that is adequate to studying either success or failure in television shows. For that, we shall require a vocabulary for talking about all of the story space and all of the physicality that brings that story space to viewers. No doubt, that vocabulary will emerge eventually. Our sense of the inadequacy to television of the analytical systems that were invented for prose fiction and for feature films is an indication that we are all finding the experience of watching television shows far different from what we thought it would be when television first appeared. If the paperback bookscape teaches the tactics of thick reading, television teaches the parallel tactics of thick viewing. It may be that this style of viewing yields rewards no richer than thick reading does, but those rewards are different and it may be that they are no less worth thoughtful attention.

I spoke of the paperbacks as offering readers a literature without texts. As we have just seen, I might have said that of literary scholarship, too, and of television, which has so far been content to offer us an art without masterpieces. Most of the other vernacular traditions give little honor to monumentality, of course. Still, most of us continue to read or to view the forgettable objects these vernacular traditions generate and to find pleasure and profit in them—"sweetness" and "usefulness" (Horace's *dulce et utile*); Robert Frost's "delight" and "wisdom." The reception models of the past, though sophisticated, have been making it difficult for us to understand how this can be. Those models were designed to account for equally mysterious but qualitatively different dramatic situations: our encounters with the monumental.

Centuries of literary and philosophical and scientific commentary have shown us that studying is a productive strategy for the reader. Reading is productive, too. Does reading harvest smaller rewards than studying? We have always assumed that it does, and perhaps it does—but it may be its equal. We know so little about thick reading, viewing, listening, that we hardly know how to begin to compare them with studying.

Our examination of the people who are both amateurs and experts in literature does indicate, however, that some of the people who have the highest and most diverse forms of reading intelligence feel incomplete if they do not study monumental texts but incomplete, too, if they do not involve themselves with dynamic systems, with genres. Most of them have studying and reading appetites too complex to be easily characterized, but we do see some of them alternating between literature and learning and others alternating between literature and the vernacular genres.

Since the observations and reports and speculations on these pages have focused on thick reading at the expense of study reading, a caveat is due. The study model of reading still is appropriate to the monumental in art, and we could not abandon it even if we wished to do that. Those learned artscapes are not the invention of teachers. If all institutionalized study of the arts were to disappear, readers would still find the works of Shakespeare and Goethe and Manzoni and Mozart and Raphael; and those monumental objects from the past would still teach them studying. Study, and not reading, is the appropriate response to the monumental. It is appropriate not because it is respectful of greatness but because it is the response that most richly repays us. Studying handicaps us only when we begin to feel that anything that does not elicit that kind of attention from us is worthless. There are materials that do not reward us when we attempt to study them but do reward us very richly indeed when we are content to read them.

works cited

· · · · · · · · · · ·

Where it has been possible, I have given the real names of the writers who have been using pen names, collaborative names, or house names. Some of the writers remain masked, however, and in one or two instances, it is probably best for all concerned that they do.

I am grateful to my sources of this information, not only for their help but also because they provided some serendipitous bits of pleasure of their own. Here and there the idly wandering eye finds nestled in a list of the writers who shared a publisher's house name the names of writers who were later to win recognition in their own right. There are oddities, too. Thus, Susannah Bates lists as a pseudonym of James E. Gunn the name "James A. Gunn"; and Allen J. Hubin tells us that "Lionel Derrick" is a house name used alternately by Mark K. Roberts and Chet Cunningham, that Roberts has written the odd-numbered titles of The Penetrator series and Cunningham has written the even-numbered titles. Paging through the volumes, we get odd glimpses of the life of the professional storyteller in our own time.

The sources do not always agree with one another, and they are least informative on house names. Still, they do provide many answers. A good start for those who want to look beneath the disguise of a pen name is *The Writers Directory*, though it is helpful only if the writer is still active. Bates's *PENDEX* is useful on both living and dead writers and on many different genres. Hubin is excellent on crime fiction; Myron J. Smith is good on spy fiction; James Vinson, on the westerns; E. F. Bleiler, on science fiction. I also got some of the help I needed from Barzun and Taylor's *Catalogue of Crime*, from the scrupulous bibliographies in John J. Pierce, and from Jon Tuska and Vicki Piekarski's work on westerns.

Adams, Andy. *The Log of a Cowboy*. 1903. London: Corgi, 1962.
Adams, Douglas. *Hitchhiker's Guide to the Galaxy*. 1979. Rpt. in *The Hitchhiker's Quartet*. New York: Harmony, 1986.
Aldiss, Brian. *Billion Year Spree: The True History of Science Fiction*. 1973. New York: Schocken, 1974.

————. *The Malacia Tapestry.* 1976. New York: Ace, 1978.

————, ed. *Galactic Empires.* 2 vols. New York: St. Martin's, 1976. Vol. 1.

Aldiss, Brian, with David Wingrove. *Trillion Year Spree: The History of Science Fiction.* New York: Atheneum, 1986.

Ambler, Eric. *A Coffin for Dimitrios.* 1939. Rpt. in *Intrigue: Four Great Spy Novels of Eric Ambler.* Intro. Alfred Hitchcock. New York: Knopf, 1943.

Archer, Jeffrey. *Not a Penny More, Not a Penny Less.* 1976. New York: Crest-Fawcett, 1981.

Aristotle. *On the Art of Fiction* [*The Poetics*]. Trans. L. J. Potts. 2d ed. 1959. Cambridge: Cambridge UP, 1968.

Arnold, Matthew. "The Function of Criticism at the Present Time." *Lectures and Essays in Criticism.* Vol. 3 of *The Complete Prose Works of Matthew Arnold.* Ed. R. H. Super and Sister Thomas Marion Hoctor. 11 vols. Ann Arbor: U of Michigan P, 1960–77. 258–85.

————. "The Literary Influence of Academies." 1864. *Lectures and Essays in Criticism.* Vol. 3 of *The Complete Prose Works of Matthew Arnold.* Ed. R. H. Super and Sister Thomas Marion Hoctor. 11 vols. Ann Arbor: U of Michigan P, 1960–77. 232–57.

Asimov, Isaac. *I, Robot.* 1941–50. New York: Signet-NAL, 1956.

Asprin, Robert. *Thieves' World.* New York: Ace, 1979.

Atwood, Margaret. *Lady Oracle.* New York: Simon, 1976.

Auden, W. H. "The Guilty Vicarage: Notes on the Detective Story, by an Addict." 1948. Rpt. in *The Critical Performance.* Ed. Stanley Edgar Hyman. New York: Vintage-Random, 1956. 301–14.

Bargainnier, Earl F. *10 Women of Mystery.* Bowling Green, Ohio: Bowling Green State U Popular P, 1981.

[Barks, Carl.] *Uncle Scrooge in* Only a Poor Old Man. Rpt. in *The Best of Walt Disney Comics.* Racine, Wisc.: Western, n.d.

Barlow, Joel. *The Columbiad.* London: Phillips, 1809.

Barzun, Jacques, and Wendell Hertig Taylor. "A Catalogue of Crime." *Armchair Detective* 18 (1985): 220–21.

————. *A Catalogue of Crime.* New York: Harper, 1971.

————. Editors' Introduction. Brochure for *Fifty Classics of Crime Fiction.* New York: Garland, n.d.

Bates, Susannah. *The PENDEX: An Index to Pen Names and House Names in Fantastic, Thriller, and Series Literature.* Garland Reference Library in the Humanities 227. New York: Garland, 1981.

Beagle, Peter S. *The Last Unicorn.* 1968. New York: Ballantine, 1969.

Beardsley, Monroe C. "The Concept of Literature." *Literary Theory and Structure: Essays in Honor of William K. Wimsatt.* Ed. Frank Brady, John Palmer, and Martin Price. New Haven: Yale UP, 1973. 23–39.

Bennett, Arnold. *Anna of the Five Towns.* 1902. London: Methuen, 1912.

———. *Denry the Audacious [The Card].* New York: Doran, 1911.

———. *The Loot of Cities: Being the Adventures of a Millionaire in Search of Joy: A Fantasia.* 1903. Philadelphia: Train, 1972.

———. *The Old Wives' Tale.* New York: Grosset, 1911.

Bennett, Donna. "The Detective Story: Towards a Definition of Genre." *PTL: A Journal for Descriptive Poetics and Theory of Literature* 4.2 (1979): 233–67.

Bentley, E. C. *Trent's Last Case.* 1913. Avon Crime Classic Collection. New York: Avon, 1970.

Berkeley, Anthony [Anthony Berkeley Cox]. *The Poisoned Chocolates Case.* 1929. New York: Dell, 1980.

"Best All-Time Novels." *Locus: The Newspaper of Science Fiction* Aug. 1987: 32–33.

Bester, Alfred. "Fondly Fahrenheit." 1954. Rpt. in *The Science Fiction Hall of Fame.* Ed. Robert Silverberg. 1970. New York: Avon, 1971. 570–90.

Binyon, T. J. Rev. of *Twentieth-Century Crime and Mystery Writers,* ed. John M. Reilly. *Times Literary Supplement* 5 June 1981: 639.

Bleiler, E. F., ed. *Science Fiction Writers: Critical Studies of the Major Authors from the Early Nineteenth Century to the Present Day.* New York: Scribner's, 1982.

Bloch, R. Howard. "Wasteland and Round Table: The Historical Significance of Myths of Dearth and Plenty in Old French Romance." *New Literary History: A Journal of Theory and Interpretation* 11.2 (1980): 255–76.

Bloch, Robert. "That Hell-Bound Train." 1958. Rpt. in *A Treasury of Modern Fantasy.* Ed. Terry Carr and Martin Harry Greenberg. New York: Avon, 1981. 295–306.

Block, Lawrence. *The Burglar Who Studied Spinoza.* New York: Random, 1980.

Booth, Wayne C. *The Rhetoric of Fiction.* Chicago: U of Chicago P, 1961.

Brand, Max [Frederick Faust]. *Rogue Mustang.* 1932. New York: Dodd, n.d.

Brown, Fredric. *What Mad Universe.* 1949. New York: Bantam, 1950.

Bruce, Leo [Rupert Croft-Cooke]. *A Case for Three Detectives.* Philadelphia: Stokes, 1937.

Brunner, John. *Stand on Zanzibar.* 1968. New York: Ballantine, 1969.

Buchan, John. *The Thirty-Nine Steps.* 1915. Rpt. in *Adventures of Richard Hannay.* Boston: Houghton, 1939.

Budrys, Algis [Algirdas Jonas Budrys]. "On Writing." *Locus* Nov. 1977: 12.

———. "Paradise Charted." *Ti-Quarterly* 49 (1980): 5–71.

Burgess, Anthony [John Anthony Burgess Wilson]. "The Apocalypse and After." Rev. of *Terminal Visions: The Literature of Last Things,* by W. Warren Wagar. *Times Literary Supplement* 18 Mar. 1983: 256.

———. "Modern Novels: The 99 Best." *New York Times Book Review* 5 Feb. 1984: 1+.

Burke, Kenneth. "Literature as Equipment for Living." *The Philosophy of Literary Form.* Rev. ed. New York: Vintage-Random, 1957.

Burke, Peter. *Popular Culture in Early Modern Europe.* New York: Harper, 1978.

Burnett, W. R. *Little Caesar.* 1929. New York: Avon, 1945.

Burroughs, Edgar Rice. *A Princess of Mars.* 1912. New York: Ballantine, 1963.

————. *Tarzan of the Apes.* 1912. New York: Ballantine, 1963.

Cain, James M. *Cain X 3: The Postman Always Rings Twice; Mildred Pierce; Double Indemnity.* 1934, 1941, 1936. Intro. Tom Wolfe. New York: Knopf, 1969.

Calder, Jenni. *There MUST Be a Lone Ranger: The American West in Film and Reality.* 1974. New York: McGraw, 1977.

Calvino, Italo. *Invisible Cities.* 1972. Trans. William Weaver. 1974. New York: Harvest-Harcourt, 1978.

Cameron, J. M. "Between the Character and the Role." Rev. of John Bayley's *Shakespeare and Tragedy. Times Literary Supplement* 3 July 1981: 743.

Campbell, John. "Twilight." 1934. Rpt. in *The Science Fiction Hall of Fame.* Ed. Robert Silverberg. 1970. New York: Avon, 1971. 40–61.

Capps, Benjamin. *The Trail to Ogalalla.* New York: Duell, 1964.

Carr, John Dickson. *The Three Coffins.* 1935. Gregg Mystery Series. Boston: Gregg, 1979.

Carr, Terry, and Martin Harry Greenberg, eds. *A Treasury of Modern Fantasy.* New York: Avon, 1981.

Carter, Forrest. *The Outlaw Josey Wales.* 1973. New York: Dell, 1980.

Carter, Paul A. *The Creation of Tomorrow: Fifty Years of Magazine Science Fiction.* New York: Columbia UP, 1977.

Cawelti, John G. *Adventure, Mystery, and Romance: Formula Stories as Art and Popular Culture.* Chicago: U of Chicago P, 1976.

Céline, Louis Ferdinand [Louis Ferdinand Destouches]. *Death on the Installment Plan.* Trans. Ralph Manheim. New York: New Directions, 1966.

Champigny, Robert. *What Will Have Happened: A Philosophical and Technical Essay on Mystery Stories.* Bloomington: Indiana UP, 1977.

Chandler, Raymond. "Nevada Gas." Rpt. in *Great Action Stories.* Ed. William Kittredge and Steven M. Krauzer. New York: Mentor-NAL, 1977. 266–308.

Chaucer, Geoffrey. *The Canterbury Tales.* Ed. A. Kent Hieatt and Constance Hieatt. 1960. New York: Bantam, 1981.

Chesterton, Gilbert K. *The Father Brown Omnibus.* New York: Dodd, 1939.

Childers, Erskine. *The Riddle of the Sands: A Record of Secret Service Recently Achieved.* 1903. London: Rupert Hart-Davis, 1955.

Christie, Agatha. *The Murder of Roger Ackroyd.* 1926. New York: Bantam, 1983.

Clark, Walter Van Tilburg. *The Ox-Bow Incident.* 1940. New York: Readers Club, 1942.

Clement, Hal [Harry Clement Stubbs]. *Mission of Gravity.* 1954. New York: Pyramid, 1962.

Coleridge, Samuel Taylor. "Shakespeare's Judgment Equal to His Genius." *The Selected Poetry and Prose of Samuel Taylor Coleridge.* Ed. Donald A. Stauffer. New York: Modern Library-Random, 1951.

Conrad, Joseph. *The Secret Agent: A Simple Tale.* 1907. Garden City, N.Y.:
Anchor-Doubleday, 1953.

Coppel, Alfred. "The Rebel of Valkyr." 1950. Rpt. in *Galactic Empires.* Ed. Brian
Aldiss. 2 vols. New York: St. Martin's, 1976. 1: 149–93.

Cunningham, John M. "The Tin Star." Rpt. in *The Western Story: Fact, Fiction, and
Myth.* Ed. Philip Durham and Everett L. Jones. New York: Harcourt, 1975.

Dante Alighieri. *Dante's Inferno.* Trans. Mark Musa. Bloomington: Indiana UP, 1971.

Davis, Kenneth. *Two-Bit Culture: The Paperbacking of America.* Boston: Houghton,
1984.

De Camp, L. Sprague. *Lest Darkness Fall.* 1941. New York: Pyramid, 1963.

Delaney, Samuel R. *The Einstein Intersection.* New York: Ace, 1967.

Del Rey, Lester. "Helen O'Loy." 1938. Rpt. in *The Science Fiction Hall of Fame.* Ed.
Robert Silverberg. 1970. New York: Avon, 1971. 62–73.

Derrick, Lionel [Chet Cunningham]. *Death Ray Terror.* Penetrator series *34.* Los
Angeles: Pinnacle, 1979.

Dick, Philip K. *The Divine Invasion.* New York: Timescape, 1981.

———. *The Man in the High Castle.* New York: Popular, 1962.

Dick, Philip K., and Roger Zelazny. *Deus Irae.* 1976. New York: Dell, 1977.

Dickson, Gordon R. *The Dragon and the George.* New York: Del Rey-Ballantine, 1976.

Doyle, Sir Arthur Conan. *The Complete Sherlock Holmes.* 2 vols. Garden City, N.Y.:
Doubleday, 1930.

Dryden, John. "An Essay of Dramatick Poesie." *Prose 1668–1691: An Essay of
Dramatick Poesie and Shorter Works.* Ed. Samuel Holt Monk et al. Vol. 17 of *The
Works of John Dryden.* Ed. Edward N. Hooker and H. T. Swedenberg. 19 vols.
Berkeley: U of California P, 1956–87. 3–81.

Dryer, Stan. "The Conquest of the Washington Monument." Rpt. in *Great Action Stories.*
Ed. William Kittredge and Steven M. Krauzer. New York: Mentor, 1977. 113–19.

Dubrow, Heather. *Genre.* New York: Methuen, 1982.

Easton, Robert. *Max Brand: The Big "Westerner."* Norman: U of Oklahoma P, 1970.

Eddison, E. R. *The Worm Ouroboros.* 1926. New York: Ballantine, 1962.

Edwards, Jonathan. "Sinners in the Hands of an Angry God." 1741. Rpt. in *The
American Tradition in Literature.* Ed. Sculley Bradley, Richmond Croom Beatty, and
E. Hudson Long. 2 vols. New York: Norton, 1967. 1: 109–24.

Effinger, George Alec. "The Ghost Writer." 1973. Rpt. in *From Here to Forever.* Ed.
James Gunn. Vol. 4 of *The Road to Science Fiction.* 4 vols. New York: Mentor-NAL,
1977–82. 341–51.

Eliot, T. S. "Tradition and the Individual Talent." *Selected Writings: New Edition.* New
York: Harcourt, 1950.

Ellis, Edward S. *Seth Jones; or, The Captives of the Frontier.* Oct. 2, 1860. Beadle's
Dime Novels 8. Dime Novel Club facsimile reprint of 1877 edition. New York:
C. Bragin, 1946.

Ellison, Harlan, ed. *Dangerous Visions.* 1967. New York: Berkley Medallion, 1972.

————. "I Have No Mouth, and I Must Scream." 1968. Rpt. in *From Heinlein to Here*. Ed. James Gunn. Vol. 3 of *The Road to Science Fiction*. 4 vols. New York: Mentor-NAL, 1977–82. 431–46.

Escarpit, Robert. *Sociology of Literature*. 1958. Trans. Ernest Pick. Lake Erie College Studies 4. Painesville, Ohio: Lake Erie College P, 1965.

Evans, Tabor [house name]. *Longarm, No. 1*. New York: Jove, 1983.

Fair, A. A. [Erle Stanley Gardner]. *The Bigger They Come*. 1939. Quill Mysterious Classic. New York: Quill, 1984.

Farmer, Philip José. "Sail On! Sail On!" 1952. Rpt. in *A Treasury of Modern Fantasy*. Ed. Terry Carr and Martin Harry Greenberg. New York: Avon, 1981. 273–85.

Farnsworth, James. *The Lash of Vengeance*. New York: Manor, 1978.

Fitton, Toby. "Murder on the Market." Rev. of *Outbid*, by David Hume. *Times Literary Supplement* 30 Mar. 1984. 354.

Fleming, Ian. *Casino Royale*. 1953. London: Pan, 1974.

————. *You Only Live Twice*. New York: NAL, 1964.

Forrest, Williams. *White Apache*. Greenwich: Gold Medal-Fawcett, 1966.

Forsyth, Frederick. *The Day of the Jackal*. 1971. New York: Bantam, 1972.

————. "No Comebacks." *No Comebacks: Collected Short Stories*. New York: Viking, 1982.

Forward, Robert L. *Dragon's Egg*. New York: Del Rey-Ballantine, 1980.

Fraser, John. *Violence in the Arts*. Illustrated ed. Cambridge: Cambridge UP, 1976.

Frost, Robert. "The Figure a Poem Makes: An Introduction." 1939. Rpt. in *Robert Frost: Poetry and Prose*. Ed. Edward Connery Lathem and Lawrance Thompson. New York: Holt, 1972. 339–96.

Frye, Northrop. *Anatomy of Criticism: Four Essays*. Princeton: Princeton UP, 1957.

Gardner, Erle Stanley. *The Case of the Lame Canary*. New York: Morrow, 1937.

Gardner, Martin. *Mathematical Puzzles and Diversions*. 1959. London: Penguin, 1965.

Garfield, Brian. *Recoil*. New York: Morrow, 1977.

Gash, Jonathan [John Grant]. *The Grail Tree*. 1979. New York: Dell, 1982.

Geis, Richard. Rev. of *The Final Circle of Paradise*, by Boris and Arkadi Strugatski, trans. Leonid Ranen. *Science Fiction Review* 21 (1977): 74.

Gibson, Walker. "Authors, Speakers, Readers, and Mock Readers." *College English* 11 (1950): 265–69.

Glendinning, Victoria. "His Dog and Himself." Rev. of *My Sister and Myself: The Diaries of J. R. Ackerley*, ed. Francis King. *Times Literary Supplement* 30 Apr. 1982: 478.

Gombrich, E. H. *The Sense of Order*. 1979. Ithaca: Cornell UP, 1984.

Greene, Graham. *The Human Factor*. 1978. New York: Avon, 1979.

Grey, Zane. *Five Complete Novels: Riders of the Purple Sage, To the Last Man, The Thundering Herd, The Hash Knife Outfit, West of the Pecos*. 1912, 1921, 1924, 1929, 1931. New York: Avenel, 1980.

Guinness Book of World Records: 1986. Ed. Norris McWhirter et al. New York: Bantam, 1986.

Gunn, James, ed. *From Gilgamesh to Wells.* Vol. 1 of *The Road to Science Fiction.* 4 vols. New York: Mentor-NAL, 1977–82.

———, ed. *From Heinlein to Here.* Vol. 3 of *The Road to Science Fiction.* 4 vols. New York: Mentor-NAL, 1977–82.

———, ed. *From Here to Forever.* Vol. 4 of *The Road to Science Fiction.* 4 vols. New York: Mentor-NAL, 1977–82.

Guthrie, A. B. *The Big Sky.* New York: Sloane, 1947.

———. *Trouble at Moon Dance* [*Murders at Moon Dance*]. 1943. New York: Popular, 1951.

Haldeman, Joe. *The Forever War.* New York: Ballantine, 1976.

Hall, Adam [Elleston Trevor]. *The Quiller Memorandum.* New York: Simon, 1965.

———. *The Striker Portfolio.* 1968. New York: Pyramid, 1970.

Hall, Austin, and Homer Eon Flint. *The Blind Spot.* 1921. New York: Ace, n.d.

Hamilton, Donald. *The Intriguers.* London: Coronet, 1973.

———. *The Mona Intercept.* New York: Gold Medal-Fawcett, 1980.

Hammett, Dashiell. "The Gutting of Couffignal." Rpt. in *Great Action Stories.* Ed. William Kittredge and Steven M. Krauzer. New York: Mentor-NAL, 1977. 174–204.

———. *The Maltese Falcon.* 1930. Rpt. in *The Novels of Dashiell Hammett.* New York: Knopf, 1965.

———. *Red Harvest.* 1929. Rpt. in *The Novels of Dashiell Hammett.* New York: Knopf, 1965.

———. *The Thin Man.* 1934. Rpt. in *The Novels of Dashiell Hammett.* New York: Knopf, 1965.

Harding, D. W. "The Notion of 'Escape' in Fiction and Entertainment." *Oxford Review* 4 (1967): 23–32.

Hare, Cyril [Alfred Alexander Gordon Clark]. *When the Wind Blows.* 1949. New York: Perennial-Harper, 1978.

Harrison, Harry [Henry Maxwell Demsey]. *Bill, the Galactic Hero.* 1965. New York: Medallion-Berkley, 1966.

Harvard Lampoon [Henry N. Beard and Douglas C. Kenney]. *Bored of the Rings: A Parody of J. R. R. Tolkien's* "The Lord of the Rings." New York: Signet-NAL, 1969.

Haycox, Ernest. *Bugles in the Afternoon.* 1943. New York: Signet-NAL, 1973.

Healy, Raymond J., and J. Francis McComas, eds. *Adventures in Time and Space.* New York: Random, 1946.

Heinlein, Robert. *Starship Troopers.* 1959. New York: Signet-NAL, 1961.

———. *Stranger in a Strange Land.* New York: Avon, 1961.

Herbert, Frank. *The Dragon in the Sea.* New York: Avon, 1956.

———. *Dune.* New York: Ace, 1965.

Heyer, Georgette. *Arabella.* Melbourne: Heinemann, 1949.

Higgins, George V. *The Digger's Game.* New York: Knopf, 1973.

———. *The Friends of Eddie Coyle.* 1971. New York: Bantam, 1973.

———. *The Rat on Fire.* New York: Knopf, 1981.

Highsmith, Patricia. *The Talented Mr. Ripley.* New York: Coward, 1955.

Himes, Chester. *The Big Gold Dream.* 1960. New York: Signet-NAL, 1975.

———. *For Love of Imabelle.* 1965. New York: Dell, 1971.

Hoban, Russell. *Riddley Walker: A Novel.* 1980. New York: Pocket, 1982.

Holman, C. Hugh, and William Harmon. *A Handbook to Literature.* 5th ed. New York: Macmillan, 1986.

Homer. *The Iliad of Homer.* Trans. Richmond Lattimore. 1951. Chicago: Phoenix, 1961.

Horace [Quintus Horatius Flaccus]. "The Art of Poetry." *The Complete Works of Horace.* Trans. Charles E. Passage. New York: Ungar, 1983. 359–71.

Hospers, John. "Aesthetics, Problems in." *The Encyclopedia of Philosophy.* 8 vols. 1967. New York: Macmillan, 1972.

Howard, Robert E. *Conan the Warrior.* 1936. Ed. L. Sprague de Camp. New York: Lancer, 1967.

Hubin, Allen J. *Crime Fiction, 1749–1980: A Comprehensive Bibliography.* New York: Garland, 1984.

Husband, Janet. *Sequels: An Annotated Guide to Novels in Series.* Chicago: American Library Association, 1982.

Huxley, Aldous. *Brave New World.* 1932. New York: Harper, 1946.

Jakubowski, Maxim, and Malcolm Edwards. *The SF Book of Lists.* New York: Berkley, 1983.

James, Clive. "That Old Black and White Magic." Rev. of *The Work of Atget,* ed. John Szarkowski and Maria Morris Hambourg. *New York Review of Books* 17 Dec. 1981: 37+.

Jason, Heda. *Ethnopoetics: A Multilingual Terminology.* Jerusalem: Israel Ethnographic Society, 1975.

Jessup, Richard. *The Cincinnati Kid.* 1963. New York: Dell, 1965.

Johnson, Douglas. "Crypto-Christian with a Pipe." Rev. of *Maigret: Enquête sur un enquêteur,* by Jean Fabre. *Times Literary Supplement* 1 Oct. 1982: 1058.

Jonas, Gerald. "Onward and Upward with the Arts (Science Fiction)." *New Yorker* 29 July 1972: 33–52.

Kaye, Marvin. "The Toy with One Moving Part." Rpt. in *Fields of Writing: Readings Across the Disciplines.* Ed. Nancy R. Compley et al. New York: St. Martin's, 1984.

Kelton, Elmer. *The Time It Never Rained.* New York: Ace, 1973.

Kerr, Elizabeth Margaret. *Bibliography of the Sequence Novel.* Minneapolis: U of Minnesota P, 1950.

King, Stephen. *The Shining.* 1977. New York: Signet-NAL, 1978.

Kipling, Rudyard. *Kim.* 1901. Rpt. in *The Collected Works of Rudyard Kipling.* 28 vols. New York: Doubleday, 1941. 16: 179–525.

————. "With the Night Mail: A Story of A.D. 2000." 1908. Rpt. in *The Collected Works of Rudyard Kipling*. 28 vols. New York: Doubleday, 1941. 8: 401–51.

Knight, Damon. "Chuckleheads." *In Search of Wonder: Essays on Modern Science Fiction*. Rev. and enl. ed. Chicago: Advent, 1967.

Kroeber, A. L. "The Superorganic." *American Anthropologist* ns 19.2 (1917): 163–213.

Labov, William. *The Social Stratification of English in New York City*. Washington, D.C.: Center for Applied Linguistics, 1966.

Lafferty, R. A. *Past Master*. 1968. New York: Ace, 1982.

L'Amour, Louis. *Heller with a Gun*. Greenwich, Conn.: Gold Medal-Fawcett, 1955.

Laumer, Keith. *Galactic Odyssey*. New York: TOR, 1967.

Le Carré, John [David John Moore Cornwall]. *The Spy Who Came in from the Cold*. 1963. New York: Coward, 1964.

————. *Tinker, Tailor, Soldier, Spy*. New York: Knopf, 1974.

Le Guin, Ursula K. *The Dispossessed: An Ambiguous Utopia*. New York: Harper, 1974.

Leiber, Fritz. "Four Ghosts in Hamlet." 1965. Rpt. in *A Treasury of Modern Fantasy*. Ed. Terry Carr and Martin Harry Greenberg. New York: Avon, 1981.

Leonard, Elmore. *Glitz*. 1985. New York: Warner, 1986.

Lewis, C. S. *The Allegory of Love: A Study in Medieval Tradition*. 1936. London: Oxford UP, 1959.

————. *An Experiment in Criticism*. 1961. Cambridge: Cambridge UP, 1965.

————. *Out of the Silent Planet*. New York: Collier, 1962.

Lewis, Ted. *Get Carter [Jack's Return Home]*. 1970. New York: Popular, n.d.

Linebarger, Paul M. A. *Psychological Warfare*. New York: Duell, 1954.

"Locus Survey Results." *Locus: The Newspaper of the Science Fiction Field* Aug. 1985: 24+.

Logan, Jake [house name]. *Slocum's Debt: #41*. New York: Playboy, 1982.

Lovecraft, H. P. *The Dream-Quest of Unknown Kadath*. 1943. Ed. Lin Carter. New York: Ballantine, 1970.

Lowes, John Livingstone. *The Road to Xanadu: A Study in the Ways of the Imagination*. Boston: Houghton, 1927.

McBain, Ed [Evan Hunter]. *Ice*. 1983. New York: Avon, 1984.

McClure, James. *The Gooseberry Fool*. New York: Harper, 1974.

MacDonald, John D. *Cinnamon Skin*. New York: Harper, 1982.

————. "The Corpse Rides at Dawn." 1948. Rpt. in *7 Westerns of the 40's: Classics from the Great Pulps*. Ed. Damon Knight. New York: Harper; Barnes, 1978. 73–92.

————. "Escape to Chaos." 1951. Rpt. in *Galactic Empires*. Ed. Brian W. Aldiss. 2 vols. New York: St. Martin's, 1976. 2: 8–51.

————. Foreword. *The Good Old Stuff: 13 Early Stories*. By MacDonald. Ed. Martin H. Greenberg et al. 1972. New York: Gold Medal-Fawcett, 1983.

————. *Free Fall in Crimson*. New York: Harper, 1981.

————. *On the Run*. New York: Gold Medal-Fawcett, 1963.

————. *The Scarlet Ruse*. New York: Lippincott, 1980.

Macdonald, Ross [Kenneth Millar]. *The Chill.* 1964. New York: Bantam, 1965.

McLaughlin, Dean. "Locus Letters." *Locus: The Newspaper of the Science Fiction Field* Mar. 1981: 14.

Malcolm, Norman. *Ludwig Wittgenstein: A Memoir.* London: Oxford UP, 1958.

Margolies, Edward. *Which Way Did He Go? The Private Eye in Dashiell Hammett, Raymond Chandler, Chester Himes, and Ross Macdonald.* New York: Holmes, 1982.

Marshall, William. *The Far Away Man.* New York: Holt, 1984.

———. *The Hatchet Man.* 1976. New York: Popular, 1978.

———. *Yellowthread Street.* New York: Holt, 1975.

Mather, Cotton. *Bonifacius: An ESSAY upon the GOOD.* 1710. Ed. David Levin. Cambridge, Mass.: Belknap-Harvard UP, 1966.

Meyers, Richard. "TAD on TV." *Armchair Detective* 18 (1985): 202.

Miller, Wade [Robert Miller and Robert Wade]. *Devil May Care.* New York: Fawcett, 1950.

Miller, Walter M., Jr. *A Canticle for Leibowitz.* 1959. New York: Lippincott, 1960.

Milne, A. A. *The Red House Mystery.* 1922. New York: Dell, 1980.

Milton, John. *Paradise Lost.* Rpt. in *The Complete Poetical Works of John Milton.* Ed. Douglas Bush. Boston: Houghton, 1965. 211–459.

MLA (Modern Language Association). "Allied Organization Meetings." *PMLA* 102 (1987): 952–53.

———. *General Literature and Related Topics.* Vol. 4 of *1986 MLA International Bibliography of Books and Articles on the Modern Languages and Literatures.* 5 vols. New York: MLA, 1987.

———. "MLA Divisions and Discussion Groups." *PMLA* 102 (1987): 449–50.

———. "Trends in Scholarly Publishing." *MLA Newsletter* 16.2 (1984): 10.

Moore, Ward. *Bring the Jubilee.* 1955. New York: Equinox-Avon, 1976.

Mulford, Clarence Edward. *Bar-20: Being a Record of Certain Happenings That Occurred in the Otherwise Peaceful Lives of One Hopalong Cassidy and His Companions on the Range.* New York: Outing, 1907.

O'Brien, Robert, et al. *Machines.* Life Science Library. New York: Time-Life, 1968.

O'Donnell, Peter. *Modesty Blaise.* 1965. London: Pan, 1966.

Olsen, Theodore V. *The Stalking Moon.* 1965. New York: Avon, 1968.

Oppenheim, E. Phillips. *The Great Impersonation.* Boston: Little, 1920.

Ortega y Gasset, José. *The Dehumanization of Art and Other Writings on Art and Culture.* Trans. 1948. Garden City, N.Y.: Anchor-Doubleday, 1956.

Orwell, George [Eric Blair]. *Nineteen Eighty-Four.* New York: Harcourt, 1949.

Overholser, Stephen. *A Hanging in Sweetwater.* Garden City, N.Y.: Doubleday, 1974.

Parker, Robert B. *Looking for Rachel Wallace.* 1980. New York: Dell, 1981.

———. *Promised Land.* 1976. New York: Dell, 1987.

Pierce, John J. *Foundations of Science Fiction: A Study in Imagination and Evolution.* Contributions to the Study of Science Fiction and Fantasy 25. New York: Greenwood, 1987.

Plato. "Ion." *Critical Theory Since Plato*. Ed. Hazard Adams. New York: Harcourt, 1971. 12–19.

———. *Laws*. Vol. 5 of *The Dialogues of Plato Translated into English*. Trans. B. Jowett. 3d ed. 5 vols. New York: Macmillan, 1892.

Pohl, Frederik, and C. M. Kornbluth. *Gladiator-at-Law*. New York: Ballantine, 1955.

———. *The Space Merchants*. 1952. New York: Ballantine, 1953.

Pope, Alexander. *Dunciad. Poetical Works*. Ed. Herbert Davis. London: Oxford, 1966. 425–623.

Porter, Joyce. *Dover One*. London: Cape, 1964.

Pound, Ezra. *ABC of Reading*. 1934. New York: New Directions, 1960.

Puzo, Mario. *The Godfather*. New York: Putnam's, 1969.

Queen, Ellery [Frederick Dannay and Manfred Lee]. *The Chinese Orange Mystery*. New York: International Readers League, 1934.

Radway, Janice A. *Reading the Romance: Women, Patriarchy, and Popular Literature*. Chapel Hill: U of North Carolina P, 1984.

Réage, Pauline. *The Story of O (Histoire d'O)*. New York: Ballantine, 1981.

Reilly, John M. "Margaret Millar." *10 Women of Mystery*. Ed. Earl F. Bargainnier. Bowling Green, Ohio: Bowling Green State U Popular P, 1981.

Rendell, Ruth. *An Unkindness of Ravens*. New York: Pantheon, 1985.

Rhode, John [John Charles Street], et al. *Ask a Policeman*. New York: Morrow, 1933.

Rhodes, Eugene Manlove. *The Rhodes Reader: Stories of Virgins, Villains, and Varmints*. Ed. W. H. Hutchinson. 2d ed. Norman: U of Oklahoma P, 1975.

Roaf, Michael. "Braving the Basalt." Rev. of *Jawa: Lost City of the Black Desert*, by S. W. Helm. *Times Literary Supplement* 18 Sept. 1981: 1078.

Roberts, Thomas J. "The Critics' Conceptions of Literature." *College English* 31.1 (1969): 1–24.

———. "Fiction Outside Literature." *Literary Review* 22.1 (1978): 5–21.

———. "The Network of Literary Identifications." *New Literary History* 5.1 (1973): 67–90.

Robin, Kathe. "Tete a Tete." *Rave Reviews* 13 (June/July 1988): 73.

Rogers, Rosemary. *Sweet Savage Love*. New York: Avon, 1974.

Rohmer, Sax [Arthur Salsfield Ward]. *The Insidious Doctor Fu-Manchu*. 1918. New York: Pyramid, 1961.

Rosenberg, Betty. *Genreflecting: A Guide to Reading Interests in Genre Fiction*. Littleton, Colo.: Libraries Unlimited, 1982.

Ruehlmann, William. *Saint with a Gun: The Unlawful Private Eye*. New York: New York UP, 1974.

Runyon, Damon. "The Hottest Guy in the World." Rpt. in *Great Action Stories*. Ed. William Kittredge and Steven M. Krauzer. New York: Mentor, 1977. 205–15.

Russell, Bertrand. "On Denoting." 1950. Rpt. in *Problems in the Philosophy of Language*. Ed. Thomas M. Olshewsky. New York: Holt, 1969. 300–311.

Sandoz, Mari. *Cheyenne Autumn*. New York: McGraw-Hill, 1953.

Sapper [Herman Cyril McNeile]. *The Return of Bulldog Drummond*. London: Hodder, 1932.

Sayers, Dorothy. *The Nine Tailors: Changes Rung on an Old Theme in Two Short Touches and Two Full Peals*. New York: Harcourt, 1934.

Sayers, Dorothy, and Robert Eustace [Robert Eustace is pseud. for Eustace Robert Barton]. *The Documents in the Case*. 1930. London: Gollancz, 1978.

Sayles, John. "I-80 Nebraska M.490–M.205." Rpt. in *Great Action Stories*. Ed. William Kittredge and Steven M. Krauzer. New York: Mentor, 1977. 229–46.

Segre, Cesare, with Tomaso Kemeny. *Introduction to the Analysis of the Literary Text*. Trans. John Meddemmen. Advances in Semiotics. Bloomington: Indiana UP, 1988.

Sencourt, Robert. *T. S. Eliot: A Memoir*. Ed. Donald Adamson. New York: Dodd, 1971.

Shea, Michael. *Nifft the Lean*. New York: DAW, 1982.

Sheldon, Sidney. *Rage of Angels*. New York: Morrow, 1980.

Shelley, Mary Wollstonecraft. *Frankenstein; or, the Modern Prometheus*. 1818. Ed. James Rieger. New York: Bobbs, 1974.

Sheridan, Richard B. *The Rivals*. *The Dramatic Works of Richard Brinsley Sheridan*. Ed. Cecil Price. Oxford: Clarendon, 1973. 72–148.

Sidney, Sir Philip. *Defense of Poesy*. Ed. Lewis Soens. Lincoln: U of Nebraska P, 1970.

Silverberg, Robert, ed. *The Science Fiction Hall of Fame*. 1970. New York: Avon, 1971.

Simenon, Georges. *A Maigret Omnibus*. London: Hamish Hamilton, 1962.

Singer, Jerome L. *The Inner World of Daydreaming*. 1975. New York: Colophon-Harper, 1976.

Sjöwall, Maj, and Per Wahloo. *The Laughing Policeman (Den skrattande polisen)*. Trans. Alan Blair. New York: Pantheon-Random, 1970.

———. *Roseanna*. 1965. Trans. Lois Roth. New York: Pantheon-Random, 1967.

———. *The Terrorists*. 1975. Trans. Joan Tate. 1976. New York: Vintage-Random, 1978.

Sladek, John. "Clichés." *The Science Fiction Encyclopedia*. Ed. Peter Nicholls. Garden City, N.Y.: Dolphin, 1979.

Smith, Cordwainer [Paul Linebarger]. "Dead Lady of Clown Town." 1964. Rpt. in *The Best of Cordwainer Smith*. Ed. J. J. Pierce. New York: Ballantine, 1975.

———. *Norstrilia*. 1964, 1968. New York: Ballantine, 1975.

———. "Prologue." *Space Lords*. New York: Pyramid, 1965.

———. "Scanners Live in Vain." 1948. Rpt. in *The Science Fiction Hall of Fame*. Ed. Robert Silverberg. New York: Avon, 1971.

Smith, E. E. *Skylark DuQuesne*. 1965. New York: Avon, 1966.

———. *The Skylark of Space*. New York: Pyramid, 1958.

———. *Skylark Three*. 1948. New York: Pyramid, 1963.

———. *Spacehounds of the IPC*. 1931. New York: Ace, 1947.

Smith, H. Allen. *Low Man on a Totem Pole*. Garden City, N.Y.: Doubleday, 1941.

Smith, Myron J. *Cloak-and-Dagger Bibliography: An Annotated Guide to Spy Fiction, 1937–1975*. Metuchen, N.J.: Scarecrow, 1976.

Sparshott, F. E. "On the Possibility of Saying What Literature Is." *What Is Literature?* Ed. Paul Hernadi. Bloomington: Indiana UP, 1978. 3–15.

Spillane, Mickey [Frank Morrison Spillane]. *I, the Jury.* 1948. New York: Signet, 1969.

———. *The Tough Guys.* 1963–64. New York: Signet-NAL, 1969.

Stapledon, Olaf. *Last and First Men and Star Maker: Two Science Fiction Novels.* 1931, 1937. New York: Dover, 1968.

Stout, Rex. *Full House: A Nero Wolfe Omnibus.* New York: Viking, 1955.

Symons, Julian. *Mortal Consequences: A History—From the Detective Story to the Crime Novel.* 1972. New York: Schocken, 1973.

Thomas, Ross. *The Eighth Dwarf.* 1979. New York: Avon, 1980.

Thompson, Jim. *The Getaway. The Killer Inside Me. The Grifters. Pop. 1280.* London: Zomba, 1983.

Thurber, James. *My Life and Hard Times.* 1933. Rpt. in *Vintage Thurber: A Collection in Two Volumes of the Best Writings and Drawings of James Thurber.* 2 vols. London: Hamish, 1963. 2: 159–213.

———. "The Secret Life of Walter Mitty." 1939. Rpt. in *Vintage Thurber: A Collection in Two Volumes of the Best Writings and Drawings of James Thurber.* 2 vols. London: Hamish, 1963. 1: 27–30.

Tolkien, J. R. R. *The Lord of the Rings.* 3 vols. New York: Ballantine, 1965.

Trevor, Elleston. *The Theta Syndrome.* Garden City, N.Y.: Doubleday, 1977.

Trilling, Lionel. *The Liberal Imagination: Essays on Literature and Society.* 1940–49. New York: Viking, 1950.

Trout, Kilgore [Philip José Farmer]. *Venus on the Half Shell.* New York: Dell, 1975.

Turco, Lewis. *The Book of Forms: A Handbook of Poetics.* New York: Dutton, 1968.

Tuska, Jon, and Vicki Piekarski, ed. *Encyclopedia of Frontier and Western Fiction.* New York: McGraw, 1983.

Upfield, Arthur. *Death of a Lake.* 1954. London: Heinemann, 1967.

Van Dine, S. S. [Willard Huntington Wright]. *The Greene Murder Case.* 1927. Gregg Press Mystery Fiction Series. Boston: Gregg, 1980.

Van Vogt, A. E. *Slan.* 1940. Garden City, N.Y.: Doubleday, 1946.

———. "The Weapon Shop." 1942. Rpt. in *The Science Fiction Hall of Fame.* Ed. Robert Silverberg. 1970. New York: Avon, 1971. 183–225.

Varley, John. "The Persistence of Vision." *The Persistence of Vision.* New York: Dial, 1978.

Verne, Jules. *Mysterious Island.* New York: Scribner's, 1919.

Vinson, James, ed. *Twentieth-Century Western Writers.* Detroit, Mich.: Gale Research, 1982.

Vonnegut, Kurt, Jr. *Player Piano.* 1952. New York: Bard-Avon, 1972.

Walker, Benjamin. *Encyclopedia of Metaphysical Medicine.* London: Routledge, 1978.

Walker, J. K. L. "Damming It Up." Rev. of *The Centre of the Universe Is 18 Baedkerstrasse,* by Jonathan Gathorne-Hardy. *Times Literary Supplement* 22 Mar. 1985: 327.

Wallechinsky, David, and Irving Wallace. *The People's Almanac*. Garden City, N.Y.: Doubleday, 1975.

Watson, Colin. *Snobbery with Violence: Crime Stories and Their Audience*. London: Eyre, 1971.

Watson, Ian. *The Embedding*. New York: Scribner's, 1973.

Webster's Seventh New Collegiate Dictionary. 1963.

Weinbaum, Stanley G. "A Martian Odyssey." 1934. Rpt. in *The Science Fiction Hall of Fame*. Ed. Robert Silverberg. 1970. New York: Avon, 1971. 13–39.

Wellek, René, and Austin Warren. *Theory of Literature*. 3d ed. New York: Harvest-Harcourt, 1956.

Wells, H. G. "The Country of the Blind." 1904. Rpt. in *The Famous Short Stories of H. G. Wells*. Garden City, N.Y.: Garden City, 1938.

————. *The Island of Dr. Moreau*. 1896. Rpt. in *Seven Famous Novels by H. G. Wells*. New York: Knopf, 1934. 67–157.

Wertham, Fredric. *The World of Fanzines: A Special Form of Communication*. Carbondale: Southern Illinois UP, 1973.

White, Steward Edward. "Buried Treasure." 1907. Rpt. in *The Omnibus of Adventure*. Ed. John Grove. New York: Junior Literary Guild, 1930.

Whitten, Leslie H. *Progeny of the Adder*. New York: Ace, 1965.

Williams, Charles. *The Sailcloth Shroud*. 1960. New York: Pocket, 1972.

Williamson, Jack. "With Folded Hands." Rpt. in *The Science Fiction Hall of Fame, Vol. IIA*. Ed. Ben Bova. 1973. New York: Avon, 1974. 527–72.

Wilson, Edmund. "'Mr. Holmes, They Were the Footprints of a Gigantic Hound!'" Rpt. in *Classics and Commercials: A Literary Chronicle of the Forties*. 1945. New York: Farrar, 1950.

————. "Why Do People Read Detective Stories?" Rpt. in *Classics and Commercials: A Literary Chronicle of the Forties*. 1944. New York: Farrar, 1950.

Wimsatt, W. K., Jr. *The Verbal Icon: Studies in the Meaning of Poetry*. New York: Noonday, 1954.

Winn, Dilys. *Murder Ink: The Mystery Reader's Companion*. New York: Workman, 1977.

Wister, Owen. *The Virginian: A Horseman of the Plains*. New York: Macmillan, 1902.

Wodehouse, P. G. *Meet Mr. Mulliner*. 1927. Harmondsworth: Penguin, 1967.

Wollheim, Donald A. *The Universe Makers: Science Fiction Today*. New York: Harper, 1971.

Woodhouse, Martin. *Tree Frog*. 1966. New York: NAL, 1967.

Woodiwiss, Kathleen E. *Come Love a Stranger*. New York: Avon, 1984.

Wright, Andrew. Rev. of *The Trollope Critics*, ed. N. John Hall. *Times Literary Supplement* 19 Mar. 1982. 322.

The Writers Directory, 1988–90. Chicago: St. James Press, 1988.

Wyss, [Johann] David. *The Swiss Family Robinson: or, The Adventures of a Shipwrecked Family on an Uninhabited Isle Near New Guinea*. 1812–13. Enl. Baroness de Montolieu. 1826. New York: Harper, 1909.

Zelazny, Roger. "For a Breath I Tarry." *Survival Printout*. Ed. Total Effect [Leonard Allison et al.]. New York: Vintage-Random, 1973. 68–107.

———. *Lord of Light*. 1967. New York: Avon, 1969.

———. *Road Marks*. 1979. New York: Del Rey-Ballantine, 1980.

index

• • • • • • • • • •

. . . .